Sayler, Oliver Martin, 1887-
    Revolt in the arts; a survey of the
creation, distribution and appreciation
of art in America.

REVOLT IN THE ARTS

BY OLIVER M. SAYLER

Russia White or Red
The Russian Theatre Under the Revolution
The Russian Theatre
Our American Theatre
Inside the Moscow Art Theatre

EDITED BY MR. SAYLER

The Moscow Art Theatre Series of Russian Plays, First Series
The Eleonora Duse Plays
The Moscow Art Theatre Series of Russian Plays, Second Series
Max Reinhardt and His Theatre
The Plays of the Moscow Art Theatre Musical Studio

REVOLT IN THE ARTS

A SURVEY OF THE CREATION, DISTRIBUTION AND APPRECIATION OF ART IN AMERICA

BY

OLIVER M. SAYLER

With Contributions by
Thirty-six Representative Authorities
in the Several Arts

BRENTANO'S

PUBLISHERS   NEW YORK

To

IDA LOU SAYLER

Who May See the Realization
of the Dreams Herein Set Forth

PREFACE

IF a book could speak, the preface would probably be the logical place for it to do so. But since it can not, perhaps the author may be permitted in this spot to perform the task of presumptive autobiography.

"Revolt in the Arts" had its birth in the general recognition of a state of revolution in our contemporary American theatre during the past season. Realization that all of the arts have a common fountain-head in the human imagination and that whatever profoundly influences one of them is likely to affect the others, dictated a survey to discover whether revolt was present, incipient or impending in the cinema, in music, in the dance, in literature, in painting and sculpture, in architecture, in the craft arts. The result of this survey pointed to a chaotic condition in all of the arts comparable in many ways to the overt revolt in the theatre, a condition which has assumed in the intervening months an increasingly revolutionary aspect.

Originally conceived simply as a coordinated symposium on the subject by typical workers in the several arts, the book suddenly enlisted the author's own interpretive interest when he detected unmistakable trends and feasible goals emerging from the general chaos. These trends and these goals might have intrinsic interest and significance besides serving as a pattern to assure coordination of the reports of the contributors.

Hence, instead of a mere field-survey, "Revolt in the Arts" became an attempt to analyze the multiple forces at work in the several arts, to determine the relative importance of esthetic, economic and moral factors and their reciprocal interplay, to inquire causes and to formulate implications. With these motives and from this point-of-view, it becomes possible to study the field of the arts as a whole and to realize that they form an intricate network of busy canals in close contact with our daily lives instead of a series of individual ruts hermetically sealed from one another and from life. It is even possible, thus, to conceive of the arts as handmaids to science in the effort to explain life, replacing religion and metaphysics for those who have lost faith in these aids to cosmic understanding and supplementing their service for those who still retain faith in them.

Perhaps the most stimulating conclusion to which this survey leads, however, is that, in our Machine Age, intimate art may exist alongside mass-production art, deriving support from the latter in return for serving as its laboratory, testing ground and inspiration. It would seem possible, therefore, if we wish it earnestly enough, to preserve the personal touch in the arts, no matter what inroads the machine may make.

In expressing my deep gratitude to the distinguished contributors to this volume, I hardly need say that they are not to be held responsible for my opinions any more than I am for theirs. They were chosen not only for their commanding position in the particular art which each of them professes but also for their mature and independent understanding of the present posture of that art, whether they are the victorious strategist or the innocent victim of revolution.

To list all those who have borne with the persistent rehearsal of this book as it grew into its final shape, would be to compile a list of all whom I count friends. I can not, however, forego acknowledging specifically my debt to my professional associate, Jessie Cowin Goldsmith, without whose executive skill at my elbow I would never have undertaken a task of such manifold and exacting personal contacts.

New York City   OLIVER M. SAYLER
September, 1930

CONTENTS

PART ONE
by Oliver M. Sayler

Contents

PART TWO

A Field Survey

Contents

xiii

Contents

PART ONE

by Oliver M. Sayler

I

THE FACT OF REVOLT

In this age of sudden and violent change we are frequently confronted with the necessity of adjusting ourselves to the consequences of an event before we have had fair warning of the event itself. Disturbing as such a technique of living and working might have been to our ancestors, we have so far reconciled ourselves to the apparent inevitability of this regime, that we have schooled ourselves to blink our eyes, promptly make the essential contacts with the new situation and carry on. No sooner have we made our peace with radio and acclimated ourselves to the strange circumstances which it has introduced into our daily round, than we find ourselves face to face with television and the need for further readjustments. In the same way, other inventions, scientific hypotheses, economic theories, popular philosophies, political panaceas and esthetic fads pass in procession, treading on one another's heels, until at times we are tempted to stand aside, assume a bland indifference and wait for the shifting scene to settle down into something stable, ordered, dependable.

But there is no standing aside. We ourselves are organic parts of this enveloping chaos, destined to whirl dizzily with it until modern prophets out of our own ranks detect new and convincing patterns, paths, meanings and motives, new orientations in a world which has lost most if not all of its age-old sign posts. Meanwhile, pending the birth of a new and durably valid philosophy of

3

life, a new and revealing cosmogony, even a new and compelling religion, it behooves each of us for his own peace of mind to plot tentative paths in that portion of the chaos where his lot is cast, and, if those trial paths afford him any security and consolation, to share them with others.

As such a sharing of experience, of working-conclusions, and not as anything dogmatic, final or prophetic, these notes of my own and of my collaborators are directed to no narrowly professional audience. In such a tentative and experimental spirit, I suggest that we agree that *art is anything which the human imagination conceives and the human hand contrives out of words, sounds, colors, forms and material substance to appeal to the human emotions or the human intellect, or both, in such a way as to reproduce in the auditor or spectator an emotional or mental state, or both, similar to that which the artist himself experienced.*

Unlike most previous revolutions in the arts, the present upheaval is no mere tempest in a studio teapot. Its ramifications are well-nigh universal. Few, in fact, are fully aware of the fact that few are immune from the consequences of this revolt, so intrenched is the traditional idea that art has little to do with the general run of mankind. Most of us are still laboring under the inherited impression that art is all very well for those who have the time, the skill or the resources to create it or appreciate it, but that after all it is a luxury. But, like so many other luxuries of our fathers and grandfathers, art has become our necessity. Through the distributive agencies of our Machine Age, it has so insinuated itself into the remotest recesses of our daily lives that it is more indispensable to us than religion, politics or sport and second only to the fundamental requirements of food, shelter and sex.

If anyone doubts these sweeping statements, let him stop to consider the professions, crafts, industries and trades whose members are habitually in contact with the creation and the distribution of the several arts in America today, in addition to the millions who, as looking, listening and reading audience, are engaged in the process of appreciation. Even if complete statistics were available or approximately calculable, they would bewilder rather than clarify an attempt to comprehend the extensive and intensive significance of the arts in our daily life. Rather, let us consider what occupations would be affected if the arts were suddenly to disappear from life, pushing our inquiry into more or less remote detail in one of the arts and sketching the rest in the large.

If we select the theatre for detailed examination, we see at a glance that occupations directly involved include playwrights, actors, scene designers and painters, carpenters, producers, stage directors, house managers, electricians, stage hands, architects, legal staffs and press representatives. But that is not all. Indirectly, but hard by around the corner, are many more. Play brokers and their staffs and play readers enter the list on the heels of the playwright. Costumers, and makers and dealers in wigs and cosmetics attend the actor. Manufacturers and salesmen of paint, brushes, drawing paper and canvas are the attendants of the scene designer. Beholden to the carpenter are lumber dealers, saw mills, loggers and wood cutters, hardware makers and dealers, trucking corporations and chauffeurs. Satellites of the house manager include box office treasurers, bank tellers, ushers, charwomen and ticket agencies. The electrician accounts for glass blowers and lamp makers, fixture and wire manufacturers, copper miners and, behind them all, the research scientist in illuminating engineering. Outside the door of the architect and builder await the engineer, the draftsman, the contractor, the wrecking expert, the pneumatic

5

driller, the structural steel worker, the steel millhand, the iron and coal miner, the mason and bricklayer, the plasterer, the upholsterer, the ventilation authority and all of the scores of trades and crafts associated with the building industry. Important on the legal staff is the tax expert. And finally, among the manifold communicants of the press department are printers, publishers, lithographers, photographers, photo-engravers; magazine and newspaper dramatic staffs, compositors, proofreaders and pressmen; telegraph and cable companies and the Post Office Department of the United States Government. In addition, as long as a remnant of "the road" is left, the railroads, including both the passenger and baggage departments, share with all these other industries and occupations a vital interest in the health and vigor of the art of the theatre.

With a far larger audience, the cinema repeats most if not all of the theatre's innumerable collaborators, adding still others characteristic of this art alone, while the dance shares, too, on a greatly restricted scale.

Music, on the other hand, besides counting an audience in tens of millions, is justified in listing not only composers and professional performers, vocal and instrumental, and managers and their staffs, but also the personnel of the nation's radio broadcasting stations and the manufacturers and distributors of phonograph instruments and records, player pianos and rolls, and radio receiving apparatus.

Considering only those directly implicated, the art of literature accounts for authors, publishers, booksellers, librarians and readers; while painting and sculpture suggest numerous subsidiary crafts and trades.

Architecture engages the active interest of an incredible figure

6

until we stop to consider that not merely the architect but the entire range of the building trades as well as the millions of tenants of more or less significant buildings whose lives are molded by the structures they inhabit, are daily influenced by the architect's original dream to the extent to which he has been able to realize it.

And finally the craft arts cap the structure with almost our entire adult population, including designers, manufacturers, merchants and users, an overwhelming testimonial in itself to the universality of art in America today.

Here is proof prompt and irrefutable that vast numbers of our adult population are concerned simultaneously with more than one of the arts. Here is proof, too, that, while we as a people may not yet be art-conscious, in the terminology of the social engineers, we are already art-susceptible and art-involved. For a country widely reputed to know little, care less and do still less about art, America is a strange case either of smoke without fire or of fire so unprecedented in hue and heat that observers with traditional instruments have been unable to detect, measure or understand it.

Perhaps it is this lack of consciousness of what the arts already mean to us which has delayed a general realization of how revolt is running rife among them and how the implications of this revolt penetrate and help to illuminate some of the most stubborn problems which confront us today.

Of course, if there were a modern Temple of Janus to serve as symbol of peace or insurrection in the arts, its doors would probably never have been closed within our time, certainly never since the dawn of the Twentieth Century. It was about then that the "isms" of esthetic unrest began to reach us from Europe to ruffle the complacency of the Mauve Decade—realism and naturalism in literature, impressionism in painting and music, symbolism in poetry and drama. But, for the most part, these were family spats to which the vast mass of the public was indifferent after fad interest waned. As the century wore on, futurism, cubism and vorticism kept the painters under arms in their esthetic trenches. Free verse and imagism split the poets into bitterly rival camps. Jazz vied with neo-classicism to harry the slumbers of conventional music. The skyscraper, that upstart coxcomb of the gay nineties, pushed onward and upward. Expressionism and constructivism undermined the security of the well-made play after it had successfully adapted itself to realism; and the new movement in the theatre left us wondering whether scenery is the most important element in that art or a factor beneath contempt.

Meanwhile, as foretaste of the sweeping economic convulsions of our own time, the theatre was called upon to defend itself against the mutiny of the motion picture, while the performing musician had to meet the competition of the phonograph and the player-piano. That both the theatre and music survived the struggle with these rivals and came back stronger than ever, should encourage the machine-beleaguered defenders of the same and other artistic citadels today in the new and even more ruthless struggle in which they are involved.

In view of the almost continuous nature of these esthetic forays and because armistice or peace-without-victory rather than decisive conquest prevailed between the theatre and the cinema, between produced and reproduced music, it is perhaps natural that the omens of a new, universal and catastrophic revolution in the arts should have been generally disregarded. Even yet there may be some who believe that they can maintain a complacent neutrality. But as the struggle reaches its climax and the conference table looms in the offing, the right to participate in the negotiations is likely to outbid the advantages of neutrality.

It was during Christmas week, 1929, that this new revolt began to be frankly recognized as inevitable if not already in existence. Omens there had been for a year or more, omens which a more leisurely civilization would have heeded. But then a more leisurely civilization would never have bred them. Born of an age of engrossing intensity, they attracted attention only in their own limited spheres, like new tenants in an apartment house, with no one to correlate them and reveal their cumulative significance. Most of these omens were preponderantly economic. If esthetic, they partook of the mechanical and technical side of esthetics rather than the spiritual, thus verging toward the economic. And economic omens are much more ominous than esthetic, just because they are more imperative and more comprehensive in their implications. They grip life, all life, at its primitive core. They will not be gainsaid.

In the theatre, for example, "the road" had been shrivelling for a decade. The competitive pastime of the automobile had conspired with mounting production, operation, transportation and exploitation costs in the theatre itself to close the playhouses across the continent, one by one and community by community, leaving the spoken drama successfully on the defensive in four major oases— New York, Chicago, Philadelphia and Boston. Exceptional players like Ethel Barrymore and George Arliss, exceptional productions like "The Miracle" and the Ziegfeld "Follies," exceptional plays like "Journey's End" and "Strange Interlude," merely proved the rule of an ever-contracting field for operation.

Within the year, civil war had broken out in the cinema. The parent silent film, grown complacent with easily-won wealth, suddenly found itself banished to suburban and rural stages by its hoarse-voiced, lisping offspring, the sound film, only to have to retreat still further, before the year was out, to the fire-proof vaults of the warehouse, leaving millions of dollars' worth of equipment valueless and terminating the careers of hundreds of artists in mid-air.

About the same time, so unobtrusively that few awoke to its potentialities, the concert dance became something more than a sporadic novelty and gained a permanent foothold on our stage, utilizing theatres darkened for Sunday evenings and pointing the way to a genuine native American Ballet.

Music, still recuperating from the rivalry of the earliest reproductive mechanisms, had short shrift before girding to withstand the growing competition of a new machine, the radio, a machine more flexibly reproductive and with incredibly broader distributive faculties than its predecessors. Concurrently, the growing pains of the opera, physical and economic as well as esthetic, found ready record in a press chronically suspicious of society intrigues whenever this form of musical expression is mentioned.

The art of letters, too, contributed its omen of revolt, an omen brazenly economic, for no topic in the book world in years remotely approached in controversial bitterness the arguments for and against the book clubs. Holding the front pages of the newspapers for a few days, however, this controversy soon receded from public view, leaving the impression that it was a technical and professional affair without general purport.

The painter and the sculptor, long-suffering victims of specious curiosity ever since Duchamp's "Nude Descending a Staircase," Chabas' "September Morn" and Brancusi's "Bird in Space," enjoyed respite of temporary oblivion, but the architect became whipping-boy for the plastic arts in the factitious race for height on the part of publicity-crazed builders.

Unrest, confusion, chaos. Intrusion of new factors, new forces, new inventions, new points of view. Expansion of the ranks of appreciation at certain points, contraction at others, but enormous expansion in grand total. A few traditional channels of distribution rendered obsolete, sterile; many others taxed far beyond their normal capacity. The demand for creation at a standstill, even retrogressive in more than one of the arts. In other words, a vastly larger audience served through an inept and makeshift system of distribution by a bewildered and shrinking staff of creative artists.

This is the inevitable conclusion which anyone must have reached who took the trouble to survey the entire field of the arts as a unit. As specialists, however, we are not prone to the making of broad surveys. Preoccupied with our own profession, or even our subdivision of a profession, we seldom have time to look beyond its limits. So with the arts. And if, as audience, we are patrons of more than one of the arts, the same process of preoccupation leaves us scant time to analyze our experiences and observations and draw conclusions from them.

An extraordinary jolt was necessary, therefore, to provide the premises for a broad inductive judgment. One art had to reach across its natural boundary and deliver another art a body blow to remind us that the arts, after all, are intricately interrelated; that they spring from a common inspirational source; that, apart from strictly occupational and technical considerations, they serve similar ends in life; and that whatever happens to one of them is happening or may happen to the rest.

Such a jolt, bewildering at first and then clarifying, was the frontal attack of the new sound film against the dramatic stage. Whether this assault was deliberate or unintentional need not bother us at this juncture; the effect on the theatre was the same. Staving off admission of these effects through the fall of 1929 and blaming the theatre's traditional rivals for unprecedentedly bad business, the dramatic stage had to confess the efficacy of this new competitor when, during Christmas week, 1929, the time-honored annual high-water mark of theatrical attendance, twenty-nine theatres on Broadway were "dark." If safe and secure calculations like this were no longer to be relied upon, perhaps other axioms, other accepted relationships, were in similar danger. Beset with confusions and harsh readjustments of its own, each of the arts had been conscious only of its own problems. Was it possible that other arts had similar problems, the same problems? Could anything be learned by comparing notes, by trading experiences? Might the locked horns of the sound film and the dramatic stage be repeated between two other arts? What other surprises had the Machine Age in store for the arts? What, after all, is the function of the arts in a Machine Age? How can that function be most satisfactorily fulfilled?

Once the arts were started on mutual interrogation, the questions have unrolled like the cross-examination of a Senatorial Investigation Committee. Little by little a map of general chaos in the arts has been plotted, replacing those of isolated sectors. By and large, it corresponds with my survey a moment ago of "unrest, confusion, chaos." But map reading is another and more exacting art than map making. Too hasty conclusions are likely to be sensational and misleading. We must feel our way calmly, patiently, dispassionately, with all of the experience, insight and mutual respect at our command. Successful orientation in esthetic chaos depends on determining fixed points of reference, just as surely as it does in geography or astronomy. Satisfactorily as the map reader may have oriented himself in an individual art—and no one has any right today to be too proud of his achievement even in so limited a field—he will find old fixed points of reference inadequate in the larger field. New ones must be sought and agreed upon. And, when found and acknowledged, they are altogether likely to invalidate many of the old fixed points of reference in the smaller fields even for local use in those fields.

Tentative as the new fixed points of reference in the field of the arts as a whole may be and subject to more accurate placement, as study, experience and use perfect our first rough calculations, I am convinced that they indicate such a speeding up of evolutionary processes as to justify the employment of the term "revolutionary." In other words, what seems at a glance like mere chaos is in reality a vast, overwhelming readjustment of values, involving not alone the arts as such but our whole understanding and conception of life. If this indeed be revolt and not just aimless confusion, it is our duty and privilege to study and acquaint ourselves with its nature, its extent, its causes and its implications, in order that we may control it and direct its unseen and incommensurable forces toward humanly desirable ends.

II

THE NATURE OF REVOLT

THREE types of revolt engage our attention—esthetic, economic and moral. The general character of the first two is self-evident. By moral revolt, I understand the protest against external censorship in behalf of literature, the cinema, the theatre and, more rarely, painting, sculpture and the dance in order to preserve their freedom of expression. We are dealing primarily, therefore, with revolt *in* the arts, *within* the arts, especially in the first two types, although all vital art, of course, is a protest, a battle-cry, against human lethargy, indifference and ignorance, a summons to sentiment and significant living.

It will help us, I think, to understand these three types of revolt if we allocate to each of them one of the three phases of the artistic process—creation, distribution and appreciation. Such an allocation will not be exclusive, but it will recognize preponderant interests and responsibilities. Let us assume, then, that Esthetic Revolt is the Problem of Creation; Economic Revolt, the Problem of Distribution; and Moral Revolt, the Problem of Appreciation.

If we apply this classification literally and rigidly, it would appear that, with the exception of moral revolt, assigned to the audience or general public, the revolution in the arts is an intramural problem, a question of professional readjustment only remotely concerning the public at large. But that is an utterly false assumption. Just as the three phases of the artistic process are organically interrelated, so their several problems are inextricably interwoven and significant to the public as well as to the artist.

1. Esthetic Revolt, the Problem of Creation

Esthetic revolt is one of the most familiar and time-honored phenomena in the history of the arts of civilized man. Its perennial character and its tendency to recur in cycles have been vividly described by Henry Hazlitt, literary editor of *The Nation,* in his contribution, "Humanism and Value," to the symposium, "The Critique of Humanism," edited by C. Hartley Grattan:

"Just as a period of traditionalism is succeeded by one of revolt, so revolt in turn is succeeded by revolt from revolt, i. e., by another wave of traditionalism. . . . Behind this endless see-saw are two main causes. Either traditionalism or revolt, when it reaches a high point, tends to discredit itself by its own excesses. And even if it does not, critics tire of the old theories and the old gods, and want new theories and new gods, if only for the sake of something fresh to talk about."

I can not agree with Hazlitt, however, that we are now on the threshold of a wave of traditionalism, or, as I prefer to call it, a wave of counter-revolution. Esthetic revolt, it seems to me, has merely paused here and there to take breath for a further advance, to adjust positions which have gotten out of line, to reduce the stubborn resistance of certain outposts of defensive traditionalism which have suddenly cropped up under a mask of counter-attack, and, possibly, to replace leaders whose freshness and flexibility in attack have gone stale. I can conceive, as Hazlitt does, of shouts of down with Mencken, down with Dreiser, down with Lewis, down with Cabell, without necessarily tracing these shouts exclusively to Professors Babbitt and More and their callow and spineless protégés. A revolutionary army sometimes moves faster than its leaders, sometimes casts them off whimsically and without just cause. Witness Trotsky in Russia; Mirabeau, Marat, Danton and Robespierre in France.

Esthetic revolt in the arts will not have run its course and gone to seed, will not have committed those excesses which render it defenseless against counter-revolution, until all the arts have extended their conquests more equally; until they have recognized, as they do not yet recognize, the fact that their separate campaigns are directed to a common goal which, united, they are bound to achieve before their day's work is done; until contemporary life itself, whose interpreters and prophets they are, ceases its revolutionary readjustment and resolves its chaos into a new order. For esthetic revolt is the concomitant of social revolt, just as esthetic traditionalism is the companion of social order.

As a perennial visitor in human affairs, esthetic revolt and its recurring cycles could be made to tell the entire story of civilized mankind, for the cycles have coincided with the cycles of revolt in life and thought. The golden age of Greek tragedy, a revolt against the meager and primitive traditions which preceded it, paralleled the burgeoning of Athens from a provincial city-state to a world power. Enduring nearly a century, it disclosed a succession of leaders in Aeschylus, Sophocles and Euripides, each related organically to the revolt and to the changing political and social scene. Though differing greatly from one another, they provided the possibility of a long-continued period of varied but essentially homogeneous esthetic revolt under a changing leadership.

Other cycles of revolution and counter-revolution, coincidentally esthetic and political or social, ensued in classic and medieval times.

And then came the Renaissance with its simultaneous revolt of life and art against the dead traditionalism of the Schoolmen. For two centuries, under leadership bewildering in its intensity, variety and fundamental homogeneity, the fires of this revolt burned in one corner of Europe or another.

What I am getting at in stressing the duration of the esthetic revolt in Athens in the Fifth Century B.C. and that of the Renaissance is a precedent for belief that our contemporary revolution in the arts, instead of rapidly nearing the end of its cycle, as the new Humanists and even the more timid of their opponents seem to believe, is really only on the threshold of an unsuspected and almost incredible career. Unless we keep these two periods clearly in mind, we are likely to be misled by the rapidly successive cycles of revolt and counter-revolt of the last hundred and fifty years and take it for granted that our own is destined for the same short and fitful existence.

These brief cycles, it seems to me, were only the rehearsals for the present age of revolt, clearing the ground step by step for its unimpeded progress. Eighteenth Century classicism, the romanticism which rose in mutiny against it, the decay of romanticism into an arbitrary routine against which realism was the healthy protest, were all the short-lived children of a century and a half which vacillated, seldom knew its own mind and got off to several false starts socially, economically, politically—and of course esthetically. Feudal and imperial Europe received a mortal blow in the French Revolution, but the dying agonies were protracted by deceptive convalescences through the Nineteenth Century and required the World War and the Russian Revolution to deal them the *coup de grace.* Discovery and invention inaugurated the Machine Age with the steam engine but permitted it to develop at a leisurely and

halting pace before arming man with electricity and giant power
to accelerate that pace beyond the wildest dreams of prophet and
visionary. Science disturbed a complacent religion, threatened to
displace it as a guide to the understanding of human destiny, and
frightened it into a drastic and temporarily successful revision of
its tenets. Latterly, however, science, the first to admit its help-
lessness in trying alone to solve the riddle of the universe, has
seen its ancient enemy fade away as a dominant force in modern
life, almost without a struggle and largely by abdication.

It would appear, therefore, that, politically, economically, mechanically and philosophically, mankind has eliminated most of
the traditional barriers to unrestricted inductive progress for which
it will need the arts in sustained esthetic revolt as interpreters.
Rehearsals are over; the play begins.

Esthetic revolt, roughly speaking, is equally concerned with
both of the two main subdivisions of the creative process in the
arts—content and form. What the artist chooses to say, and how
he chooses to say it. What the public wishes and permits him to
say, and how it wishes and permits him to say it. For both of
these functions—the "what" and the "how"—there has always
existed a more or less flexible repertory from which the artist can
choose, and a more or less imperative repertory of tabus. The accepted content and form of one epoch may fall under the ban of
the next, and vice versa.

Since the characteristic gestures of the chaotic, machine-ridden
age in which we live are an extreme busyness, a frantic running
round in circles, punctuated by rare moments of self-questioning
or importunate reaching for the unattainable, it is only natural
that our arts partake freely of these gestures. Esthetic revolt directs
itself against the last remaining barriers and tabus of a conserva-

tive tradition. The mere presence of a barrier, no matter what its importance, is reason for upsetting it to see what is on the other side. The walls around the unmentionable are assaulted, not only for the enlargement of the repertory of sense stimuli but for the mere sake of assault. If certain facts, impressions and stimuli prove on conquest to be unworthy of the cost of the assault, and if they are thereupon abandoned, that is no reason to suspect that esthetic revolt is slacking its pace but rather that, with all its headlong character, it retains a sense of discrimination, a sound, if hasty and approximate, measuring stick for determining values.

As with content, so with form. The entire repertory of physical phenomena, those accepted by convention as well as those under traditional ban, is claimed by the artist for use at will. Owing to the highly formal connotations of the Machine Age, it is spiritually as well as physically in keeping for the artist who interprets that age to be absorbed in trying out new patterns, new mechanisms, new sense-languages, new arrangements and applications of old patterns, mechanisms and communicative media. Tabus in the realm of form have seldom been as sacrosanct as in that of content, although they have ruled entire generations of poets and play-wrights, novelists and painters and composers. Woe betide the poet in Racine's France who dared use anything but the Alexandrine! Witness the obloquy heaped upon Wagner for tampering with the musical conventions of the mid-Nineteenth Century! Rare courage was required throughout Europe to overstep the regulations of the "well-made play."

Our age has taken particular delight in exploring all of the proscribed physical phenomena for conveying sense impressions and in pressing into immediate service the new media discovered or suggested by science and the machine. Here, too, we should not be thrown off the track by the fitful rejection of once-favored forms or antitheses of forms. There should be no solace to reactionaries in such repudiation and in the subsequent return to less extravagant forms, for here, too, as in content, it is a case of trial and error with the urge toward a richer and more varied freedom still unquenched. Form, after all, stands or falls on its communicative utility. A form which requires a key is already weighted for descent into oblivion.

On the positive side, esthetic revolt today is directed toward the absorption and interpretation of every skein and every crumb of our tangled and chaotic existence. Nothing in life is too great or too small to escape this consuming curiosity. The arts challenge the infinite in both directions, just as science does, and life spurred by science—particularly the infinitely important and the infinitely insignificant within the human consciousness and subconsciousness.

2. *Economic Revolt, the Problem of Distribution*

Economic revolt in the arts, on the contrary, is so new, so without previous parallel, that we have never yet fully understood or thoroughly appraised either the economic factor itself nor the revolt which disturbs its smooth and orderly procedure, not to mention its interrelated bearings on the other types of revolt.

In making that broad assertion, I am not unmindful of the economic aspects of past civilizations which have conditioned their esthetic creation directly or indirectly. To the slave economy of ancient Egypt and classic Greece is undoubtedly attributable the leisure of their upper classes which fostered the golden ages of their arts. The unpaid labor of the bondsman was the only limitless dynamic reserve in human history comparable to the modern machine. To the craft guilds of the Middle Ages, with their rigid subdivision of labor and their chain systems of buying and selling, like the Hanseatic League, we may trace the homely and realistic character of the arts and crafts of the time. And to the wealthy patron of the Renaissance, whether he was courtier, King, Emperor, Pope or merchant prince, we owe the glories of its artistic achievement almost as much as to the artists themselves. In other words, the arts of the past have been aware of economics, often singularly and intimately aware. But until our own day, they have never had an economics of their own.

That the arts have such an independent economic structure today is one of the distinctive phenomena of the Machine Age. Whether it is to be deemed a blessing or a burden, an asset or a liability, will depend on whether we choose to look upon the arts as the precious possession of the few or the common property of the many. Regardless of which of these two views we may prefer as an ideal, we are confronted by the fact of the latter; and if we wish to restore and preserve the peculiar virtues of possession by the few, we shall have to contrive this restitution by arrangement with the regnant mass economics.

It would lead us too far afield into general social, cultural and economic history to trace in detail the processes whereby the arts, like so many of the other luxuries of our forebears, became the present necessities of the masses. In brief, the transformation is due to the liberation of the masses which has come in the wake of the machine. When we think of the machine as an engine of impoverishment, stealing from us the casual leisure our forefathers enjoyed, we are taking into account only the privileged classes. The average man and woman of today have both more time and more money to spend than they ever had before in history. And, as we have seen, they are freely spending both upon the arts, whether or not they consciously apply that term to the object of their quest.

A separate and independent economics of the arts has sprung into existence, therefore, in answer to an insistent demand. Mass appreciation calls for mass distribution. The artist can no longer maintain the traditional personal contact with his patron, his audience. The middleman becomes an increasing necessity. The business of bringing artist and patron together, of bridging the gap between them, of serving both, each according to his own needs, grows by leaps and bounds, enlisting thousands and tens of thousands in the pursuit of an essentially new profession. This new calling presents great opportunities and greater responsibilities, both directly traceable to the profession and the public which it serves and the commodity in which it deals.

Contradictory elements enter into the successful pursuit of this new calling. Inevitably, it is a business, owing to the often enormous amount of the capital investment. Theatres, opera houses, concert halls, exhibition galleries and museums; theatrical, lyric and cinema productions all require heavy underwriting. The builder, serving as middleman for the architect, must be prepared for an outlay of millions in materials and labor. The publisher's investment is small for a single book, but not inconsiderable for scores and hundreds of books over a year's time. Whether these various projects are profit-making enterprises or maintained at public or private cost with no profit expected and even a deficit taken for granted, they must be administered soundly according to at least the primary tenets of good business if they are to persist and achieve their purposes. Executive skill must be employed and economic laws must be respected, or they will end in fiasco.

Inevitably, too, the business of the distribution of the arts is partly a gamble. So is all business, but that of the arts more so than the average. The whims of public taste are more volatile here than elsewhere. The productive reserves of the artist are less calculable than the ore reserves of a copper mine or the life tenure of a machine. Furthermore, the potential profits and losses compared with the original investment resemble the ratio under which the gambler operates rather than that of general business.

Ideally, at least, the business of artistic distribution also partakes of a cultural profession. There is something that marks off transactions in the arts from the buying and selling of stocks and bonds, of cars and cabbages, something that consciously or subconsciously influences those who are engaged in such transactions. Men of culture often flaunt the dignity of that culture in their shops and offices, using it as an excuse for failure to keep up with the times. Upstarts and illiterates, attracted by the opportunities of this new calling, are overawed by their new surroundings and assume the extravagant trappings of a culture they do not possess.

In like manner, this calling involves social responsibility, a fact which has hardly begun to dawn upon the vast majority of those who have enrolled in it. If the arts are to serve as the interpreters of life, those who stand between the producers and the consumers of art are in a strategic position to stimulate and control both the supply and the demand. That we are barely on the threshold of fulfilling this responsibility is proof alone that economic revolt in the arts is just as far, and farther, from running its course than esthetic revolt.

We have, in this latter point, a striking hint as to the fundamental difference between economic and esthetic revolt. The latter, as we have seen, with an age-old history, consists largely of protest against inhibitions. Economic revolt, on the other hand, has practically no inhibitions or traditions to bar its way. Its task is to conquer chaos and to build new roads through uncharted territory. Paradoxical as the elements of efficient distribution of the arts may seem, they can and must be fused into an entity before the arts can hope to fulfill their potential service to mankind. If any one of these paradoxical elements receives undue emphasis, the profession of distribution falls short of this potentiality. If too little attention to business tenets makes for instability, too much attention incurs risk of exploitation. If over-indulgence in the gambling element tends to make the arts a sportsman's foot-ball, indifference to the element of risk will leave many of the most thrilling and stimulating opportunities still-born. If the dead hand of a superior culture can stifle a virile and healthy art, the false glitter of a pretentious culture can give us art that is specious and mawkish. And finally, if over-zealous social responsibility tends to the dangerous emphasis of art as propaganda, social irresponsibility saps the virile energies of the arts and leaves them a prey to the more violent forms of moral censorship.

We have heard a great deal during the past year about art in industry. That is one of the logical fruits of our realization of the importance of the arts in contemporary life. But we should not confuse that popular slogan with the implications of art as industry. Art as industry is irrevocably related to general economics. The industry of the arts yields to the same broad stimuli which expand or depress industry in general. In so far as the arts are still a luxury, they are likely to yield first to depressing stimuli and last to those which are favorable, although, as we have seen, the arts are becoming more and more the necessities of civilized man.

Apart from the higher ethical code which follows logically from the cultural and social responsibilities of the profession of artistic distribution, the economics of this calling differs from general economics most strikingly, it seems to me, in the growing recognition of endowment and subsidy as a legitimate policy. Endowment and subsidy are not unknown to general economics, but they usually appear as temporary expedients to foster desirable infant industries. In the arts, however, we are gradually coming to the comprehension and natural acceptance of endowment as a permanent process. Understanding and acceptance of endowment has been delayed by the false assumption that it is the artist who is being endowed; and a realistic philosophy quite rightly contends that to endow the artist frequently enervates him. It has remained for Eva Le Gallienne with her Civic Repertory Theatre, operated with practical capacity at a deficit of one hundred thousand dollars annually, to awaken us to the fact that endowment need not endow and therefore debilitate the artist but endow the public, leaving the difference between the purchase price of art and its cost of production in the pocket of the purchaser. All unawares, this theory of endowment has been practiced for years with our public libraries, our art museums and our symphony orchestras; but, now that it is seen in its true light, its application is likely to be extended far more widely, not only in the theatre but in all of the other arts.

Art as industry is a concept which has made variable progress in the several arts. Acutely recognized in the theatre, its growing pains find expression in such an odd lot of specific problems as theatre ticket prices, over-supply of theatres, prohibitive ground rents, excessive production costs, contractual difficulties with the actors and the stage hands, and exorbitant transportation rates. The keen realization of the pressing nature of these multiple problems is half of the battle toward their solution.

With clear eye the cinema sees and therefore half-solves many of these same problems, problems less ominous on the whole than for the theatre. But the mushroom growth of its economic structure, the insignificant cultural foundation of many of its leaders and the wide spread between its social opportunity and its social achievement tend to discount its success in solving its specific economic problems and leave it far from efficiency and stability in its distributive function. Music is an economic house divided against itself, but a house with a good record for patching up misunderstandings and with a high and alert idealism withal. Of the old established arts, with a modest and compact economic structure dating to modest beginnings far back of the Machine Age, literature has made perhaps the least progress in bringing its economics abreast of the times. A "gentleman's" calling, it has only itself to blame for deferring house-cleaning until the intrusion of the book clubs and "dollar books" ripped off the mask of its complacency and gave it the embarrassing task of reforming its domestic affairs in public view. As for the other arts, the dance, painting and sculpture, architecture and the craft arts, their independent economics are still so rudimentary that the terminus of their reconstruction lies in an indefinite future.

3. Moral Revolt, the Problem of Appreciation

Before we attempt to sketch the backgrounds of moral revolt, it will be well for us to understand just what we mean by revolt in this connection. Since the two sides of the struggle for and against censorship are so evenly matched, with the tide of battle now swinging in one direction, now in the other, it is difficult at first to detect who is revolting and who is defending. My personal sympathies are probably revealed in my choice of the term revolt for those who are attacking categorical control of the arts and that of counter-revolt for the proponents of censorship. At the moment, the latter are creating more sound and fury than the former and might appear to the unguarded judgment as the side in revolt against the freedom and laxity which many of the arts have managed to appropriate for themselves amid the confusion of the war years and after. The point of view of these counter-revolutionists, however, is negative, repressive and traditional in character and therefore at cross purposes with the forward-looking forces of esthetic creation and distribution, so that I prefer to consider the opponents of censorship as the blood-brothers in revolution of creative artists who are tilting at convention and the pioneers of artistic distribution who are plotting paths through the wilderness.

It is a singular fact that, while moral revolt most directly benefits the creative artist, keeping horizons clear of meddling impediments, the burden of supporting it and keeping its defenses intact against counter-revolution rests on the general public. The artist himself, of course, can shoulder this burden. When the public relaxes its vigilance and becomes indifferent, he sometimes has to do so or retreat before the advancing restrictions of bigotry. But it should not be his task. He is ill-equipped to perform it, for he is expert in expressive media far removed from that of logic and ethical pleading; and, appearing in his own defense, he is all too likely to descend to emotional excuses which only damage his case.

Opposition to reaction at the hands of the general public, however, is not a safeguard on which we can depend with assurance. In a century and a half of democratic government, we have learned all too painfully that the mass mind moves slowly, that it tolerates inconvenience and imposition with a supine patience, that it has to accumulate righteous wrath slowly before it will take overt action, and that, in the meantime, it suffers various busybodies to think and speak and act in its name. For years, the American public permitted a piratical minority of brewers and saloon-keepers to direct its sumptuary legislation. Then, becoming disgruntled at the high-handed impudence of this minority, it bestowed its proxy for managing the same sumptuary affairs on the equally high-handed and equally impudent minority of the professional prohibitionists. Finally, after nearly half a century of abdication in favor of minority rule, the American public seems to be taking the matter into its own hands.

As long as the arts were looked upon as the pastime and the luxury of the few, the public, apathetic to their importance and universal significance, could not be expected to disturb itself greatly over the domestic affairs of the arts. Now that it is becoming slowly aware of the enormous potential importance of the arts in the daily life of everyone in the body politic, it will probably bestir itself a little more, but another generation or two may be required before we can trust this public to think and act for itself on artistic problems.

Meanwhile, such questions as moral standards in the arts and the various forms of censorship for the protection of those standards have been and still are delegated to minorities. If we were quite as logical as we pretend to be, we should not be as shocked as we are at the political dictatorship of the proletariat in Russia, for we in America are living today under an esthetic dictatorship of an even smaller minority. As a matter of fact, we are living under a shifting esthetic régime which is the resultant of two diametrically opposed minority groups who serve as a check and balance on each other, with now one, now the other, gaining the upper hand. One of these dictatorial minorities consists of the bitter, self-righteous and austere standard-bearers of Puritan intolerance, to whom all of the arts, except as moral propaganda, are anathema. The mere fact that man finds pleasure in them is sufficient to suspect and condemn them. That this minority does not dare any longer to urge the complete application of its program of suppression is due not so much to the whittling away of its ranks and the growing indifference of the younger generation to its fulminations, as it is to the presence of another alert and powerful minority. This second minority, composed more of immigrants and sons and daughters of immigrants from an esthetically freer Europe than it is of the offspring of pioneer Anglo-Saxon blood, tends to the other extreme of utter libertarianism. Between the two policies of no art at all and that of complete *laissez-faire,* what art we have produced has managed to slip through.

The fact that moral counter-revolution is displaying an unwonted and unexpected vitality at a time when esthetic and economic revolt are scoring enormous gains is an interesting phenomenon. We have always had this form of counter-revolution in America. Waldo Frank, Everett Dean Martin and others have probably rightly traced its source to the fact that the founders of American civilization escaped most of the beneficent esthetic emancipations of the Renaissance by their early flight from Europe, freighted only with the sombre teachings of the Reformation. The present flare-up of intolerance is probably due to three causes. The minority guardians of a free art, acting in the name of a lethargic public which, I am convinced, is in truer sympathy with them than with their opponents, have probably grown slack in watchfulness, thinking the battle for tolerance practically won. In the second place, individual creative artists and over-zealous distributors of their products have probably, here and there, overstepped the privileges of freedom. Flamingly immoral today by the most liberal standards, they may be serenely moral tomorrow, for morality has been proved a fickle jade by the researches of modern science. But their unconventional performances have been startling enough to call the hounds of censorship to their heels. Neither of these explanations, however, seems to me so pertinent as the probability that intolerance, challenged all along the line, is making a last determined stand against a new and freer generation.

While sex censorship is probably the one of which we hear most often, it is not the only stricture against which the artist has to contend and which the public or its spokesmen must oppose in his name. Sex censorship has rallied more defenders and aroused larger attacking hosts, not only because of the dominant place of sex in life, but also because lingering intolerance on that subject on the part of those who are otherwise liberal-minded has stimulated equally determined revolt on the part of those who believe that compromise on this score endangers freedom in other respects. In the furor over sex censorship, however, we should not forget that the artist can be just as seriously enslaved by a bigoted and intolerant religious, economic, social and narrowly national censorship.

The evils of censorship and the corresponding advantages to the arts, as well as to life in general, of free and tolerant moral standards have been so fully elucidated in recent volumes by Morris L. Ernst, Everett Dean Martin, H. I. Brock, Leo Markun, and others, that I do not feel justified in dwelling too long on them here. The important point which I have tried to establish is the responsibility of the public rather than of the artist for creating and maintaining an atmosphere conducive to creative freedom for the arts as interpreters of life. It is probably sufficient here to recall the absurd temporal, geographical and functional relativity of moral standards and the inequality of the censorships set up to defend them; the hypocrisy, the opportunities for graft, and the premium on parasitic bureaucracy which naturally follow in the trail of that relativity and inequality; the tendency of censorship, if given an inch, to take a mile; and the unseen threat of censorship which stifles bold and perhaps invaluable concepts at their source in the imagination of the artist.

All these dangers, and many others naturally attendant upon them, threaten the very life of the revolt of the arts in America in their attempt to understand, interpret, and resolve the chaos under which we live. Sometimes I think that successful opposition to these threats is more important than the further immediate progress of esthetic revolt and economic reconstruction, for they stand like stretched wires across the road of progress, often invisible like such wires. In their book, "Censored, the Private Life of the Movies," Ernst and Lorentz have plausibly absolved the executives, directors, authors and actors of the screen from most of the responsibility for the snail-like progress of the film out of the nursery into an adult art, and have convincingly laid the burden of that responsibility at the doors of the censorship. Battening for years on their prerogatives in the motion pictures and drunk with the power which they have arrogated to themselves in that art, the censors are all too likely to preempt the control of that new art which looms on the horizon, television, unless a vigorous frontal attack is made upon them.

Next to the cinema, the most censor-ridden of the arts are the theatre and literature. It is perhaps only natural that these three customarily representational arts should be singled out by the intolerant as the chief targets for their heavy guns, for censorship is almost exclusively concerned with content rather than with form, and with realistic content. The expressionistic and presentational are either beyond the censor's mental and emotional grasp or he thinks they are beyond the danger of harming the public for whom he is so solicitous. Almost every season the guardians of artistic freedom in New York and elsewhere have to repel all over again the threats of a censorship of the theatre and a so-called "clean books" law, besides conducting the defense of books and plays haled into court by those who would lose their jobs if they found nothing in contemporary literature or on the current stage to arouse their suspicion and shock their liberally rewarded sensibilities. Of the two, the theatre is harried probably more than literature, for it is a notoriously inconsistent fact that the unexpurgated acting versions of plays ridden out of town on a rail continue on sale unmolested in the book stores.

Modern athletic sports have done as much as anything else to relieve the dance of the snooping interference with the undraped body to which it was subject not so long ago. And painting and sculpture ceased to interest the censor the moment their unrealistic technique passed beyond his realistic comprehension. The craft arts and architecture, of course, are ethically and morally apathetic. I have no doubt, though, that impassioned music is just as reprehensible as erotic literature and drama to the congenitally or professionally censorious, but how could they frame a case to which a jury would listen seriously?

4. *The Types of Revolt Interrelated*

It is theoretically possible, in some of the arts at least, to conceive of creation without appreciation—of a dancer dancing, of a composer writing music or a performer singing or playing, of an author writing, of a painter or sculptor executing his canvas or his statue, just for himself. But the arts would never have developed into a vital and indispensable function of human life if they had been thus restricted. Creation needs appreciation, not only for material but for spiritual reasons.

It is theoretically possible, also, to conceive of creation and appreciation without the mediation of distribution. The dancer by her own arrangement can dance for an audience of one or more. The musician, likewise, can sing or play his own composition to a hearer of his own choosing. The poet can read his own lines to the one for whom he wrote them. The painter or sculptor can, and often does, fulfill without intermediary aid a commission for a patron. But by such simple and primitive processes we could never have had the arts of the theatre and the cinema, and the other arts would have remained in a rudimentary state.

And, of course, distribution alone, appreciation alone and distribution with only creation or appreciation, are inconceivable.

In like manner, the problems which crystallize out of the three types of revolt and which we have roughly assigned to these three phases of the artistic process, dovetail into one another. Esthetic revolt can move forward to its logical and potential goal only if economic revolt clears the way for its proper and efficient presentation to the public. Economic revolt with the consequent construction of smooth-running channels of distribution is futile, a hollow shell, unless esthetic revolt keeps pace with it, providing significant artistic creation to route through those channels. And moral revolt, the constant vigilance on the part of the public against a stifling censorship, is not only indispensable to true and untrammeled esthetic revolt but it tends to atrophy unless esthetic revolt exerts constant pressure and manifests a genuine need for creative freedom.

Generally speaking, too, apart from the specific responsibility of the public for keeping the censor's claws clipped, the hosts of appreciation can not afford to remain indifferent and uninformed regarding the problems, the progress, the motives and aims of esthetic and economic revolt. Keen curiosity and alert attention to these matters sharpen the experience of appreciation, enable the public to bestow or withhold favor and custom, and, through the law of supply and demand, control and stimulate or retard the creative and distributive processes and the solution of their allied problems. Just as the ideal program for the artistic process at peace is sound and valid creation served by just and efficient distribution in behalf of eager and intelligent appreciation, so the most satisfactory program for the artistic process in a period of upheaval like our own is esthetic revolt closely paralleled by economic revolt in behalf of a public on its toes to see that no ulterior factors interfere with the logical course of revolution on its way to a new stability in keeping with the demands and opportunities of a new day.

Hitherto, as long as the artistic process was simply comprised of creation and appreciation, these two phases were usually treated separately and distinctly. The bookshelves of our parents and of our own youth disclosed such titles as "The Appreciation of Music," "The Foundations of Musical Composition," "The Fundamentals of Art Appreciation," "The Problems of the Painter," "How to Enjoy Literature," or "The Principles of English Composition." After all, why study the two subjects together? The artists gave us what they pleased, and we got the most we could out of what they gave us. When public demand overreached the capacities of this primitive process of give and take and called into existence the vast, intricate and still growing mechanism of artistic distribution, the entire process underwent a revolutionary transformation. The plane geometry of the arts of an elder day became the solid geometry of the present, with corresponding complications, permutations and combinations.

Soon outgrowing the role of mere go-between, the distributor, with an eye to business and a legitimate ambition to establish his calling as a reputable profession, cast about for new uses for the arts and new outlets for artistic talent. History will probably assign to this metamorphosed middleman of the arts a great deal of the credit for their phenomenal growth and expansion in our times, a growth whose breathless pace we have chosen to call revolutionary rather than evolutionary.

Chaotic as this growth has been, it is so sensitively articulated that nothing can happen in any one of the arts or to any one of the three phases of the artistic process without the emergency nerve centers of this inchoate and seething organism carrying the message to its manifold motor outlets. The linking of art to art, of process to process, and of problem to problem could be made to tell almost the entire story of our contemporary civilization, but a glimpse of what has happened under this régime to several of the most familiar types of creative artists will visualize the essential homogeneity and unity of the arts.

The author of today, for example, is not merely the author of a book which may often have three lives:—as a magazine serial, as a book, and as a newspaper feature, with a possible fourth life as a popular-priced reprint book; but he is also potentially a dramatist and a film scenarist, if he adapts his own work to stage or screen, or a collaborator in those fields, if he resigns the actual task of adaptation to others. On occasion, he is even called upon to transpose the success of stage or screen into fiction form. Not only, as author, must he keep abreast of his primary audience through the economics of his own art, but it behooves him to understand the economics of the theatre and of the motion picture. It is for that reason, among others, that the Authors' League came into being and grew in power. In a primitive, peaceful and stable society the artist can walk alone, but in a time of chaotic expansion and revolutionary readjustment, he seeks his kind.

The same principle motivates the banding of the actors into Equity. And the same interweaving of interests, perplexing enough in the days of the silent film, has resulted, with the coming of the sound film, in the vexatious and still hotly-debated problem of whether Equity Shop, corresponding to the closed shop of labor in industry, can or should be extended to include the actor for the screen.

The birth of the sound film is likewise responsible for the extension and aggravation of the dramatist's economic problems. Welcome and at the same time bothersome as was the discovery that his product often had substantial values for the screen beyond its run as a stage play, he would probably have laughed not so long ago at the suggestion that the motion picture rights, once the tail of the dog, would expand to the point of wagging the dog itself. But such is the case today, for the sound film overnight has rendered obsolete the basic agreement between the producing managers and the Dramatists' Guild of the Authors' League, whereby the dramatist is prevented from making a separate sale of the motion picture rights to his work before stage production. Time alone will tell whether this typically economic problem, a thorn in the side of the artist until it is solved and a blocking of traffic which should command the intelligent attention of the public as audience, will be settled by the motion picture companies becoming theatrical producers and subscribers to the basic agreement or by a radical revision of that agreement.

An interesting aspect of the problem, revealing the gambling instinct in the artist, is that which appears in the contrast between the methods of remunerating the author for stage and screen. The time-honored tradition of the stage is to take the dramatist in as partner, effectually as fellow-capitalist, by paying him a percentage of the receipts, or royalty, for his author's rights. The screen, on the other hand, treats the dramatist as a tradesman, rather than as a partner, in paying him a flat and final sum for his rights. Plausible as is the dramatist's resentment at this method, he will probably have to accede to it, for the motion picture industry is organized by block-booking, by pooling of production costs and by annual salaries to its executive and producing staffs to such an extent that no known process of auditing could unscramble the books and provide a tangible basis for computing royalties.

Of all the familiar types of creative artist, however, the singer is probably most affected by economic and mechanical developments in the arts today. Almost any singer with an established reputation can recall the time when his channels for expression comprised the concert platform and the light or grand operatic stage. The casual music lover might suppose that the additional outlets of the radio and the sound film, with television in the offing, might be eagerly acclaimed by the singer, but the resultant complications are not only baffling but tend to curtail the total range of opportunity.

That the arts of the dancer, the painter, the sculptor, the architect and the handcraftsman present few comparable quandaries is not, as might be supposed, an evidence of their stability amid surrounding chaos, but proof of the fact that individual economic developments in these arts are so immature, so hardly initiated, that most of their problems lie, unguessed, in the future.

Not only the creative artist, therefore, but the administrators of distribution—the producer, the manager, the publisher, the builder and the manufacturer—as well as the hearing, seeing and reading public, should all understand equally what revolt is directed against and toward what it is aimed. I might as well admit at this point that no time will be wasted on those specious manifestations of dissatisfaction which often pass for true revolt. Superficially vivid and dramatic as they may be, sentimental persecution complexes and the sympathy they frequently evoke only distract a situation already sufficiently complicated by legitimate and inescapable enigmas. The world owes no one engaged in the artistic process a living. The artist who comes before his time is the exception to the rule that the time creates its artists. And in the rare instances when the exception occurs, the time is more the loser than the artist, a misfortune which the world as knit together today is less and less likely to permit to happen.

Nor do I propose to waste any tears or fears over bad or meretricious art or the appreciation it commands. Energy devoted to revolt or protest against these conditions is energy misapplied, for good art is the only effective antidote for bad art and great art the only dangerous rival for good art.

At this point, too, I may as well clarify my attitude toward so-called social revolt in the arts. Those whose chief interest in the arts is to make them subserve propagandist purposes, whether fundamentalist or radical, would probably demand the addition of this type of revolt to the three I have listed. They might even consider it the chief type of revolt, for, having no interest in the arts on their own account, they would enslave them as they would education and other human functions, to further their fanatic programs. To me this seems like a serious displacement of values, a false and misleading determination of the fixed points of reference which we are seeking. Equally false and misleading it would be to deny to the arts and their revolt any social significance or implications. That is just the point. The arts in revolt have numerous implications, and one of the most far-reaching is social implication. In that connection and in due course the subject will be considered.

III

THE EXTENT OF REVOLT

REVOLT usually connotes a leader. And like anything organic, it may be expected to have structure—a beginning, a middle and an end; and extent—extent in time, extent in space, extent in character.

The present revolt in the arts in America appears to be without a leader. Perhaps that is one reason why it has taken us so long to recognize it as revolt. But, though it should put us on our guard, the lack of leadership is no sufficient reason for us, by the book, to rule out the contemporary upheaval as revolt. In the first place, modern life is so complex, its processes so specialized, and its pressure so relentless, that the chance is seriously reduced for a leader to impress his personality and his faith on millions of people. That, of course, is the definitive requirement of leadership, whether the actual leader be a man of action or a man of thought which provokes action. Even in the individual arts, outstanding and exclusive leadership is rare. So much the rarer it is bound to be in the larger field where the several arts have attained varying stages of revolt, complicated as well by the triple nature of the revolt. Spontaneous mass movement, then, seems to be the order of the day, and it is likely to serve us here as it already does in so many other channels of life, unless a leader is unexpectedly born to the task when the true lines of revolt become more specific and coherent.

The extent of the revolt, both actual and presumptive, is much simpler to chart and forecast. As I have already inferred, it has been in process much longer and has progressed much farther in some of the arts than in others, while its character has likewise differed greatly. Comparable trends, nevertheless, are visible, and others are predictable, so that it will repay us to attempt to date the beginnings of revolt in each of the arts and to appraise the extent of its development.

In several cases premature revolt anticipated the fundamental one, after the manner of the 1905 Revolution in Russia, the Boston Tea Party and John Brown's raid on Harper's Ferry. Thereafter, gains were lost and losses recouped and life went on much as before. While these preliminary risings are not to be ignored, neither should they be over-emphasized.

It was with such a premature uprising that the theatre had to contend when the first full-length motion pictures began to attract a widespread audience, denuding the galleries of the dramatic playhouses and relieving their stages of responsibility for western melodramas, slapstick farces and plays dependent on mechanical tricks. That the perfected motion picture marked the birth of a new and independent art form rather than a secession from an existing art, became evident not only directly in the presence of such early masterpieces of the screen as "The Birth of a Nation," but indirectly in the renewed vigor and vitality of the dramatic stage. Despite the onward march of the cinema, the American theatre embarked in 1915 on a phenomenal decade studded with the foundation and growth of the Provincetown Players, the Neighborhood Playhouse, the Washington Square Players and their heirs, the Theatre Guild; the discovery of Eugene O'Neill; the extraordinary collaboration of Arthur Hopkins, producer, and Robert Edmond Jones, designer; and the advent of Norman Bel Geddes; not to mention the hospitable welcome to the Moscow Art Theatre, and Max Reinhardt and other stimulating artists from overseas.

For base line of serious unrest involving the theatre, I prefer to turn to two other events, far removed from each other in time or obvious contact, but, I hope to prove, intimately correlative. The first of these events was the invention of the progenitor of the sound film, confidently installed in B. F. Keith vaudeville theatres throughout the country, but precipitately withdrawn for years of further laboratory experiment. Few saw this as a portent of the first order. Fewer still realized, when Eva Le Gallienne founded the first true repertory theatre in America in the fall of 1926, that our theatre was being inoculated thereby against the impending ravages of the sound film, perfected and armed for conquest. Only time, of course, will prove that true repertory is the theatre's best weapon of defense, though not necessarily its sole safeguard, but at the present stage of revolt it appears to be the most likely champion.

Genesis of the revolt in the cinema is clear, as I have just indicated, but present status and terminus are more difficult to assay because the art itself is so new, so free from inhibiting traditions and so enormously powerful that it can afford at a moment's notice to scrap whatever traditions it has built up for the sake of a new experiment. Just now it is engaged in finding out whether the sound film is primarily a coherent and self-dependent art or a mass-production means of "canning" and distributing the art of the theatre. That it is likely to serve both purposes as well as permit the ultimate resumption of the silent film and the perfection of the latter which seemed to be just around the corner when it was packed off to the warehouse, is at least a tenable hypothesis.

Revolt in the art of the dance is much tardier, much more embryonic. When Isadora Duncan, after a lifetime crowned with the renaissance of her art in Russia and other European countries, largely due to her inspiration, wrote in 1927 "I see America dancing," she was not reporting but prophesying. America has not lacked stimulus or example. In addition to Isadora herself, whom we humiliated and ignored to our lasting shame and irreparable loss, we have played passing host to Diaghileff and his Russians and harbored indefinitely the dynamic talents of Pavlova and of Fokine and Bolm and Mordkin. And yet the dance as a native art lags, shuffles, dallies, instead of moving, dancing. Possibly true revolt from this lethargy is incipient in the current vogue of the concert dance, solo and in groups, in the feeble gesture toward a Dance Repertory Theatre and in the experiments of the Neighborhood Playhouse. But far more vigor and imagination, both creative and executive, are needed before revolt flowers in a truly native ballet, before the dance attains its civic and communal possibilities, before Isadora's vision is realized.

As in the theatre, so in music, esthetic revolution developed concurrently with economic and mechanical upheaval. Beginning humbly with the forgotten pioneers of popular jazz, the esthetic revolt was deemed beneath notice until Walter Damrosch in December, 1926, dignified George Gershwin's "Concerto in F" with full orchestral presentation in Carnegie Hall. Conservative music thereupon gave grudging admittance to the mutineer, only to be stung to self-defense on another tack by the almost simultaneous intrusion of George Antheil, trailing echoes of Schoenberg, Honneger, Prokofieff and Stravinsky from the neo-classic concert halls of Europe. If the curve of modernist esthetic revolt in paint-

43

ing and poetry is any criterion for music, the obsession with form or formlessness, the orgy of cacophony and the scorn for melody will run their course in time, and both jazz and neo-classicism will leave residue of flexibility, sharpened senses and a more catholic taste than the Brahmins of music permitted before the storm broke.

As in the theatre, too, serious economic revolt in music was preceded by a flash in the pan. I have already recalled how mechanical reproduction put musical production on its mettle from the early years of the century. But to that challenge, just like the theatre to the challenge of the motion picture, music adjusted itself. It even reaped in time, by the curiosity thus aroused, substantial allegiance from hitherto dormant sources. The real upheaval, of course, came with the extraordinary improvement of the microphone, the receiving set and loud speaker, for thereby radio broadcasting could carry the concert, vocal, instrumental or symphonic, on a magic carpet of ether to the farthest farm house on the continent. While the casualties of this campaign are still being calculated, music is warned of another and rapidly approaching uprising known as television. Is it any wonder that musicians are in panic, pleading through paid advertising for public boycott of their mechanical rivals?

The art of literature, too, knows the bitter fruit and the anxieties of both esthetic and economic revolt with the additional burdens of moral attack and defense. Fortunately, for the peace of mind of both author and reader, the esthetic battles in both prose and poetry were mostly fought and won, with victory generally on the side of the latitudinarian, before economic revolt began or moral revolt became intense. It was the sudden expansion about five years ago of the lending library and the rise, in 1926, of the book club, both of them already dominant in the economic structure of British and continental letters, that disclosed the unhealthy state of distribution in American literature. That state has been still further exposed by the frantic expedient of the dollar book. All of these are symptoms of a maladjustment to the times in strange contrast with the other arts, calling forth courageous leadership if the specter of censorship, manipulated by moral counter-revolutionists, is to be withstood and utter chaos avoided. In other words, orderly revolt, deferred in literature longer than in the other arts, may reap the whirlwind of all readjustments, esthetic, economic, social and political, which are kept in check too long with a gloze of well-being hiding a festering discontent.

Ever the parade-ground of rival factions and the scene of sharp skirmishes between extremists, painting and sculpture have not yet fully awakened to the consequences of a general revolt in the arts or to the part they are able and will probably be called on to portray in that revolt. In probably no other art is it so possible for the ultra-conservative and the ultra-radical to work simultaneously, each catering to creative urge and appreciative market on a personal basis almost untouched by the factors of a Machine Age which have placed most of the other arts at their mercy. Perennial guerilla sniping is one of the fruits of this condition, but so is the absence of any powerful forces mustered in camps determined upon mutual annihilation. Creation is spasmodic, distribution primitively simple and ineffectual, and appreciation a matter of coteries and cliques. Esthetic revolt of a significance superior to the strident caterwauling of the "isms" is brewing, however, in the steadily growing realization that the easel painting, product of an anemic era in bondage to the theory of art for art's sake, is losing ground to the mural painting executed on and for the spot where it is to remain. Simultaneously, the statue, carved without reference to its setting on the same theory, is yielding to a structural and fundamental collaboration with architecture. It is hard to see how painting and sculpture can avoid economic consequences of an esthetic revolt along these lines, but their exact nature is still extremely problematic.

Economic and esthetic revolts are more nearly equalized in architecture. Beneath the cheap, vulgar and disgusting race for mere height in our skyscrapers and the irresponsible individuality still rife in our city planning, a profound uprising is gathering momentum. Prophets and exhorters of architectural revolt have long been thundering in a chaos of conglomerate borrowings from all styles, times and climes and of gerry-built structures which infrequently last long enough to become landmarks. As permanent buildings increase in number, however, the principle of significant form, of functional justification, is winning new adherents. We are beginning to realize that use should dictate form, rather than that form should have a free hand, letting use get along the best way it may. Strangely enough, as foreign critics of our building achievements have proved in reserving their highest praise for our grain elevators and other commercial structures erected without benefit of art-conscious architect, the solution of a functional need is the soundest assurance of satisfying esthetic taste, a secret which the other arts would do well to heed in these days when standards and values are in flux and susceptible of right modification as well as wrong.

Economic revolt in architecture, on the other hand, marks time as far as actual results are concerned, although its tenets are hotly debated. The stone wall against which these arguments are directed is the prohibitive ground rent which the builder must shoulder until his structure is ready for occupancy—a consideration which handicaps the architect not only in the thoughtful development of his plans but dictates constructional compromises which will speed the undertaking. True economic revolt in that larger field of architecture, regional and city planning, faces the pyramided total of the obligations and commitments of all the individual builders concerned, and is that much farther from realization. But the overwhelming scope of the vision it holds out for mankind is one of those gauntlets which no one can fling down to the American people with certain impunity.

Revolt in the craft arts, finally, is still in that vague state one might expect in an art newly reborn or rather in those branches of industry newly recognized as an independent group art. Buried and forgotten under complete mechanization before this recognition took place, the craft arts are now struggling to regain those privileges long ago surrendered to the machine, with attention divided between a revival of actual handcraft and an effort to guide the machine in the reproduction of good design. The potentialities of the craft arts as a group are so momentous, not only intrinsically but for the analogy they suggest for the future of all the arts, that I shall use them to point the climax of this survey.

Probably no two observers will agree as to the relative progress of the several arts toward a new stability by way of revolution and readjustment. For my part, taking esthetic, economic and other factors into consideration, I would rank music in the van, despite its troubled economic status, for I am confident that it will turn to good account in the present emergency the lessons it learned in its previous encounter with mechanization. The theatre stands second in my list and literature third, largely because of their high coefficients in esthetic revolt. In fourth place is the cinema, on account of the uncertainty as to how much farther revolt can carry this new art, both esthetically and economically. Architecture, painting and sculpture, the dance, and the craft arts trail in that order, due to the rudimentary state of their economic reconstruction.

These ratings, of course, are only approximate and arbitrary, and they are susceptible of quick and drastic revision in the light of sudden and unexpected accelerations in the pace of revolt in one or more of the individual arts. By these revisions, wide divergences are almost certain to narrow and in time to disappear, for the arts at last are getting acquainted with one another, comparing notes and profiting by each other's experience.

THE CAUSES OF REVOLT

It is impossible to canvass the fact, the nature and the extent of revolt in the arts, as we have been doing, without implying between the lines the presumptive causes of revolt or occasionally referring specifically to them. But it has seemed best to defer explicit examination of this subject until we had built up a clear picture of the phenomena, the causes of which we would seek to determine.

Only the most perversely conservative sophist would contend that the present upheaval of all three phases of the artistic process in America has its source in a petulant and temperamental dissatisfaction. That this revolt was inevitable, brewing ominously under the complacent surface of American life throughout the Nineteenth Century, must have been obvious to any sociologist with a broad enough conception of human nature to realize that no nation can persist and grow and achieve its potential greatness without the inspiration of the arts freely created and eagerly appreciated. Van Wyck Brooks, Lewis Mumford, Thomas Beer and other biographers of American artists of that period and Matthew Josephson in his recent composite "Portrait of the Artist as American" have indicted dispassionately and conclusively the smug parochialism and brutal indifference of that America which sent into exile Henry James, Henry Adams, Lafcadio Hearn, Isadora

Duncan, Whistler, Bierce, Crane, Ezra Pound, T. S. Eliot and others. The same America built spite fences round the genius of Poe, Thoreau, Emerson, Whitman, Howells, Melville, Mark Twain, Emily Dickinson, Louis Sullivan, MacDowell, Steele MacKaye and a host of lesser talents. With a bitterness born of fear for the loss of its power, that America crippled the formative years of Theodore Dreiser, Sherwood Anderson, Edgar Lee Masters and their fellow-leaders of the revolt which burst at last like a clearing thunder-storm.

With fury still unspent, this thunder-storm is still washing away the last vestiges of the Nineteenth Century. But its salutary results are already evident in the roster of outstanding American artists of today whose creative span has been reasonably free from the frustrating forces that disheartened and stunted their artistic forebears. Among many others that roster includes: Eugene O'Neill, Paul Green, Ernest Hemingway, Sinclair Lewis, Louis Bromfield, Thornton Wilder, Conrad Aiken, Carl Sandburg, George Gershwin, Maurice Sterne and Thomas Benton.

American life is not yet made to order for the artist, for it is not yet ordered itself. But only those who are pathologically sensitive find it impossible to work here, while to many the American tempo is now a positive stimulus to creation. It may be creation of a nervous, transitional type, seeking understanding rather than providing it, but it is bothered little by the inhibitions of "the stammering century."

If the Nineteenth Century with its insularity and its materialistic preoccupations was the primary objective, the hated target, of the revolt, it may also be considered as its latent cause. Its more immediate, specific and kinetic causes, therefore, may be analyzed out of the salient concrete characteristics of that century, and will take political, social, economic, ethical, religious and mechanical form.

Politically, America thanked God for its isolation throughout the Nineteenth Century and well into the Twentieth. Indispensable as that isolation may have been on strictly political and materialistic grounds, America paid an enormous price for it. The cost is not to be computed in dollars and cents but in the loss of true culture and genuine civilization. We were conquering a continent and we didn't want anyone to meddle in the job. But we got behind the procession in the arts, except a few rare souls whose instincts or travels kept them abreast of world-thought and world-feeling. Political problems are rarely solved except by political means. And so it was the World War with its abrupt leveling of international political walls which hurled us violently and irrevocably into world affairs. With political barriers down, esthetic intercourse has free play, serving in turn as insurance against the rebuilding of those political barriers. Once we saw the esthetic achievements of the rest of the world and caught a glimpse of how the rest of the world viewed our own lack of artistic progress, the seeds were planted for emulating that achievement and speeding up our own progress even if revolutionary methods were needed to do so.

Socially, American life during the Nineteenth Century presented similar aspects of isolation and insularity, just as discouraging to significant creation of the arts as it was to their appreciation. The feudal South, Brahmin New England and a thin crust of pioneer first families in the middle and far West were poor soil for the seeds of art. The arts have thrived before in a tame and pallid way under a stable and stratified culture. But American social strata were not integrated even from city to city, while the masses

51

suspected the very word "artistic" as evidence of the pretentious and the effete. Again, it was the World War which integrated America, both geographically and socially, hastening and completing a process already under way.

It was in 1916, nearly a year before our entry in the war, that Winthrop Ames, at a dinner to E. H. Sothern and Julia Marlowe, illustrated with an anecdote his contention that our once aristocratic theatre audience had already become democratic. "A month ago," he said, "I drove to a New York theatre in a taxi and when I paid my fare the driver asked: 'Boss, what time does this show begin?' 'Half-past eight.' 'Just got time to make the garage and get the wife,' said he. 'I'm going, too.' Well, there you are! The taxi-driver and Mrs. taxi-driver—or, to be more accurate, the class just above him in the social scale—outnumber any other in the average modern audience four or five to one. This is what we have grown to call the General Public: the public that pays the piper and therefore calls the tune."

In other words, and increasingly since 1917, this General Public has become our patron of the arts, whether or not it is yet fully aware of the fact that its theatres, its motion pictures and its novels are specimens of art, good, bad or indifferent. Such a public, it may be, is watered stock, for whom cultural standards had to be reduced and spread thin. But the appreciation of this public, though often wrongly bestowed on bad art, is natural, spontaneous, genuine and susceptible of unlimited growth and improvement. To the incursion of this public is unquestionably due the huge expansion in the demand for the arts in America and the consequent revolutionary expansion of the economic channels for their effective distribution.

Wider political and therefore wider esthetic horizons, combined with an almost complete social democratization of the appreciation of art, would not have been enough to nourish sustained revolt. The economic wherewithal had to be present to satisfy aroused desires. The whole trend of American industry since the turn of the century had been preparing the ground for this enabling factor of revolt, a process which the war only stimulated and perpetuated. As Paul M. Mazur pointed out in "American Prosperity, Its Causes and Consequences" and reiterated in "America Looks Abroad," the distinguishing doctrine of our industrial structure, marking it off from all others past and present, is the payment of wages on such a scale as to enable the worker to buy freely the products of his own and his fellow-workers' hands, and the limitation of the working day and the working week to give him leisure to spend and enjoy his wages.

One physical and two abstract inhibitions remained in the path before revolt in the arts could attain real momentum. The abstract inhibitions were ethical and religious. The Nineteenth Century in America was a curious patchwork of moral tabus traceable to the austerity of the colonists and crossed and underscored by the makeshift moral precepts of centuries of pioneering. Effective revolt in the arts could make little headway until these ethical standards were broadened and civilized by the infusion of immigrants from pleasure-loving nations and by the sudden collapse of false and hypocritical restrictions under the realistic stress of war years.

Closely allied to ethical inhibitions were the religious interdictions of the Nineteenth Century. Many a creed frowned upon art, especially upon the theatre, the novel and the dance, as the work of the devil. In his "Re-Discovery of America," Waldo Frank has advanced the theory of America as the graveyard of ideas long dead in Europe, ideas, like religion's suspicion of the arts, which were brought from their death-bed in Europe to a long and secure reprieve on our isolated continent. Nothing is surer than that the Puritan theocracy of New England and fanatic sectarianism of manifold varieties established across the continent a bigoted kill-joy attitude toward the arts that might have been dictated at a Roundhead council table under Cromwell, without even heeding the Lord Protector's warning: "My brethren, by the bowels of Christ I beseech you, bethink you that you may be mistaken!" Losing validity, almost imperceptibly, this suppression of natural instincts crumpled like a straw man when the unleashed war generation announced it would have what it wanted when it wanted.

And yet, with all of these barriers removed and with all of these causes at work, revolt in the arts would have been feeble and ineffective without the dynamic emancipation of the machine. Not so much the theme of the machine and of man's reaction toward it for realistic or expressionistic content of the arts and its rhythmic patterns for their form, although this has been more than a passing phase of the theatre, literature and music. What I refer to, rather, is the physical energizing of esthetic revolt by the machine and the analogous executive energizing of economic revolt and reconstruction. As these factors have as much to do with the implications of revolt as with its causes, I shall let them serve as the bridge to that topic.

V

THE IMPLICATIONS OF REVOLT

Meanings come last. The implications of a project or movement begin to clarify with any degree of certainty only after it is well under way. The fact that motives do not always coincide with meanings has been neatly tucked away in the old adage about the best laid schemes o' mice an' men. Even when the wheel of an event has come full circle, its true significance is not always immediately apparent, often requiring the perspective of years and generations for a complete understanding. In a case so confusing as the present revolt in the arts, a case, moreover, which appears to be still far distant from the terminus of its cycle, we shall probably be fortunate if we detect a few of its implications, or the hints of implications, which we can use at least tentatively and approximately as the fixed points of reference which we set out to determine in the first chapter.

So many people today seem to be so without anchor or sense of direction that I am emboldened to pass on for what they may be worth the two main implications, as I see them, of revolt in the arts. The first of them has to do with the use to which we can put the arts, now that we have become so generally aware of their existence; while the second concerns the steps we must take if we wish to preserve for ourselves and posterity the full values of the arts against the inroads of the self-same Machine Age which has called our attention to those values. Let me state these two implications as theories, which I shall develop separately, owing to their divergent nature and ramifications:

(*a*) *To those of us who have been deprived, by the processes of modern thought, of an untroubled faith in any existing religion or philosophy and who are deeply impressed by the achievements of science, though unwilling to depend upon science alone for a solution of the riddle of the universe, I propose the arts as collaborators with science in the attempt to interpret human destiny.*

(*b*) *Realizing that the Machine Age has destructive as well as constructive potentialities, such as the displacement of personally-performed art by its mechanical reproduction, and that the clock of progress can not be turned backward, I propose that "machine-made" art should subsidize "hand-made" art, both for the intrinsic value of the latter and for its service as an independent laboratory and testing ground.*

1. The Implications of Art

Before we undertake to develop the first of these two implications of revolt, however, let us inquire into the implications of art itself and examine the function of art in the Machine Age. What is art? What fundamental kinds of art has man created and utilized? What kind is most compatible with the Machine Age and most appropriate to its needs and conditions?

Probably no other abstract concept invented by the human mind has been defined in so many ways as "art." A sizeable handbook could be compiled from these definitions. Each race and age has phrased its understanding of the concept, each profession, each craft, each social class and each mental and emotional stripe of each race and age. Even the artists themselves do not agree on where art begins and where it ends or what aims it is supposed to fulfill. What is the relationship of beauty to art? What has art to do with ethics and morals? Entire volumes, shelves full of volumes, have been devoted to the coldly analytical or passionate discussion of these eternal and apparently insoluble questions.

For our purposes, it seems best to avoid these controversies wherever we can and to establish our understanding of art on the simplest and at the same time the broadest possible basis. We shall have such a basis if we retain my tentative definition from Chapter I that *art is anything which the human imagination conceives and the human hand contrives out of words, sounds, colors, forms and material substance to appeal to the human emotions or the human intellect, or both, in such a way as to reproduce in the auditor or spectator an emotional or mental state, or both, similar to that which the artist himself experienced.*

Ignoring the lesser dilemmas and the subtleties of the subject, we may consider the kinds of art on the same broad and simple basis. Art as interpreter and art for art's sake between them comprise practically the entire field, as Walter Lippmann has pointed out most recently in "A Preface to Morals." In all the great ages of art, the former kind has predominated, while the theory of art for art's sake has commanded practitioners and converts most readily as a means of escape in periods when the arts have lost contact with life. There is probably no hard and fast line of demarcation between these two kinds or theories of art. The attempt to set up exact boundary lines, here as elsewhere, fails to take into account the usual presence of a minimum of one theory in the practice of the other.

In discussing art for art's sake, Lippmann admits his belief "that any theory of art is inevitably implicated in some philosophy of life, and that the only question is whether the artist is conscious or unconscious of the theory he is acting upon. For unless the artist deals with purely logical essences, provided he observes and perceives anything in the outer world, no matter how he represents it or symbolizes it or comments upon it, there must be implicit in it some attitude toward the meaning of existence. If his conclusion is that human existence has no meaning, that, too, is an attitude toward the meaning of existence."

Likewise, as Dr. Ducasse contends in "The Philosophy of Art," there is a large share of art for the artist's sake, if not of art for art's sake, in the clearest cases of art as interpretation. The artist does not work on order like the manufacturer. No matter how much of a prophet an artist may be, his urge for expression through his art, for the mere sake of expression, is a factor which can not be wholly controlled and which should not be ignored. If this factor of art for the artist's sake were irrelevant, the artist as prophet would probably be content with prophecy and cease to bother about being an artist.

It is unfortunate that Lippmann has limited his illustration of the two antithetical theories of art to the painter, for the painter is probably a less likely prophet than the practitioners of some of the other arts. Even in the case of the painter, however, Lippmann strangely undervalues the artist's most powerful tool as prophet. "It is reasonable to ask," he contends, "whether the analysis and abstraction which thinking involves are not radically different sociological processes from the painter's passionate appreciation of the appearance of things." But need the prophet be a great thinker? Can he not be, is he not usually, a great feeler? "The passionate appreciation of the appearance of things" is not to be belittled. Even in the case of Leonardo and Goethe, whom Lippmann admits were original and important thinkers, it is not their thinking so much as their feeling, their power to experience deep and profound emotion and to stimulate emotion and thereby the intellect in others, which has sustained their prophetic role through the centuries.

Whether or not the artist can fulfill the responsibility of prophet as often as I believe he can, it seems to me that there can be no argument as to which of these two kinds of art, which of these two theories, is the more pertinent in the Machine Age. Art for art's sake may result in a mildly titillating decoration of an era in which the clock-springs of life are running down. But art as interpretation is the crying need of an age in creative flux. Art for art's sake may provide a means of escape from the confusions of such an age, but only the lesser artists will be thus tempted. The artist with imaginative and emotional stamina, the artist who has in him the gift of prophecy, will rise to the challenge of the Machine Age.

In any case, there is no turning backward. Nor too far forward. We can not reverse the wheels of civilization for the sake of the artist who is irritated by the pace of life today, any more than we can for the scientist who yearns for the simplicities of Aristotle's laboratory or for the sociologist who dreams of the naive innocence of prehistoric pastoral life. Only the sensationalist or the weakling deplore mass production, mass distribution, mass appreciation. Man made the machine. He can destroy it if he will. But he won't. It has given him too many things which he values. If it pinches here and there, he must adjust it so that it will run smoothly and accomplish all that he wishes it to accomplish. Man can, must and will master the machine. Paraphrasing the great German industrialist, C. Hartley Grattan has written: "Rathenau saw that there can be no retreat from mechanization. It must be accepted as an irreducible fact. We must proceed to turn it to the service of man. Man must master things, a not impossible task logically viewed." To do otherwise, would be like a driver abandoning his car by the roadside or peevishly grumbling about it just because it rattled instead of investigating and correcting the cause of the trouble.

The heart of the matter is clearly expressed by John Dewey in these combined statements from two different sources: "The machine is the authentically embodied *Logos* of modern life, and the import of this fact is not diminished by any amount of dislike to it. . . . Escape from industrialism on the ground that it is unesthetic and brutal can win only superficial and restricted successes of esteem. It is a silly caricature to interpret such statements as meaning that science should devote itself directly to solving industrial problems, or that poetry and painting should find their material in machines and in machine processes. The question is not one of idealizing present conditions in esthetic treatment, but of discovering and trying to realize the conditions under which vital esthetic production and esthetic appreciation may take place on a generous social scale."

Acceptance of the Machine Age in this spirit is not the act of a Pollyanna. No mere placid acquiescence in present conditions will suffice just because an intrenched minority has benefited by them. Another minority, more important to the well-being and progress of the race, is not satisfied. And, however proud of the machine the bulk of mankind may be, it can not be satisfied either, when it has tired of the novelty of the toy and has been awakened by its prophets to the human values which it is missing. Accepting the machine, therefore, not as a finished product, but as a working drawing which may be altered at will, we must study and work to improve it, remembering with Charles A. Beard that "under the machine and science, the love of beauty, the sense of mystery, and the motive of compassion—sources of esthetics, religion, and humanism—are not destroyed. They remain essential parts of our nature. But the conditions under which they must operate, the channels they must take, the potentialities of their action are all changed. These ancient forces will become powerful in the modern age just in the proportion that men and women accept the inevitability of science and the machine, understand the nature of the civilization in which they must work, and turn their faces resolutely to the future."

If we can not turn backward from the machine, it is equally futile to think and plan too far ahead. Petulant clamor against the Machine Age or ecstatic acceptance of it without revision are surpassed in futility and lack of realistic judgment only by the construction of utopias. Indulgence in the fashioning of the ideal state is a pleasant romantic pastime but one with small significance for the practical reconstruction of life today. Anyone's guess is as good as Bernard Shaw's when he contends that the artist will have vanished from the human scene when we have gone "As Far As Thought Can Reach." And if Leon Samson is so sure that there will be no artists in the perfected society which he sketches in "The New Humanism," he will have to focus more exactly the vague substitutes which he proposes for the arts before we have any right to let him undermine our faith in the value of the artist today.

2. *The Function of Art in the Machine Age*

I can not see why the artist should be raising more clamor about the restrictions of the Machine Age than anyone else. Unless we have been hypnotized by the whirling wheels of that age into a craven worship of all its manifestations, none of us is any too happy with the confusions and the readjustments which it has forced upon our mode of living and thinking. Possibly the artists have been the first to protest because they are by nature the most sensitive. If this is true, they are likely to forestall the rest of us by using this same sensitiveness in coming to an understanding of the Machine Age and to a cogent and convincing emotional or intellectual interpretation of it.

It is conceivable that certain types of artist will never be any more at home in the Machine Age than were the inhibited artists of the Nineteenth Century in their day. But these nonconformists will not have the same justification as their forebears for indicting the age in which they live. Nineteenth Century America ignored its artists, gave them no life which art could interpret significantly. Machine Age America, on the contrary, is an age rich in opportunity for interpretation, an age pleading for interpretation. The Nineteenth Century artist was a sailor becalmed and fretful. The artist of the Machine Age is on a craft racing with the wind. If wind and wave terrify him, he may be an object of amused pity but not of profound sympathy. A shaming challenge to the recalcitrant artist of the Machine Age has been delivered recently by Sherwood Anderson in one of his sketches of the Southern factories: "Suppose an artist were to come into this mill, to design cloth. Let him accept the limitations of the machine as the poet accepts the limitations of the sonnet form. Here is something gay that might be done, something joyous."

There is no corresponding complaint on the part of the public against the art which the Machine Age has brought it. The artist naturally and rightly feels that there should be more complaint, that the public should not accept so readily the standardized, usually commonplace, and often ugly product of the machine. But we must remember that untold millions have been suddenly introduced to the arts by the machine and the Machine Age, that they are like a child with a new toy, beguiled by obvious and superficial aspects, fascinated by the mere turning of wheels and flattered by their acquisition of something which their forefathers considered beyond the realm of possibility. They have few standards for judging what has been put within their reach. Many of them do not yet even realize that it is art. But standards can be taught. Judgment and discrimination can be acquired. Art and the standards of good art are not unnatural. They are born in nature and they live and have their being in nature. Curiosity, that quality which more than any other characterizes America's millions today, will seek and find those standards if given half a chance. No one has expressed so profound and convincing a faith in such an outcome as Professor Dewey when he wrote recently: "Interest in art, science and philosophy is not on the wane; the contrary is the case. There may have been individuals superior in achievement in the past, but I do not know of any time in our history when so many persons were actively concerned, both as producers and as appreciators, with these culminating aspects of civilization. There is a more lively and more widespread interest in ideas, in critical discussion, in all that forms an intellectual life, than ever before. Anyone who can look back over a span of thirty or forty years must be conscious of the difference that a generation has produced. And the movement is going forward, not backward. . . . A characteristic culture will come by turning a machine age into a significantly new habit of mind and sentiment, or it will not come at all."

In Sherwood Anderson's challenge to the artist there is implicit a corresponding challenge to the distributor—to the manufacturer, salesman, producer, manager and builder. The same Machine Age which has created a profession and a livelihood for the distributor or middleman in all of these guises in the several arts has placed upon him an enormous and all but impossible burden. Not only has he incurred the responsibility of establishing satisfactory relationships with the creative artist and with the purchasing public, but he labors constantly under the suspicion of exploiting one or the other or both against each other. What shall he feed the machine? Not only the actual machine, but the far vaster and more intricate if invisible and intangible machine of mere distribution? But the distributor knows in a vague way that he is dependent on the artist for the sustenance of the machine. It is folly to fear this machine as a Frankenstein or a salt mill grinding out its uniform products without ceasing just because the magic word for stopping it has been forgotten. The machine, as I have said, was made by man and it can be controlled by man. If man loses control momentarily, the blind forces of economics will step in and call a halt.

If it is folly to fear the machine, it is not folly, however, to insist that every ounce of intelligence, every gleam of vision, should be mustered to feed the machine for the maximum benefit to mankind. No matter how difficult it may be for the distributor to understand the peculiar psychology of the artist, he must learn to do so. He must learn to respect the artist as the Prime Giver. He must establish and maintain conditions conducive to the free and joyous output of the artist.

Neither is it folly to insist that the distributor must play fair with his public. If he plays fair with the artist, half of the problem of playing fair with the public will be solved. He is in a position, however, to induce the public by the use of all of the stratagems which he has worked out for arousing desire on its part, to demand finer and still finer performance on the part of the artist.

It is too soon yet to balance the books on the art of the Machine Age resultant from the still confused interrelationships of artist, distributor and public. A little of it is good art, much of it is bad, more of it is indifferent. That much we can say, though it would be rash to estimate the exact proportions. But it is not too soon to see that the age has given indication of its vitality by stamping the mark of its specific character on both the content and the form of art.

The machine as content has naturally appeared most freely in those arts in which content usually consists of concrete ideas— literature and the drama; while the machine as form has impressed itself first upon music, drama and poetry, owing to the obvious importance of pattern in their makeup. Only the Machine Age could have given us, to cite a few examples, such plays as Eugene O'Neill's "The Hairy Ape," "Dynamo," and "The Great God Brown," Sophie Treadwell's "Machinal," Elmer Rice's "The Adding Machine" and John Howard Lawson's "Processional"; such a ballet as John Alden Carpenter's "Skyscrapers"; such a poem as Nicholas Vachel Lindsay's "The Santa Fé Trail"; such a novel as Theodore Dreiser's "An American Tragedy"; such musical compositions as Gershwin's "Rhapsody in Blue," and George Antheil's "Ballet Mechanique"; such architectural achievements as the Telephone Building and the Daily News Building in New York.

Thus far, the art of the Machine Age, whether it uses the machine as content or as form or both, has usually been content to echo the machine. Gingerly, but with consuming curiosity, it has picked up the machine, handled it, pulled it apart. Now and then it has ventured to express a comment, a judgment, on the machine, usually from the proletarian viewpoint. But we still await anything really interpretive, anything which would justify the term prophecy. If it comes—and come, it will; in which of the arts first, no one can foretell—we shall begin to realize the first rich fruits of art using its own chaotic soil for the resolution of chaos. Such a truly prophetic art may utilize realistically the tempos, the rhythms, the imagery of the machine, or it may transmute these values in terms which we do not yet suspect. But when it comes, art as interpretation will have justified itself whether it accepts, condemns, or transforms the Machine Age which gave it birth.

Meanwhile, to the extent that the arts comment on the machine and whatever follows in its wake, they are bound to assume social as well as esthetic significance. The reader will recall that in an earlier chapter I denied social revolt a separate category in the examination of the types of revolt in the arts. To me, the social significance of the arts is a by-product, often a profound by-product, one which may rock civilization to its foundations, as when "Uncle Tom's Cabin" emotionally energized the intellectual abhorrence of slavery in the North. But these connotations of the arts seem to me to belong in the field of sociology and political economy rather than in that field which we are attempting to survey, especially when the motive of propaganda overtops the disinterested aim of art to see all life and see it whole. Apart from art as propaganda and so-called "class-art," which to me is a contradiction in terms, the arts can no more escape social implications than they can avoid personal and cosmic implications. Confronting life as their raw material, the very pattern which they impose on this raw material is a commentary on it, an interpretation of it, a prophecy regarding it.

3. The Arts as Collaborators with Science in the Understanding and Interpretation of Life

Man has, or has had in the past, five keys for unlocking the mystery of life—pure science, the social sciences, religion, philosophy and the arts. At different stages of civilization, these several keys have been variously favored, have proved variously efficacious. The ancient Hebrews reposed almost their entire confidence in the religious key. The classic Greeks depended primarily on philosophy and the arts, doing little more than lip service to their religion. Rome of the republic and the empire got along with a modicum of philosophy of a practical and pragmatic sort, but for the most part appeared to bother little about life's mystery. Religion and the arts were the twin solaces of the Middle Ages, giving way to philosophy, the arts and the beginnings of pure science under the Renaissance. Retaining philosophy but relaxing its passion for the arts, the Eighteenth Century zealously cultivated pure science and first awoke to the possibilities of the social sciences. Pure science still overshadowed the social sciences in the Nineteenth Century, spurring to rivalry a threatened religion, especially in America, though all but oblivious to the key of the arts.

The dawn of the Machine Age discovers thinking man in this country almost wholly engrossed in science, pure and social, and tolerant but indifferent toward an impassive religion and a futile philosophy. It is my contention that, before this age proceeds much farther, the key of the arts will be polished off to serve with the sciences in the attempt to interpret human destiny.

Before elaborating upon that contention, let us glance in turn at each of the five keys for unlocking the mystery of life in order to discover, if possible, why they are pertinent or irrelevant in Twentieth Century America.

It is easy to see why pure science exerts such a universal and almost hypnotic spell over the mind and the imagination of Machine Age man. Science is the father—or at least the grandfather through its offspring, invention—of almost everything which he sees, hears, touches and uses in his daily existence. Science measures. Science proves. Science works in the open. Science takes nothing for granted. Applied science as engineering has given us the structures in which we live and work; the railroads, ocean liners, harbors, airplanes and dirigibles by which we travel; and the telegraph, telephone, and radio by which we communicate with one another. Applied science in other guises has metamorphosed the industries whereby we are fed and clothed. In fact, no all-giving God of primitive races, to whom was accredited the light of day and the bounties of nature, ever bestowed such largess upon his children.

Nor is there anything vague or elusive about science's acquisition of this rôle as Giver. As Whitehead in "Science and the Modern World" admits: "The reason why we are on a higher imaginative level is not because we have finer imagination, but because we have better instruments. . . . A fresh instrument serves the same purpose as foreign travel; it shows things in unusual combinations. The gain is more than a mere addition; it is a transformation." Then, too, the invention of invention has been largely responsible. Instead of waiting for someone to discover some new fact, formula, equation or process, we systematically set out to find the desirable unknown in laboratories superbly equipped for the purpose.

In a very real sense, modern science has become the victim of its own astounding progress. It has done so much, has unlocked so many secret doors, has armed man with such incredible powers, that man, the child, feels that science, the father, knows everything. Trading upon this credulity, pseudo-scientists have promised man the Philosopher's Stone, the mystic key of the riddle of the universe.

Meanwhile, however, true, patient science is much less certain today than it was in the time of Darwin and Huxley of its ability to solve that riddle. Science measures. Quantity can be measured. But quality can't. Furthermore, the farther pure science pursues the unknown into the infinitely great or the infinitely small, the more elusive the unknown becomes. If Huxley honestly thought that science in time could explain all life, might even create life, Whitehead and Millikan and Michelson and Einstein now know that it is extremely unlikely to be able to do so.

Younger than pure science but with an ancient and honorable heritage, the social sciences run pure science a close race for allegiance in Machine Age America. Dealing with man rather than with inert matter, with man in all of his infinite and unpredictable variety, with all of the untraceable whims that motivate his action, psychology, sociology, anthropology, ethnology and their allied and subsidiary sciences are at a grave disadvantage as compared with the exactitude and dependability of pure science. But these sciences, too, can claim many of the tangible and intangible aspects of our life today as their offspring, and, when we remember man's intense yearning to know about himself, whence he came, why he is here and whither he is going, it is not strange that the social sciences have exercised an enormous appeal to his imagination. That they are legitimate science, we should not doubt when we recall what progress they have made in the comparatively short duration of their intensive application, but it is not improbable that they, too, like pure science, will have to revise the sweeping claims which they have made.

When I maintain that the thinking American of today is tolerant but indifferent toward religion, I am recording a general observation, not a criticism or a judgment. Others may argue whether it is deplorable or fortunate that the key of religion has been somehow mislaid, that religious faith has ceased to sway even the nominally believing masses with its old-time power and vigor, has ceased utterly to serve the deepest needs of countless thousands who have not taken the trouble to admit publicly their agnosticism. Unless something can be found to take its place, the most confirmed agnostic would probably consider it unfortunate that the key of religion has grown rusty. He may even envy the faithful their faith, but if he has it not, he can not honestly or effectively simulate it. Moreover, the agnostic of the type of Joseph Wood Krutch, Walter Lippmann, Everett Dean Martin and others, differs radically from the type represented by Colonel Ingersoll. Theirs is a reasoned and even reluctant surrender of traditional supports because those supports appear to be grounded in a supernaturalism which they can no longer accept; while Ingersoll's renunciation of faith was a passionate and emotional experience. Chastened and even despondent over inevitable loss, theirs is not the impulse to undermine the conviction of those who can still believe, while Ingersoll flung his invitation to follow him from every platform in the land.

Tolerant but indifferent. Such an observation of contemporary

America's attitude toward religion does not take into account either of two extremes, simply because neither seems to me to be truly representative. Extreme atheism seems to be merely an appendage of American communism, and, compared with the Russian variety, it is as unrealistic as our communism when ranged side by side with that of Moscow. That the opposite pole of devout faith is likewise in a minority is evident from the fact that it begs and pleads instead of threatening and thundering. In between, in addition to the tolerant and unnumbered agnostics, are the masses who outwardly conform through inertia, the hope for social advantage, the fear of being thought "different." To call them Christians, to claim for them religious loyalty and fervor, would probably be considered blasphemy by the early martyrs of the church or by the devout believers of the Middle Ages if they could be brought back to life to sit in judgment.

Neither avowed agnosticism nor that atrophy of a potent religious faith which differs little from it has come as a sudden vision or by a cataclysmic emotional readjustment such as tormented pioneers of secession from the religious fold suffered in the last century. Little by little, the church has tempered its demands upon modern credulity, but not fast enough to stem the tide of silent but steady secession. Facing a practical loss of this venerable key, various voices, not always religious in motive, have argued for the restoration of religion, as Kenneth Burke puts it, "in order that religion may in turn restore society." But, as he concludes, "it would be too much like getting stick to beat dog to bite pig to make it jump over the stile," a singularly inefficient process to command confidence in an age of efficient machines.

The key of philosophy has fared little better than that of religion in Machine Age America. As a nation and a race, we have never been much given to philosophizing, resembling the ancient Romans more than any other social organism in that respect. A practical folk, saddled with the task of taming a wilderness, we have embodied our popular and extremely practical philosophy in the aphorisms of Benjamin Franklin, Artemus Ward, Mark Twain, Mr. Dooley and Will Rogers. Thoreau and Emerson dressed up that practical philosophy in more literary form, and William James commanded not only national but international attention with the same philosophy labeled pragmatism and bolstered by the technical terminology of the psychological laboratory. Even John Dewey, the nearest we can come today to claiming a philosopher, irritates those who look to philosophy for a well-oiled, smooth-running interpretation of the universe by his frank acceptance of the chaos under which we live as a working basis for a philosophy.

It seems to me that we have here a hint of one of the most profound reasons why the so-called New Humanists are fighting a futile and hopeless battle, a hint which their opponents have strangely overlooked. Forgetting that philosophy is the crystallization by a seer of the subconscious ideals, impulses and longings of his time, and that it can not be imposed arbitrarily from above or from the outside, Professors Babbitt and More and their doctrinaire camp followers have attempted fatuously to enlist support for their philosophic program of restraint and decorum. Instead of dignifying their impertinence with the scholarly refutations of "The Critique of Humanism," edited by C. Hartley Grattan, it seems to me that their opponents might better have introduced them, their tall hats, their frock coats, and their odor and bearing of supercilious superiority to the ribald mercies of Will Rogers and our indigenous philosophers round the cracker barrel in Main

Street groceries across the continent. Once and for all, Joseph Wood Krutch in "The Modern Temper" has characterized our American suspicions of philosophy imposed from above when he concluded that "metaphysics may be, after all, only the act of being sure of something that is not so and logic only the art of going wrong with confidence."

That the machine, the Machine Age and America as we know it need humanizing requires neither proof, argument nor reminder. But we shall achieve these ends by ourselves, in our own time and in our own way, utilizing the experience which has taught us and the tools and ideals which have been faithful to us under fire.

That the arts provide many of these tools which we have tried and found true is a fact which is only slowly dawning upon our consciousness. That these tools may combine to fashion a key, one of the five major keys for unlocking the mystery of life, is a conclusion in which neither Krutch nor Lippmann nor Waldo Frank nor any of the other critics of Machine Age America have dared to repose their faith. Our arts have not been notably thinking arts. But they have been feeling arts, addressing themselves freely and spontaneously, if often cheaply and sentimentally, to our emotions. No one can accept them, on the basis of what they are and what they have done thus far, as the manifold facets of the Great Interpreter which we are seeking. But their vitality is so inexhaustible and their adaptability so infinite that the only thing to prevent their becoming the Great Interpreter will be our failure to desire it.

Before we put each of the arts to the test for serious candidacy for this exhausting task, let us glance for a moment at the relationship of the arts with the other traditional Great Interpreters. If we revert to the seven ages of history which we chose early in this

73

chapter and the keys which we found they used, we see that the key of the arts was most freely employed in classic Greece, in the Middle Ages, and during the Renaissance. Once, during the Middle Ages, the arts were collaborators with religion in the attempt to interpret human destiny. Twice, in classic Greece and during the Renaissance, the arts shared this function with philosophy. Never before have they undertaken a partnership with science.

The arts were loyal and humble handmaidens of religion during the Middle Ages. With literature's exception of Dante—an exception so towering as almost to nullify the exception—painting, sculpture and architecture bore the burden of this service, for music had hardly emerged from its swaddling clothes. Europe is still dotted with evidences of this mighty collaboration, which extended from the ardent Italy of Giotto, Cimabue, Masaccio, and Fra Angelico, to the bleak Low Countries of Jan van Eyck. Lippmann has devised a plausible theory to explain the fecundity of these artist-servants of the church, maintaining that the ordered belief of that church gave them patterns and explicit instructions for them to follow, relieving them of the burden of what to say with their brush and chisel, a burden which, he maintains, weighs prohibitively on the shoulders of the artist at work in our aimless and faithless world today. But the artists of the Middle Ages did something far more than illustrate the tenets of Rome and indulge their professional fancies in line and color. By their naive use, as models, of the men and women and children and the pastoral and urban scenes under their eyes to represent the chapters of the Holy Story, they introduced a human tenderness into the austerity of the accepted faith which must in turn have humanized and inspired the ecclesiastical spokesmen of that faith and have justified their rôle as co-equal and co-eval prophets with the saints who gave them hire. In other words, religion created a culture; and the culture in turn recreated religion.

In the two great ages when the arts shared their prophetic responsibility with philosophy, the same interaction may be observed. Greek philosophy germinated Greek art, but Greek art in turn revitalized Greek philosophy, and the two keys working together gave us the unsurpassed glory of Greek civilization. It is not so simple to trace the processes of germination and re-creation in their interplay between philosophy and the arts during the Renaissance, for the New Learning and the new flowering of painting, sculpture, architecture, music and literature took place in successive waves which finally covered the European continent; but that the two Great Interpreters did so interact and exhilarate one another is more reasonable to believe than that they co-existed in isolation from one another. Nothing so conclusively condemns the various philosophies which have been suggested thus far as the Great Interpreter of the Machine Age as their failure to make contact with the arts of the Machine Age, not to mention its dominant interpreter, science.

If we shift our imagery and terminology to comport with the Machine Age and substitute the idea of the reagent for the concept of germination and re-creation and the interplay of these two forces, we shall obtain a clue to the presumptive interrelationship between the arts and science in our own day, a combination of Great Interpreters which, as I have said, is a phenomenon without previous parallel. It is the prime requisite of the chemical reagent that it possess the faculty of *combining* with another chemical for the sake of ascertaining the latter's nature or composition by means of their mutual reactions. In other words, in our present situation, the arts would be the reagent for a better understanding of science, and science the reagent for a clearer conception of the arts; both of them, thus clarified, serving man the more fully as Great Interpreters. But do science and the arts have this faculty of combining, of reacting upon one another, of complementing each other, of collaborating toward this sublime end?

I believe they do.

Science and the arts must have sufficient affinity with one another to get along together; they must differ from one another enough to avoid duplication of service, and between them they must answer human needs so fully that man will not have to seek his answer elsewhere.

Although science and the arts have been traditionally supposed to be hostile to one another, science sneering at the inexactitude and irresponsibility of the arts and the arts resentful of science's penchant for meticulous measurement, we are gradually coming to a realization that this antipathy is fallacious. With the collapse of faith in and dependence upon rigid and unalterable dogmatic theory, whether it be religious or philosophic, we are beginning to see that the reverse of that method is the common attribute of both science and the arts. Science—true, patient science—is in no haste to construct final systems. Neither are the arts, at least not the arts in a period of revolt. Science holds the door open for any new fact, is always ready to readjust its most treasured calculations to admit that new fact. Unless the arts have surrendered their independence, to become mere complacent satellites of an intrenched tradition, they, too, welcome with open arms the fresh, the new, the untried. Nor are science and the arts merely tolerant, open-minded and amenable to that revision which characterizes true growth. Instead of passively awaiting the new, they go out and seek it, no matter how it may embarrass their previous conclusions. In other words, both science and the arts are admirably equipped in spirit and in behavior to serve as interpreters of an age of chaos, of revolt, keeping abreast of the times and building their new truth step by step out of proved experience, unhampered by the dead hand of preconceived doctrine.

Nor need we fear from them a mere drifting with the wind or whimsical excursions down blind alleys. The pseudo-scientist and the faddist artist may indulge in the latter pastime, just as, in an age of religious or philosophic faith, sensation-seeking theologians and philosophers beckoned impressionable followers down misleading by-ways. But the true scientist, like the true artist, values his integrity so highly that he announces his conclusions only after long and patient proof and testing in laboratory or studio.

That science and the arts possess these congenial habits in common and that these habits are appropriate to the age in which we live, is not enough. Science and the arts must dovetail into one another, must each serve a common purpose in its individual way, must serve that purpose without the need of outside aid.

Faith in this dual service and in its combined self-sufficiency is beginning to find clear and convincing expression. Although we are only on the verge of a general acceptance of this faith and have hardly dared to dream of whither it may lead us, I have found it possible to construct the following extraordinarily comprehensive and coherent composite apologia for that faith from the recent works of seven artists, scientists and critics of both:

Art is science incarnate.[1] *Art is merely humanized science.*[2] *When you understand all about the sun and all about the atmos-*

---

[1] Jean Cocteau in "Le Secret Professionel."
[2] Gino Severini in "Du Cubisme au Classicisme."

phere and all about the rotation of the earth, you may still miss the radiance of the sunset. . . . Thus "art" in the general sense which I require is any selection by which the concrete facts are so arranged as to elicit attention to particular values which are realizable by them. . . . The habit of art is the habit of enjoying vivid values.[3] *While the artist contributes nothing scientific to the theory either of individual or social behavior, his genius for penetrating insights and intuitional glimpses of the personality, as it were, often reveal much that is within the individual that a more scientific method cannot capture or communicate.*[4] *In one sense the aim of the scientist and the aim of the artist are the same since both are in pursuit of what they call truth; but the difference between them may be said to consist in this, that while for science there is only one Truth, for the artist there are many. The scientist, that is to say, is in search of truths which owe their name to the fact that they correspond to something in the world outside himself, while the artist is in search of those which need to be true only in the sense that they seem true to him and that they hold good within the artificial universe which is inclosed within the frame of the work of art he is creating.*[5] *Without it (imagination), science and engineering become dogmatic and sterile. It must be and is being cultivated and nourished as one of the essential forces of the modern world. Imagination, informed by the known laws of nature, but unbound and free to experiment and dare, combined with the spirit of rationality, lives and flowers in the engineering age and will swing new planets into the ken of those who watch the heavens for signs of the future.*[6] *Our attitude toward life is illu-*

[3] A. N. Whitehead in "Science and the Modern World."
[4] V. F. Calverton in "The New Ground of Criticism."
[5] Joseph Wood Krutch in "The Modern Temper."
[6] Charles A. Beard in "Toward Civilization."

minated by the conviction that man through science can arrive at power. In other days one could take the world as he found it or he could turn from this world to fix his gaze on a life to come. Today we have a third choice. We believe that we can take this universe about us in our hands and within limits make it safer and freer and happier. . . . We purpose by comprehension and courage to remould it nearer to the heart's desire.[7] Evidently the honeymoon intoxication of the Machine Age will pass soonest in the countries which have been the first to experience it. I look, therefore, to the western nations, and more particularly to America, to establish first that more humane, more stable, and more truly scientific civilization toward which, as I hope, the world is tending.[8]

But if science and the arts are to fulfill the function of Great Interpreters for the Machine Age, to carry it through to a satisfactory understanding of itself and to a concentration of its incredible forces upon humanly desirable ends, both of these Great Interpreters must gird themselves to sustain their solemn responsibilities. We need have little fear for science. Equipped with laboratories, instruments, financial endowment and devoted and brilliant personnel beyond the wildest dreams of its pioneers, science has survived the chastening experiences of its adolescent years, has become expert in the use of its technical methods and has been organized for its maximum efficiency.

It is far otherwise with the arts. The theatre, the cinema, the dance, music, literature, painting and sculpture, architecture and the craft arts must build up, step by step, that cooperative driving power whereby any new glimpse of truth and beauty and significant form which any one of them discovers may be communicated

[7] C.–E. A. Winslow in "Whither Mankind."
[8] Bertrand Russell in "Whither Mankind."

to all the rest, just as, today, the slightest discovery of mathematics
or psychology is communicated to all of the other sciences. Such
an articulation among the arts, of course, presupposes a corresponding articulation within each art. As we put each of the
arts to the test for its presumptive service as interpreter, we must
ascertain to what extent it has mastered its esthetic and its mechanical technique—in other words its content and its form; to
what extent its distribution has been efficiently organized; and to
what extent it is imbued with the willingness to play the rôle of
prophet. It would be ironic, though it is altogether possible, that
the arts of the Machine Age should develop technical efficiency
and reap vast riches from that efficiency, without contributing
comparably to the understanding of human destiny. But such a
dénouement, though possible, is unthinkable, for it would be a
catastrophe without parallel in the history of the race.

4. The Visual and Auditory Arts as Interpreters

A. The Theatre

It is one of the inexplicable phenomena of civilization that the
theatre, although a composite of various arts, anticipated all of
its component arts, except poetry, in reaching its maturity in
Aeschylus, and that even in poetry the annals of Greece disclose
only Homer, Hesiod and Sappho as comparable forerunners of
Aeschylus. Both because of its venerable service to mankind and
its comprehensive integration of the arts of literature, music, the
plastic body resembling sculpture in movement, and the plastic
stage setting resembling architecture, the theatre might be suspected of having served as a Great Interpreter in ages when the
arts were one of the keys to understanding, and it might be ex-

pected to fulfill this function as notably as any of the rest in the Machine Age.

The records bear out this suspicion. Not only Aeschylus but Sophocles, Euripides and Aristophanes were the rivals and peers of Phidias among fellow-artists and of Plato and Aristotle among contemporary philosophers in the first great age when the arts undertook the burden of explaining human destiny. Likewise, in both of the other ages when the arts subserved a similar purpose, we find a golden age of the theatre. The mystery and morality plays, bearing the stamp of isolated local cultures across Europe, have come down to us alongside the cathedrals and the sacred paintings to attest to man's dependence on their prophetic and interpretive aid throughout the Middle Ages. And it is a commonplace of theatrical history that this art has never surpassed its achievements during the Renaissance, with Shakespeare, Marlowe, Jonson, Beaumont and Fletcher, and a score of lesser lights as its prophets in England; Racine, Corneille and Molière in France; Ariosto and Aretino in Italy; and Lope de Vega and Calderon in Spain.

But do the records of the theatre in the Machine Age bear out the expectation? They do, and they don't. That is, they do in Europe, but they are only beginning to do so in America. Gordon Craig and Appia would have been powerless to prophesy a new theatre and, through it, a new life, without the most mysterious and the most omnipotent gift of the Machine Age, electricity. Almost every country in Europe discloses playwrights who have sought to resolve the enigmas propounded to us by the Machine Age, whether economically, socially, or merely humanly. Ireland has given us Shaw; England, Galsworthy, at least with his "Strife" and "Justice"; Italy, Pirandello; central Europe, Wedekind, Toller and on occasion Molnar; Scandinavia, Strindberg; and Russia, Tchekhoff and Gorky, both of them prophets even before their day. Although few outstanding artists of prophetic stature have yet appeared, the stages of Soviet Russia, and, to a lesser degree, those of Central Europe are a welter of straining, plunging efforts to understand and evaluate their surrounding chaos.

It is only within the memory of true children of the Machine Age, however, that the theatre in America has thrown off the impedimenta of the Nineteenth Century and has striven seriously to become an art rather than a pleasant pastime. Even yet, it is timid about assuming the robes of the Prophet, but Eugene O'Neill, Paul Green, Elmer Rice and John Howard Lawson, among playwrights, have dared to try, and since they are all young men, the best work of all of them is probably still locked up within their imagination. Meanwhile, the playwright's fellow-worker, the stage designer, has reacted to the stimulus of Craig and to the omnipresent challenge of the machine as form to such an extent that I would be willing to sink the American theatre— playwright, actor, producer, and physical equipment—and trust to Norman Bel Geddes, Robert Edmond Jones, Lee Simonson, Joseph Urban and Hermann Rosse to direct its remaking.

Creatively, what the American theatre needs more than anything else is plays. We have an admirable body of acting talent, if at the moment no acting genius—a group of young, eager sensitive artists waiting for something significant to be put into their hands. We have writers who have something to say about life, who should be able to say it dramatically, but who have never tried the theatre. Someone should kidnap Vachel Lindsay, Robert Frost, Ernest Hemingway, James Stephens, Dorothy Canfield and Sherwood Anderson, just for a trial panel, and refuse to release them until they had written a play! Theodore Dreiser, Edwin Arlington Robinson and Thornton Wilder should be induced to try again, while Philip Barry should be encouraged to test his wings in full flight.

But the American theatre is not a very encouraging laboratory for experiment. The administrative and economic reasons for this fact I set forth at length in "Our American Theatre," and most of those reasons hold as true today as when they were first published in 1923. More recently, Roy Mitchell has analyzed these handicaps with a practical imagination in his "Creative Theatre." It is sufficient here to recall the major charges:

The American theatre, both in New York and across the continent, has been over-built by real estate speculators who sought to cash in on boom times.

It has been organized on a short-sightedly commercial basis which ignores the soundly financial as well as the artistic values of the permanent company and true repertory presentation of plays.

It has permitted greed and bad manners to rule the box office.

It has cheated its employees until they banded in self-defense and then has sold out cravenly to them without a concerted attempt at counter-attack.

Forgetting the warning of the first motion pictures, it has sneered at the latest and far more powerful rival, the sound film, without putting its own house in order, for comparison's sake, until it was too late.

It has been duly impressed by the example, in spirit and in administrative technique, of the Moscow Art Theatre and of other notable visitors brought to our stage by the world-searching Morris Gest; but when Gest proved not to be the man to rally our native forces to emulate these visitors, the example they revealed to us has all but gone by default.

And finally it has let a bigoted minority of "Meddlers," to use H. I. Brock's phrase, write into the statutes of the State of New York the impudent intimidation of the Wales Law, as well as local ordinances equally repressive throughout the country.

There is something of the hit-or-miss in the theatre. And there should be. Most of all the arts, it deals with the inspiration of the moment. Its values pass into memory as rapidly as they are achieved. There was something profoundly right, something strangely appropriate to the theatre, in the impromptu methods of the Italian *commedia dell'arte*. In other words, the law of diminishing returns soon starts operating in the theatre, and painstaking care beyond a certain point is not worth all it costs.

But that does not excuse the carelessness with which plays are written. Ill-made plays with good ideas and well-made plays with no ideas divide the bulk of the annual crop. Against my will I have been driven to the conclusion that most American playwrights who really have something to say neglect the arduous task of learning how to say it. Our actors, with few exceptions, soldier on the job and have hardly begun to realize what it means to work, a failing in which they have been encouraged by producers, who hurl a play at Broadway after mumbling a crap-shooter's spell over it.

The American theatre has richer potentialities for becoming an art theatre, an art which interprets and prophesies, than any other in the world today. But it will achieve that possible goal only if forces of revolt now at work maintain their courage and their persistence against overwhelming odds.

B. The Cinema

A radically different point of view from that which we have adopted toward the theatre is required by the cinema. A child among the arts, if an art at all, it is without a history, a tradition or a standard of comparison. Well on its way toward universal recognition as an independent art in its silent form, an art stemming from the theatre and from pantomime but contributing something all its own, the motion picture has suddenly decided to go back to the beginning and try all over again, this time borrowing more than ever from the parent theatre. More seriously than in the cinema's first infancy, the question is being asked: "Is the sound film an art on its own account or is it merely 'canned' theatre?"

In the nature of the case, all of its mechanical and technical expedients and problems, its economic factors, its esthetic form and content, and the relationship of the participating actor toward it, are issues of more immediate importance than its ultimate potentialities as an interpreter of life—issues which must be solved satisfactorily before that fundamental question can even be approached. That they *can* be solved satisfactorily and that the cinema *may* in time take its place among the traditionally prophetic arts, no unprejudiced mind will deny. Whether they *will* be so solved, assuring the cinema of a secure place among the elder visual and auditory arts, is a question which lies with the public as much as it does with those in artistic and executive control of its affairs. In other words, whereas the theatre has won recognition, and retained it for over two thousand years, of its peculiar conventions; whereas it has held titanic figures in its allegiance; whereas it has proved again and again its potency as solace and guide to the human emotions and the human intellect, the cinema is still on trial. It is well that both its most sanguine spokesmen and its most bitter and cynical opponents should remember this fact; the former lest they be too easily satisfied with its achievements, many of which already are extraordinary and spectacular, and the latter lest the laugh of future generations settle upon them as it has upon the detractors of Wagner, of Poe and of Whitman.

One of the easiest mistakes which judges of the arts, lay or professional, can make is to confuse the medium of an art and its use. The film-faithful have tended to concentrate on the medium and its potentialities; the film-heretics, on the ends to which that medium has been devoted. Meanwhile, the film-public, still beguiled as by a new toy with the mere mechanism of the cinema, especially since the introduction of sound, accepts and applauds.

In the case of an art on trial, it is well to begin with the mechanical and technical considerations on which its inner power of expression, if it has any, depends for reaching its public. Minus sound, color and the perspective of a third dimension, the old silent film had so nearly mastered its medium as to convince all but a handful of skeptics of its right to a separate place in the sun of the arts when all of its faculties were in full play. Roaming at will, not alone within terrestrial limits but to the outer boundaries of the human imagination, it shamed the tethered and pedestrian theatre as light waves shame the waves of sound. Both by this unprecedented mobility and by its consequent command of subtle intimation, its variation from the theatre was so largely a matter of kind rather than degree as to forecast its ultimate unreserved acceptance as an independent art. If the third dimension and the privilege of using color had been fully perfected while the film was in its silent state, its days on the waiting list of the arts would have been over.

But sound came first, catapulting it back toward the theatre. General use of color arrived alongside sound, thus forfeiting to its more impressive and exciting rival the attention which it would have won coming alone. The third of the long-sought mechanical improvements and extensions of the film, true perspective, is still in such a problematic and experimental stage that sound has the field of curiosity and argument all to itself, for the so-called "grandeur" film, though a big step forward from the tiny silver screen now lost in large cinema auditoriums, is a development in degree rather than in kind. Inside the studios, the concern is for more perfect synchronization of sight and sound, more perfect tonal reproduction. Outside the studios, discussion takes the form of how long the vogue of the sound film will endure, whether the film will ever return to its silent estate, what its relationship and attitude toward the theatre will be. The answer to all these questions seems to me to be dependent upon the answer to another and much more penetrating question: When and to what extent will the sound film master its unique opportunity, not to ape the theatre with consecutive dialogue, but to create illusion and heighten dramatic climax by the use of sound, words or no, as a contrapuntal accompaniment to the melody of its pantomime. The sooner this question is answered, and answered in positive achievement, the sooner we can be sure that the sound film has come to stay, that its attitude toward the theatre will be that of friendly and seldom competitive rival, and that its relationship to the theatre will be one of drawing apart from it. Under such a policy, the sound film would thrive best on stories written for its own unique facilities for expression, as the silent film did in its latter days after traversing the present path of the sound film in attempting to "can" the theatre for mass distribution.

Economic questions run those of mechanical technique a close second in professional concern and public curiosity. This is to be taken for granted in an art whose distributive structure has been developed so recently and so rapidly. Gigantic financial battles have been and still are the order of the day, struggles of Wall Street to obtain control of an enormously profitable industry. But, while the low admission price protects the cinema against seasonal or industrial depression, it has the public as audience which will call the tune for producers and exhibitors, compelling them to make of the motion picture an art or permitting them to exploit it as a business.

To ascertain, therefore, whether the cinema is a likely candidate for one of our Great Interpreters among the arts, it is necessary to examine its current and conceivable content and the likelihood of a public demand for improvement of that content or of public toleration for such improvement if it should be offered. Cynics used to maintain in the early days of the silent film that no travesty of it was possible, that it was its own burlesque. The same stricture was revamped for the sound film, but the studios have made such rapid improvement in technical methods that this criticism of the talking picture has had short life. With a few notable exceptions, however, the content of the sound film has been less interesting and significant than its still unperfected mechanism. Hiding behind the psychological estimate of twelve years as the average coefficient of the American mass mind, a dictum open to grave doubt like all of the attempts of the social sciences at exact measurement, the masters of the American cinema have laid themselves open to the Rabelaisian irony of Elmer Rice's "A Voyage to Purilia," a gay and withering glimpse of an incredibly perfect and perfectly undesirable society, the details of which the author did not have to leave a cinema auditorium to gather. But "Disraeli" and "All Quiet on the Western Front" were not made for the twelve-year-old mind, and their unexpected success may awaken film producers to the possibility of making sound pictures which are sound expressions and interpretations of life. If the American mass mind is only twelve years old, the Russian mass mind, with its still vast strata of illiteracy, can probably be set at eight or ten years. But from what we have seen of Russian films, Eisenstein and his fellow-directors have not let that deter them from crowding their films with honest observation of the life surrounding their audiences and of serious, if socially prejudiced, interpretation of it. The subtleties of philosophic argument may have to be reserved for the truly adult mind. But the cinema, after all, is no place for argument, and even the adult mind seeks in it those direct emotional conceptions and conclusions for which its technique is fitted, retiring to the library lamp or the intimate theatre for those finer distinctions of dialectic which only maturity can appreciate.

Apart from a legitimate curiosity regarding mechanical equipment and the fantastic finances of this prodigious infant industry, and in addition to grave concern over the insignificance of the subject matter of the American film, those who are seriously interested in its future as an interpretive art are concerned most over its esthetic, as apart from purely mechanical, technique. Is the art of the film condemned by its nature to be always realistic? "The Cabinet of Dr. Caligari" seemed to answer no, but where have been the successors of that extraordinary voyage beyond the boundaries of realism? It is not difficult to conceive of "Caligaris" made even more extraordinary and eloquent with sound. Is the film held to a realistic earth and to a sisterhood with the begrudged art of photography by its dependence upon the cameraman? The answer to that, it seems to me, even if photography is ruled out of the great arts as a mere copyist, is that the film is art, or may be art, by virtue of its limitless mobility and its freedom to create sequence in event as well as in character and thereby to achieve interpretation.

It is not so easy, however, to detect an escape for the actor as artist in the films from the aridity which Pirandello has thus described in "Shoot," his novel of the motion pictures: "They see themselves withdrawn, feel themselves torn from that direct communion with the public from which in the past they derived their richest reward, their greatest satisfaction: that of seeing, of hearing from the stage, in a theatre, an eager, anxious multitude follow their *live* action, stirred with emotion, tremble, laugh, become excited, break out in applause." It is George Arliss, it seems to me, who has discovered the most hopeful means of escape for the film interpreter of stage plays in his declaration: "It is my opinion that the performance of any good actor is incomplete until it has come in contact with an audience. There is no substitute for the inspiration which an actor gets from 'the public.' If this is true, then an actor who plays a part on the talking screen which he has not previously played before an audience is, at any rate, not seen at his best." When the sound film has forgotten the stage play to pursue its own characteristic and independent opportunities, this recourse of the actor will be out of the question, but by that time the development of his technique will probably provide him with exciting substitutes to make up for his loss.

While time, the scientific laboratory, and public opinion are showing what they can do in confirming the cinema as an independent and interpretive art, an excellent program will be to wait and see. The impatience of esthetes like Aldous Huxley, who thrive on the exquisite sublimation of a perfect past, is becoming almost as boresome as the claims of the electric signs outside the picture palaces. Would these esthetes have been any more tolerant of the arts they worship if they had lived in the infancy of those arts? I doubt it! Born of a continent bursting with power but devoid of tradition, of a race conglomerate in its make-up but rich in potentialities, in a time when earth-rocking decisions were made overnight, the motion picture, especially in its latest phase, the sound film, is an art in the making. Let us wait and see what the Germans and the Russians do to it. We invented the silent film; they proved what it could do to help us understand life. Perhaps we shall not have to wait so long to find out the possibilities of the sound film with numerous Germans and the Russian Eisenstein already in Hollywood.

America's masters of the film can not be charged with lethargy in the face of loss of an international market because of the coming of the sound film. Apparently they are determined to import entire national film staffs or to produce abroad themselves in order to preserve the international currency of America's message to the world. Or is it, ironically, a message that there is no message?

C. The Dance

"I see America dancing," wrote Isadora Duncan not long before her tragic death. She had seen America dancing from the earliest unconscious awakening of her talent in California childhood. It was the mysterious faculty of the greatest artist whom

America has yet given to the world to foresee, to visualize clearly, that which had not yet happened, and to cling indomitably to her vision in the face of superhuman odds, many of them of her own making.

I know of nothing more discouraging in the entire realm of the arts in America than our apparently willful decision to refuse to fulfill Isadora's vision for us. It is almost as if, chagrined at our ostracism of her genius, even after she had conquered the world and reinspired the Russian ballet, we were perversely determined to prove that we had been right by consciously continuing to be wrong. Yet that is only seeming. An entire nation does not cohere in such an emotional decision. The reason must be sought elsewhere.

But when we start seeking reasons, we find that the invitation to the dance has been extended to us by others than Isadora. The Diaghileff Ballet on one of its periodic wave crests spent two seasons with us, during one of which we were treated to the mad genius of Nizhinsky. Pavlova and Mordkin preceded the Ballet Russe in full force, and either remained or returned. Bolm tarried behind Diaghileff. Fokine came in his wake. And meanwhile in addition to Isadora from our own soil, Loie Fuller, Maude Allan, Gertrude Hoffman, Harald Kreuzberg and Ruth St. Denis and Ted Shawn beckoned us down a path toward which it would appear we were temperamentally predisposed. Had we not the primitive example of the aboriginal dancing Indian? The equally natural impulse and stimulus of the imported Negro? The urge of the physical body freely released in conquering a wilderness, kept free after that task was fulfilled by a universal devotion to outdoor sport? The challenge of the machine with its driving pace and suggestive rhythm?

And yet what is the inventory of the dance in America today? A score of isolated concert dancers and their pupils, such as Miss St. Denis and Mr. Shawn, Martha Graham, Charles Weidman, Doris Humphrey, Maria Theresa, Irma and Anna Duncan, Anita Zahn, Sara Mildred Strauss, Angna Enters, Tamiris and others, avidly snatching the crumbs of evenings in Sabbath-darkened theatres until a Blue Law is invoked against even that outlet. The Neighborhood Playhouse, closed as such after a half million outlay in a dozen years, but stubbornly carrying on at the devoted instance of the Lewisohns in permanent school and annual lyric festival. The Dance Repertory Theatre and the American Ballet Guild, naive and halting stabs at concerted endeavor. The grudgingly endowed and seldom utilized ballets of the Metropolitan and Chicago Civic operas under the aegis of Ruth Page or another native or foreign ballerina. The glib-toed cohorts of our light musical stage occasionally employing the distinctive talents of a Martha Lorber, a Harriet Hoctor, a Jacques Cartier. The dance classes of resident Russians and others which release an annual crop of students a hundred fold greater than the demands of the professional market. And all America out on the floor ceaselessly whirling to tom-tom rhythms. America dancing, but not as Isadora envisioned!

So much smoke, but so little fire!

What will fan this smoldering congeries of centrifugal effort into the concentrated flame of Great Interpretation? It may seem brutally frank to say so, but I suspect only an opportunity for commercial gain or a munificent endowment of an extraordinary genius for synthesis, organization and inspired leadership. If this is true, three lines of research are open, two of which must be closely coordinated to be of any avail.

93

Putting the art of the dance on a paying basis, a never-failing incentive to achievement when it can be uncovered and set in motion, is extremely unlikely even under the most favorable circumstances. I can conceive of the sound film making remunerative use of great dancing when it reaches its own artistic apogee, and I shall have something to say later of its responsibilities in that juncture. But the occasional public interest in a compelling dance personality is not likely to disturb the rule that substantial rewards will be reserved for stunt performers in the revues.

We must hunt a Maecenas, then. A Maecenas, because the art of the dance has rarely if ever thriven except under heavy endowment since it emerged from a primitive tribal ceremonial and became one of civilization's most costly forms of esthetic expression. Costly because of the long and arduous training required. Costly to imperial court, to private patron or to the public coffers. The Tsar spent a prince's ransom annually on the Russian Ballet. The Soviet Government continues that subsidy. Various private individuals heaped fortune after fortune in the lap of Diaghileff, the periodic signals for the successive phoenix-like rebirths of his extraordinary company. Even Isadora's vision of America dancing would have to depend upon public and private school funds for its realization.

And we must hunt a Diaghileff. A Diaghileff, because the art of the dance is also dependent upon a single, unifying, inspiring imagination, an impeccable esthetic taste, a voracious, insatiable and open-minded curiosity for fresh esthetic experience. A Diaghileff—or an Isadora. Perhaps, after all, the princely bearing of the impresario and master mind of the Ballet Russe would not find America any more congenial than we would find him. The essen-

94

tial democracy of another Isadora would probably win and keep our confidence more readily. And, bearing in mind America's prudential proclivities, it would be well to have a business manager for our project who would know how and when to give rein to creative temperament and when to hold it in leash with that same unobtrusive skill whereby the late Edmund Reinhardt served his brother, Max.

We scan the horizon without seeing a hint of these desired figures but we must not lose hope. And we may be permitted the hope that when they come, they will come together.

Meanwhile, we have ample material waiting to be touched to life. Subject material as well as personal material. Young as we are as a nation and mixed as a race, we can draw on the folklore of the Indian and of the Negro, on the legends of the pioneer north and west and of the southern mountains, and on the aspirations of democracy. What folk tale or character of an older world can rival that of Paul Bunyan as a challenge to choreography? And, before it is too late, we must not forget to husband the legends which our component races from overseas have brought along with them.

As subject material waits, so do the creative artists essential to its shaping and its interpretation—composers eager to try their hand; poets who, in the absence of a native art of the dance, entrust to the printed page tales which would lend themselves much more vividly and thrillingly to use as ballet librettos; dancers who are lone wolves today, suspicious of cooperation with their fellows only because the inspiring master, able to win their confidence, is lacking.

Nor are the outlets sparse. Varied opportunities await the coming of a greatly dancing America. The concert platform can always be adjusted to meet the supply. The opera houses, presumably, would not reject great dancing if they had the choice between it and the miserable stuff with which they now have to be content. They might even be induced to place the art of the dance as ballet, after the example of the Russian Operas, on a co-operatively independent basis with one or two performances a week, if at first it proves unwise or impossible to organize a wholly independent ballet like that of Diaghileff. Even the revue stage and the sound film would not turn up their noses at great dancing if it were available, remembering the triumphs of Diaghileff in the London music halls.

All these outlets, of course, are of interest only to the dance as consciously professional art. But when Isadora had her vision, she saw America dancing in the open air, on vast concourses, on village greens. The dance as a communal and a folk art rather than as a profession. The dance for the sake of the exhilaration and the exaltation of the dancing individual, rather than the dance as a performance for an audience. But I suspect that such a goal can be attained only after great performers have inspired and proved its possibility.

If such a birth of the art of the dance in America is possible—it can not be rebirth, for we have never had it—I should like to see it take the broadly flexible form of an Isadora Duncan Memorial, as a final expiation of our blindness to her inspiration when she brought it to us in the flesh. Not a rigidly institutionalized Memorial. Not a literal reading of her message or an attempt to copy what she tried to do. But an assurance that the upcropping of fresh genius in the art which she honored, no matter how much it differed from her own, might have its opportunities for expression without the fear of neglect, ridicule or exile.

D. Music

None of the arts compares with music in universal acceptance and practice as an art. Appealing directly to the emotions and, through them or often directly, to the intellect, music would probably be ranked first among the arts as Great Interpreters by more people than all of the other arts put together. After all, it is the almost wholly mental appeal of science which leaves us in need of something else. We understand, we are moved to action or resignation, more readily and more profoundly if not more exactly, through the emotions than through the mind. The great religious leaders knew that secret. To the extent that they have forgotten it, religion has lost its human leadership. To the extent that religion still serves as guide, solace and preceptor, it works almost wholly through the emotions. In its great days, religion capitalized the emotional power of all of the arts, but on none of them did it lean so heavily as on music. Modern music is the child of the church even more than the modern theatre through its fore-fathers, the mystery and morality plays of the Middle Ages. But religion needed music more than music needed religion, as has been proved by the world-wide independent development of the art, irrespective of its early sponsor.

Admitted, therefore, as a Great Interpreter by those who may question one or more of the other arts as suited for that capacity, music as a whole is not on trial. What concerns us, rather, is the question of musical performance, reproduction and distribution, a question which has been referred to frequently in previous pages and which will recur again in our effort to devise a way to protect the performing musician against his mechanically reproduced rival. Apart from this engrossing problem of distribution, however, several sidelights of the art of music in contemporary America deserve attention here. Among the most important of them are the interrelationship of music and the machine, the decentralization of music through the agency of the machine, the ultimate effect of jazz as a by-product of the Machine Age and the perennially debated question of the opera and its adjustment to the times in which we live.

As I have remarked before, the machine has affected the form of music most notably in the work of Gershwin, Carpenter, Antheil and Ornstein. Oddly, however, the machine seems to have stimulated the imagination of European composers more than our own. Recent seasons have given us such examples as Krenek's "Jonny Spielt Auf," Max Brand's "Maschinist Hopkins" and Eugen d'Albert's "Schwarze Orchidée." Perhaps the machine has overwhelmed them less than it has us. Possibly the machine *is* music to us. It is hard to understand why the American permits the incessant tangled rhythms of our urban noises unless he likes them.

The machine is more significant and more potent, however, in the incredible impetus which it has given to the decentralization of music in America. Basil Maine in his recent book, "Reflected Music," has sounded the rational attitude toward the question of music and the machine: "Mechanized music," he writes, "is not a retrogression, but a logical development, a development which may be called 'intensive instrumentation.' . . . The invasion of mechanized music is inevitable, and it were better to take full advantage of the advancing tide than to drown ignominiously."

Recognition of the wisdom of that policy has enabled Walter Damrosch to enlist five million school children in his weekly radio audience with three million more in sight within the next season or two. In fact, the radio, the electrically perfected phonograph, the player-piano, and the sound film stand fundamentally in relationship to music in much the same position as the printing press to literature. No one in his right mind blames the printing press for turning out cheap and meretricious books and magazines and newspapers. It is all a question of how we use the printing press—and the mechanical distributors of music. That they have not yet been used as they should be is a problem in the education of public taste, just as it is in literature. The projected Rockefeller Radio City, for instance, will be just as important as the public demands that it be—no more, no less. Encouraging signs of an improved public taste and a greater readiness to respond to it are at hand in the example of Dr. Damrosch and in the efforts of the makers of piano rolls and phonograph records to put the best of classic and modern music within the reach of all.

Those who still look with dismay upon the conquests of mechanized music would do well to remember the fate of the long-faced critics of jazz when that first-born of the musical children of the Machine Age swept across America and the world. Every art has its calamity-howlers, and music is cursed with them more than the other arts just because it has a more universal place in human affairs. By now, it is clear that the art of music has survived the jazz age; that jazz was freely written and eagerly accepted by an entirely new stratum of society simply because it was music monotonously simplified; that this same new stratum is now ready for a more mature and more complex music; and that this more mature and more complex music has profited by the rivalry of jazz in cleaning its own house of deadwood and traditional inhibitions.

The opera remains. Ancient Mariner of the esthetic seas, the opera is always dying, but it never dies. If everyone who has ever vowed that he would never enter an opera house again should carry out his threat, attendance would be sadly depleted. But the records show that it is not. Ernest Newman has recently analyzed most sagely the reason why: "Opera," he writes, "is, or at any rate sets before itself the ideal of being, not a mechanical mixture but a chemical compound, not a forced association of opportunities and incompatibles but a very subtle interfusion of elements that are instinctively groping toward each other in order to create something that has a more intense life than either can have alone. . . . It owes this vitality to the very fact that it is made up of so many elements. It will perhaps never succeed in establishing a perfect equilibrium between them all; but it is the eternal effort toward this equilibrium that gives it eternal life. . . . This oldest and apparently least rational of forms is the one form that has within itself the capacity for endless rebirth."

The vitality of opera, however, and its continuing service as an interpreting art are dependent on meeting these readjustments of equilibrium boldly and resourcefully and not by hiding behind an outworn tradition. The first responsibility rests upon the composer, and, as Francis Toye has recently remarked, "No man who bothers about good taste can, save exceptionally, write a good opera at all." But without an operatic management equally unafraid to step on someone's toes, the composer is stopped in his tracks.

Readjustment of the opera to the time in which we live seems to me to involve a frank recognition of the fact that true lyric drama is more germane to our tastes today than the traditional grand opera, that the singing actor as contrasted with the mere singer is a primary requirement for the interpretation of this lyric drama, and that, so far as the vast American public is concerned, the language of this lyric drama should be the language which we speak and understand.

Not so long ago, there was a school of professional and popular criticism which urged opera to embrace the further supposed reform of realistic interpretation. That was when realism was rampant in the theatre. Now that a slavish realism has lost its hold on the theatre, now that we see how much more exciting the theatre can be if we seek interpretively to present life rather than to represent it, we are ready to admit that realism has an even lesser place on the lyric stage and that stylization can be carried to an even higher pitch in the opera than it can in the theatre, due to the former's richer technical and expressive media.

Such an admission, however, does not relieve the opera of the responsibility for replacing dead formalism with live forms. The esthetic theories underlying this revitalization of opera as lyric drama I set forth in the chapter on the Synthetic Theatre in "Inside the Moscow Art Theatre." It was my plea then, and it is my plea still, that we should not be content with merely patching up the opera to keep a month or a year ahead of a more and more exacting clientele, but that we should boldly undertake to use it as a starting point for synthesizing all of the arts under the leadership of music and for fusing them in one supreme independent art comparable only to the Greek theatre in the annals of the race.

For this true lyric drama, which the boxholders of the existing opera houses will frankly abhor and which require millions of endowment before it can perfect its technique and train up a new and honestly appreciative public, the singing-actor is perhaps the most fundamental requirement. The singer who can act. The actor who can sing. Lip service to this ideal is all too prevalent. Too much credit is taken for the employment of a Chaliapin. Too many excuses are made for the mediocre voices of companies which have managed to solve the acting half of the problem. Vocal instruction blandly ignores the need for thorough grounding in the actor's art for all aspirants to the lyric stage, hiding behind the fallacious claim that no artist can act and sing at the same time. To that claim, David Belasco recently gave the lie direct when he said: "In the face of the most solemn pronunciamentos to the contrary, I maintain that it is eminently possible to sing and act simultaneously. Nearly all of the truly great singers have been great actors, too: Jean and Edouard de Reszke, Fyodor Chaliapin, Mary Garden, Geraldine Farrar, Maria Jeritza, Antonio Scotti. Whoever tells you that acting constrains the voice has a viciously mistaken conception of acting. The true actor conveys intensity without tensing his muscles, thus leaving his vocal muscles free for any demand that may be made on them. Any other theory is a confession of downright ignorance or laziness." Experienced in the ways of the theatre for a lifetime and invited to close collaboration with Puccini in the production of the two operas made from his own plays, "Madame Butterfly" and "The Girl of the Golden West," Belasco's verdict should be enough. But it probably won't. Sloth and the complacent theory that the public does not know the difference will have their way until other such ringing challenges awaken the public to the way it is being cheated.

Nor will opera as lyric drama ever approximate its possible service as interpreting art until English replaces languages so foreign to our masses that they all might as well be Chinese. The use of the original language is a laudable practice before an internationally cultured audience. But we shall never begin to approximate the potential service of lyric drama as Great Interpreter until every element of it, the speech, as well as the musical and poetic substance, appeals directly to our hearts and minds.

E. Television

Since it is too early yet for engineers to make definite predictions as to when and under what conditions the scientifically proved fact of television will become a practical instrument for general public use, or even whether such a development is feasible at all, the esthetic measurement of this most newly conceived of the art machines can afford to wait. Man of the Machine Age, nevertheless, has learned to be sanguine and credulous whenever science opens the crack of a new door; and, in his eagerness to anticipate the thrill of a new experience, he is already talking of what television will mean to him, if and when it comes.

Taking for granted its ultimate arrival, television at this distance looks like just another machine, a machine which will multiply almost incredibly the facilities for distribution which the arts already possess. But so did Edison's cinematograph at first acquaintance look like just another machine for distribution. With the still vivid memory of how the motion picture became, or was becoming, a distinct art, it is not surprising to hear serious discussions of a similar future for this new machine which proposes to send motion picture and sound sequences broadcast across the country without wires from the scene of the original action.

Television as the instantaneous and universal reporting of news events would be just a phenomenally speedier form of the tabloid newspaper. But television devoted to the distribution of the arts would exert an utterly incalculable influence on its presumptively component or contributing arts—the theatre, the cinema, music and the dance. That influence might be esthetic; it would certainly be economic. Until we know more about it than the most sensitive imagination can yet predict, we can not foresee whether or not, out of these component arts, television will be able to blend them in such a way as to justify its inclusion among the arts which, independently and in their own way, seek to interpret life.

5. *The Graphic and Plastic Arts as Interpreters*

A. Literature

No matter which of the arts may forge their way through to interpretive leadership in the Machine Age, the theatre has the most venerable and music the most enviable record in the past among the visual and auditory arts. To literature among the graphic and plastic arts must be granted the leadership for duration, intensity and brilliance of past service. As I have pointed out in our discussion of music, predominantly an emotional art, we are impressed "more readily and more profoundly if not more exactly, through the emotions than through the mind." As an art which almost invariably exerts its appeal directly to the mind and through it to the emotions, literature has been the great complement to music—the exact interpreter. Through the word, primarily a literal and dependable messenger to the intellect even though its audible quality may address itself directly to the emotions in poetry and ofttimes in prose, man conveys to his fellow-men the heights and depths of his living experience. Religion has employed the word for this purpose. So has philosophy. But the artist is able to use it in the same way and toward the same end without the intervention of either religion or philosophy.

In submitting literature to the test as a Great Interpreter of the Machine Age, we must not forget the key position of the word, for through it we shall discover more unresolved esthetic enigmas in the art of letters than in the tonal art and at least as many and even more aggravating problems in economics and distribution.

As reassurance against the discouragement of these contentious issues, it may be well first to canvass the major assets of our contemporary literature as interpretation. Hardly fulfilling the seemingly prophetic promise of a major literary renaissance, vouchsafed among other omens by the publication of Amy Lowell's "A Dome of Many Coloured Glass" and the first of Masters' Spoon River in *Reedy's Mirror* just before the war, our poetry has never let the impetus of that early revolt slacken completely; while Dreiser's resumption of the novel with "Jennie Gerhardt," not long before, heralded a similar continuity in fiction.

Interpreters of chaos we have; interpreters in the sense, at least, of fearlessly honest observers, even if they are sometimes blind to half the facts and therefore tend to misconstrue the rest—Dreiser, Anderson, Hemingway, Bromfield and Lewis among many others in the novel; Masters, Aiken, Sandburg, Eliot, Lindsay, Crane, and a score more in poetry.

Interpreters of eternal verities we have, standing staunch in the midst of chaos and in equally determined revolt against moribund tradition—Wilder and Cabell in fiction; Robinson, Benet and Jeffers in verse.

Interpreters of the future, not in terms of utopia but of the here-and-now—true prophets, in other words—we still await. Unless, as I suspect, Robert Frost is such an one.

Before we undertake to follow the ramifications of the word in esthetic controversy and economic predicament, it is well to make up our minds just what we mean by it. As I have said, the word is primarily the vehicle of the idea, of the mental concept. Through the imitative character of its derivative root, however, as well as through the sentimental accretions of long and varied use and through its abstract tonal and formal qualities, it possesses strong emotional potentialities apart from its meaning. It is undoubtedly these potentialities, these qualities and this character of the word—something more than mere rhetorical onomatopoeia—which have misled Gertrude Stein and her followers in their attempt to use the word as a kind of glorified musical note. It is beside the point to remind them that art which requires a key or a dictionary to be understood is futile and therefore bad art, for by deliberate intent there is little or nothing to "understand" in their work. With the best will in the world, however, it is impossible to anesthetize ourselves against the ideational connotations of their words, to the damage of their direct emotional appeal. Whatever enduring value lies in this specific esthetic revolt in literature may be observed in the employment of words by certain writers with an eye to *both* their mental and emotional appeal—notably in a few of the less fantastic, strained and pretentious poems of E. E. Cummings; in frequent passages of Conrad Aiken's novel, "Blue Voyage"; in the narrator's account of his journey under the tarpaulin on the freight car during the Italian retreat in Ernest Hemingway's "A Farewell to Arms"; and in the earlier short stories of Miss Stein herself. It is worth remarking that all of these instances deal with a highly sensitive nervous state on the border line between the conscious and the subconscious, and that for such a purpose we have hardly begun to utilize this tricky but eloquent dual faculty of the word.

It is this faculty of the word which should prove of untold value to the poet of the Machine Age, although his opportunities, responsibilities and liabilities extend far beyond this technical expedient. Shut off from certain experiences, subjects and points of view which have become obsolete, it is still his privilege as seer and visionary to hold before us the universal and eternal facts of life and death and to embody them in interpretive imagery sublimated from common experience. This new imagery is rebellious coinage, for the machine and its fruits, like the latest tenets of science regarding world-order, still have to acquire the glamour of perspective. But the true poet can distill that glamour without waiting for time to do it for him, and we are beginning to detect his success here and there. Limiting ourselves to the works of a single poet, Robinson Jeffers, although there is equally telling evidence in the pages of Carl Sandburg, Vachel Lindsay, Hart Crane and others, we find that he has successfully bent at least three products or examples of the machine to the poet's purposes:

(The dirigible—from "Phenomena")

". . . or with motor-vibrations
That hum in the rock like a new storm-tone of the ocean's to turn
   eyes westward
The navy's new-bought Zeppelin going by in the twilight,
Far out seaward; relative only to the evening star and the ocean
It slides into a cloud over Point Lobos."

(The aeroplane—in "Haunted Country")

In the dawn twilight metal falcons flew over the mountain,
Multitudes, and faded in the air;

(The battleship—in "Mal Paso Bridge")

The war-cruisers well-steerable and steel-belted
Traversing the prone sea
From eloquent round mouths in their mailed towers
Profess a metal language
Beyond the remote horizon ponderously
Significant;

The dual faculty of the word is applicable, likewise, to prose fiction, especially in the novel's growing tendency to undertake the clarification of the subconscious rather than to rest content with visible action and obvious characterization. I have already cited the instances of Aiken and Hemingway. Zona Gale experimented along these lines in "Preface to a Life," although she could have carried them even further to advantage. The same verdict seems to me to hold true for Theodore Dreiser in that extraordinary lyric passage baring the secret soul of Clyde Griffiths just at the turn of the volumes of "An American Tragedy."

Too much preoccupation with form, however, is just as serious an obstacle to a truly prophetic literature as complete indifference to form. The subtle balance of form and content—something significant to say perfectly said—is the ideal, an ideal, though, which is not likely to be generally observed in practice until we have resolved both the technical contradictions of literary expression and the chaotic life which literature sets itself to express and interpret. Meanwhile we shall have our Dreisers and our Andersons, often supercilious toward form in their revolt against a dead formalism which had nothing to say and in their passionate devotion to saying something, no matter how. Meanwhile, too, we may expect such recurrent phenomena as Elinor Wylie, Thornton Wilder and Ernest Hemingway, each in his own extremely individual way far more preoccupied with form than with content. That this latter trait is not limited to perfecting perfection in retreat from life in an Ivory Tower in necromantic Venice or ecclesiastic Lima, is evident from Hemingway's choice of the cocktail trail in Paris boulevards and studios and other downrightly contemporary alleyways as his stylistic laboratory.

While literature is gaining new strength through creative practice, controversy and growth, it is beset with formidable and even alarming problems of distribution and appreciation. Keeping in mind the primal importance of the word in the art of letters, no matter how it is distributed, we can trace its history with Carl Van Doren from the *spoken* or *chanted* word of the primitive bards, through the *written* word of the age of scroll and manuscript, to the *printed* word made possible by Gutenberg and universal by Hoe, and finally in full circle back again to the *spoken* word of radio broadcasting. Such a history ought to reassure us in troubled and revolutionary times that the word will find its way through mechanical and economic difficulties, although that way will not open up automatically nor will the difficulties of readjustment be solved by supine indifference or by hasty and panic-stricken makeshift.

If the distributive process of the theatre is in grave need of revision; of the cinema, still in course of luxuriant, spontaneous and reckless growth; of the dance, hardly as yet conceived; and of music, disturbed temporarily by the machine's preemption of services heretofore performed by man; that of literature has suddenly, tardily and hysterically awakened to the fact that it is antiquated, infirm and inadequate to the task imposed on it in the Machine Age. Publisher and bookseller alike have basked so long in a protected and scholarly paradise, aloof from the hurlyburly of a chaotic and revolutionary market place, that they have lost touch with the times; and, in the frantic effort to catch up, they are making several kinds of a fool of themselves in the eyes of those who have grown patiently and realistically with the times.

It would seem almost as if the agents of distribution in literature had looked upon the Machine Age as a bad dream from which the world would sometime awake, obviating the need for a drastic and revolutionary reconstruction of their customs and methods. Convinced at last that they had seriously misapprehended the situation, they have taken several blind leaps in the dark which have only complicated their predicament, leaving them as illequipped as ever to subserve efficiently the literary artist as prophet and the reading public awaiting his interpreting vision. After neglecting the manifest signals flashed by general industry and pointing toward the timeliness of mass distribution, publishers and booksellers let groups of outsiders organize the so-called book clubs, the profits and advantages of which they could have reserved for themselves from the start. After letting the prize escape, instead of combining to shut off the clubs' supply at its source, the publishers with few exceptions selfishly made hole-in-corner deals with the "enemy." Prodded to action by the booksellers, who found their slim profits threatened by mail-order competition, a few of the publishers withdrew from the book club field, but their action had little effect, at least upon the leading clubs which apparently fulfilled a public need. Predictions of utter disaster to the traditional channels of distribution, however, have not come true, for economic law has stepped in to check the flow toward undesirable standardization.

Lending libraries also, while incorporated in certain book shops, have grown up through outside channels, whereas foresight could have kept them at home. In the same way, the American magazine has developed into the most dangerous competitor of the American book, a competitor without parallel in Europe. A few outstanding periodicals are organically associated with book publishing concerns, like *Scribner's, Harper's, The American Mercury* and the *Atlantic,* while, conversely, the Cosmopolitan Book Corporation has grown out of the shoulders of the Hearst magazine group. But most of the golden opportunity to control and live off a formidable rival has been tossed away.

At present the entire field of literary distribution has been thrown into turmoil by the decision of a few publishers to cut prices in the Quixotic hope of stimulating sales. The "dollar book" monopolizes for the moment the economic discussion of literature, but its chance of curing deep-seated economic ills is measured by the gambler's haste and lack of careful fact-finding with which it was inaugurated.

A measure, too, of the economic crisis in book-making and book-distribution may be discerned in the fact that publishers are inclined to blame booksellers for their common ills, while the latter return the melancholy compliment. The truth is that both of them are at fault in their persistent clinging to outmoded practices of sales promotion, control of supply and incitement of demand, or in their spasmodic and sometimes suspicious and overweening efforts to correct those derelictions.

If the family rows of literary distribution can be composed and if the family can plan boldly but sanely and cooperatively for true service to the author as interpreter and to the public who can be taught to desire interpretation and not merely sedatives, literature in the Machine Age can recapture the intensity and brilliance of its past prophetic service to mankind. Compared with Europe, America neither buys nor reads books. But, as R. L. Duffus makes clear in his recent thorough survey of the subject, "Books, Their Place in a Democracy," compiled at the instance of the Carnegie Corporation, the opportunity to induce us to do so is staggering.

And the conditions are favorable. Concrete ways and means await. Compare the "best sellers" of 1930 and 1900: "All Quiet on the Western Front," by Erich Maria Remarque; "Cimarron," by Edna Ferber; "A Farewell to Arms," by Ernest Hemingway; "Roper's Row," by Warwick Deeping; "A Woman of Andros," by Thornton Wilder; and "Whiteoaks of Jalna," by Mazo De La Roche; against "David Harum," by Edward N. Westcott; "Richard Carvel," by Winston Churchill; "When Knighthood Was in Flower," by Charles Major; "To Have and To Hold," by Mary Johnston; and "Janice Meredith," by Paul Leicester Ford. There were no non-fiction "best sellers" at the turn of the century. If "The Story of Philosophy," now in its 425th thousand had sold 5,000 copies in Roosevelt's first administration or 10,000 in Wilson's, its publisher would have rubbed his eyes. The current vogue for biography can not be compared to that for the sentimental historical novel in the Mauve Decade and after, for the highest sales have been achieved by the soundest books. Then, too, the success of the "libraries" is an omen of unsated hunger—

"Everyman's," the "Modern," etc., etc., not even forgetting Haldeman-Julius's "Little Blue Books." Furthermore, it must not be forgotten that vast strata of foreign literature lie untapped by translation, while every season adds fresh literary treasure in a score or two of languages. That prompt and efficient channels of importation can not be devised is inconceivable even if those channels are more complicated than those which already provide international currency for music, painting, the cinema and the theatre.

And finally there is the almost untouched "open sesame" of books as news. For books *are* news. Trivial news, important news. The Gospels, quite literally, were, and still are to countless millions, "good news." And when books are important news, they may be informative news, stimulating news, interpretive news, prophetic news. News of what men have thought and felt. Books suspected by the average citizen as specimens of the literary art, but just that none the less, may be sold—and read—as news.

If literature does not become one of the Great Interpreters of the Machine Age, it will have only its Rip Van Winkle distributors to blame! Thus far, for all his lamentations and convulsions, Rip is only walking in his sleep!

B. Painting and Sculpture

It is the ironic fate of the venerable plastic arts of painting and sculpture that, having scarcely completed and consolidated one major revolution, they are thrust into the maelstrom of another. The prior revolt to which I refer is that long-drawn-out and bitter war, comprised of numerous distinct campaigns, whereby the painter and the sculptor won their independence from the realistic and representational shackles of the Nineteenth Century. I say "won their independence," although there are stubborn provinces which still hold out against their new authority. The fresh revolt to which they are committed is rather in the nature of winning and settling an adjoining territory which once belonged to them but which has long lain fallow. It is even possible that this latter upheaval may involve a transfer of their seat of government to the new territory, for that territory is nothing less than collaboration with the art of architecture with which painting and sculpture have not been on speaking terms for generations.

First, let me allay any doubts that may arise from my grouping of sculpture with painting instead of with architecture. It is true that sculpture and architecture are three-dimensional arts, dealing therefore directly with the problems of form and mass, while painting is two-dimensional, simulating more or less successfully the third dimension and dealing with form and mass by illusion and indirection. It is also true that, whatever the obscure genesis of painting may have been, sculpture and architecture were one and the same art in the hands of primitive man and were inseparable arts long after civilized man had learned to differentiate between their distinct but cognate functions. But ever since the Renaissance rediscovered the relics of Greek sculpture, relics which could be and were transported and placed at will like a framed canvas, the arts of painting and sculpture have shared fair days and foul, acclaim and degradation, while the esthetic controversies which rocked the one involved the other. So it has been, up to and through our own day, until the rebirth of architecture in the Machine Age beckons not only sculpture but also painting to a new but reminiscent synthesis.

Lest the two major revolts which I have mentioned be considered as independent phenomena, one of them concerned with the mode of expression and the other primarily with the site of expression, it is well to observe that both of them have their roots in the conditions of the Machine Age and that in a very true sense the second is the logical and inevitable outgrowth of the first.

Perhaps we can best establish the responsibility of the Machine Age for the revolt of painting and sculpture against realism by recalling and explaining the paradox of these arts in full tilt against the esthetic theory of copying nature at the very moment when literature and the theatre were revolting from romanticism *toward* realism. It does not speak well for the esthetic and prophetic leadership of the novel and the drama to remember that Zola and Ibsen were at the height of their influence as realists when Monet, Renoir, Manet, Degas, Cézanne, Van Gogh and Gauguin had done with realism and had impelled painting on that contentious and kaleidoscopic but brilliantly interpretive succession of "schools" which began with impressionism and has led to expressionism.

There are probably many influences which contributed to the painter's pioneer leadership of revolt while the writer lagged in the rear, among them Lewis Mumford's explanation of the mere survival of painting during the Nineteenth Century "by a complete retreat from the hurly-burly and by a willingness to forego active contemporary patronage"—not a disgruntled retreat into an enervating luxury but a stoical withdrawal to a point of vantage whence the artist, unseen, could view life at elbow reach. But an even more potent, though strangely neglected, reason seems to me to have been designated in a recent interview in New York by Henri Matisse, preeminent master of the contemporary

French school, when he said: "By mechanical means an image is now fixed on a photographic plate in a few seconds—an image more precise and exact than it is humanly possible to draw—and so with the advent of photography disappeared the necessity for exact reproduction in art."

Since the seventies and eighties, of course, thanks largely to the powerful stimulus of modern painting, stimulus both of practice and of volubly expressed theory, literature and the drama have passed through and beyond their realistic phase. Isn't it possible that the theatre was urged thereto by the coming of the cinema, the grandchild of the daguerreotype to which Matisse attributes the painter's emancipation from realism?

Far closer and more conclusive, of course, is the responsibility of the Machine Age for the contemporary decline in interest in the easel painting and portable sculpture and for their consequent rapprochement with architecture. Structural steel and modern engineering have made it compulsory for the architect to re-think his craft and its problems, and, in taking thought, he has fortunately remembered his long-forgotten natural collaborators at a juncture when his own need is their crucial opportunity. It is interesting to note and unnecessary to prove that this reunion, with its infinite challenge to great interpretation on the part of all three arts, would never have occurred to the architect or have appealed to painter and sculptor unless the latter had already adapted themselves to the interpretive needs of the Machine Age by their former revolt against realism.

I do not believe that we can easily exaggerate the importance of the sound, thorough and honest preparation by which painting and sculpture have schooled themselves to assume responsibility as Great Interpreters of the Machine Age. In the face of their great opportunity they are not compelled frantically to put their own house in order, to rid themselves of bad habits and learn right ones. They have many black sheep in their ranks, but, with an integrity and a vision worthy of their noblest prophetic service in past ages, the genuine painters and sculptors can view the prospect undismayed when Lewis Mumford thus states what is expected of them: "The artist does not illustrate science; the point is that as a living, thinking being he frequently responds to the same interests that a scientist does, and expresses by a visual synthesis what the scientist converts into analytical formulae or experimental demonstrations." It seems to me nothing short of astonishing, and a measure of what we may expect from the painter and sculptor as fearless prophets, that, through the discouraging years of the Nineteenth Century and the confusing preliminaries to the Machine Age in full swing in the Twentieth, they did not grow lax and flabby or cynical, but bravely, boldly, persistently and with high ardor pursued the truth as it unfolded before their searching mind's eye, regardless of the ridicule, scorn, obloquy or indifference of a public far behind them.

The discouraging aspect of the situation is not in the field of creation, therefore, but in that of appreciation. In spite of more voluminous and acrimonious public debate over the issues involved than all of the other arts put together have been compelled to endure, the general public in America probably still has worse standards as to what is good and what is bad in painting and sculpture than in any of the other arts. Popular music, mystery melodramas, light fiction and the rank and file of the cinema are produced, understood and consumed for just what they are— more or less harmless pastimes with no serious pretensions to being great or even good art. The poster, the average magazine illustration and advertising art in general are also fairly clearly understood to belong in the same category. But let a painter with a reputation sedulously cultivated in social circles glorify a mere poster with sufficient tubes of oil or tempera and a broad enough expanse of canvas, and his product will fool not only the public but civic art commissions and museum juries. There is still a premium on a picture which tells a literal story, especially if that story has a sentimental, patriotic or supposedly moral motive. And the premium is alluring enough to tempt many an able painter and sculptor to become Ananias, to use the apt epithet of Walter Pach for the double-dealer.

But the problem of painter-sculptor-public is far more serious and intricate than the occasional acclaim of Ananias. If that were all, we could afford to ignore the subject, as I insisted, in Chapter II, we should do in the case of all bad or meretricious art. What should give us concern, however, is the sluggishness of the public's comprehension of really significant painting and sculpture. Twenty-five years after the death of Cézanne we find otherwise alert and perceptive minds who can not grasp mentally or emotionally what he was trying to do and say. These connoisseurs—honest, at least, in their lethargy—have ceased to struggle against the earlier impressionists even if they are still unmoved by them, but when the work of one of Cézanne's successors, like Matisse or Picasso, is tardily hung upon gallery walls, they still raise the same old protest of "grotesque," "distorted," "incomplete," "bad drawing."

Now, this question of an artist having to wait for years or generations before his work is understood is a very critical one. Prophets may be without honor in their own country but if they are also without honor anywhere in their own day, both they and their day lose something infinitely valuable—the give and take, the subtle, subconscious interplay of idea and feeling which any-one with a message and his receptive audience experience in each other's presence. The present is supreme for artists because, in the words of Pach, "the time when their effort counts most is their own time. Later on they are of the past; and, if they have, indeed, the authority that only time confers, they have also the aspect of unfamiliarity caused by the changes in men's ideas."

At first glance it would seem as if the public has scant excuse for its failure to understand modern art. Sometimes an esthetic revolt breaks with tradition so suddenly and so violently that the public can not be expected to respond to it promptly and heartily. There has to be time to get acquainted, to make the inevitable read-justments and orientations. But the painter and the sculptor gave the public time. It is now between sixty and seventy years since the first secession from the literal and story-telling tradition. Nor was the break acute. It proceeded by degrees, by logical steps.

But the average man had been so thoroughly, so exclusively bred in the realistic and representational theory of art that he never even got started with the modern artists on their strange and ex-citing journeys into far lands of the human spirit. The farther modern art plunged into deliberate distortion and abstraction, the smaller its appreciative and understanding audience became. Taught to look in a picture or a statue for what the normal, uni-versal, physical human eye sees, it felt embarrassed at first, then enraged, and finally indifferent, when the modern painter and sculptor tired of the savorless task of copying nature's obvious exterior and started to present those aspects and interpretations of nature dictated by the mind's eye. That a landscape, a portrait or a study in still life disclosed qualities and values which his own physical eye had never observed or his own mind's eye had never dreamed, condemned the work of art in the court of his ingrained realistic ideology. Probably he had never even used his own mind's eye on the outer world, did not know how to use it, and so his denial of the artist's vision had nothing selfish in it. And when the artist gave him a study in lines, forms and colors without any relationship whatsoever to a concrete subject, his mystified contempt knew no bounds.

It is profoundly unfortunate that the average American today is unable to grasp and assimilate the works of the modern French masters and those of our own artists who have been inspired by that extraordinary outpouring of interpretive genius, for we are in the presence here of painting especially, and sculpture to a lesser degree, as genuine prophecy, as Great Interpreter, fulfilling as nothing since Giotto the rôle of the philosopher and the metaphysician. "All that is strange and incredible and non-existent is its subject matter," writes Mary Cecil Allen in attempting to analyze the function of the grotesque in modern art. "It takes what is not and what might be and creates with them and opposes this new imaginative world to the positive world of naturalism and science." But, thanks to the hold of a traditional idea, we shall probably have to wait for our children or our children's children to enter and roam this fertile and soul-stirring field with abandon and rejoicing.

Toward that desired dénouement, the painter and the sculptor themselves can aid. Many offshoots of modern art have abandoned a ready key to their meaning, forgetting that art which requires a dictionary is not art but insane self-indulgence. Many self-styled modern artists, too, have plunged into the tricky confusions of the newer techniques without thorough schooling in traditional methods, ignoring the fact that Cézanne, Matisse and almost all of the masters of modern art grounded themselves thoroughly in conventional practice and preparation before deciding which of the modern tacks to take to express their own vision. Is it too much to ask of painter and sculptor that they fulfill this fundamental preparation for revolt just as the human foetus rehearses the evolutional cycle in the womb? Such a preparation for revolt should not stifle it but make it all the more eager for ultimate flight and carry along with that flight a profound respect for the past, as something once true and in part eternal, to reassure those who are still loyal to that past but trying desperately to attune their senses to a new dispensation.

The new revolt of painting and sculpture in close collaboration with the architect will be just as significant as the three of them in legitimate conspiracy choose to make it. For the first time since modern art elected to plod its lonely path in strict honesty to its inner dictates, it seems to have encountered an opportunity to address itself to man in the mass and to profit by constant association with its still shy but always curious audience. As easel painting and portable sculpture, modern art had buried itself in a blind alley. It remains to be seen whether the right artists will take advantage of the open door to the open walls which the architect promises to provide for mural painting and structurally justified sculpture, and whether they will choose subjects germane to the opportunity.

C. Architecture

On the eve of his death in 1924 after a disappointed and frustrated career, Louis H. Sullivan published his architectural confessional, "The Autobiography of an Idea." In effect, it was an expansion of an article,"The Tall Office Building Artistically Considered," which he published in *Lippincott's Magazine* in March, 1896, and in the course of which occurs this crystallization of his guiding faith: "It is my belief that it is of the very essence of every problem that it contains and suggests its own solution. . . . Whether it be the sweeping eagle in his flight, or the open apple-blossom, the toiling work-horse, the blithe swan, the branching oak, the winding stream at its base, the drifting clouds, over all the coursing sun, *form ever follows function,* and this is the law."

In the January 5, 1928, issue of *The American Architect,* Thomas Hibben thus amplified Sullivan's "law," although at the time unacquainted with its original statement or its expansion into a book: "Form is determined by function and evolved in three dimensions simultaneously. The execution of this form is determined by the honest use of materials. The selection of these materials is controlled by strength, economic, climatic, color and texture factors. The manipulation of them is wholly determined by their sound structural use. The detail resulting from this manipulation can be only in the personal vocabulary of the creator, and any attempt to seek an idealization of 'beauty' or a conformity to 'style' can result only in sterility."

The dates of these utterances give no clue, however, to the fact that the theory of functionalism and significant form was America's gift to the contemporary world of architecture and that this theory dates back in practice to 1890, at least, when, on these principles, Sullivan erected the Wainwright Building in St. Louis. Meanwhile, the theory of abstract form, the archæological opponent of these principles, extraordinarily intrenched in public favor by the World's Columbian Exposition in Chicago in 1893, has not had the field to itself. Frank Lloyd Wright, Sullivan's young assistant in Chicago during World's Fair days, first recognized the value of the machine as an artist's tool at Hull House in 1903. Since then, overriding much the same indifference which drove Sullivan into retirement, Wright and a few others have written and practiced their faith until it has become possible for architects like Raymond Hood and John Mead Howells to turn from the nostalgic and reminiscently decorative Gothic of the Tribune Tower in Chicago to the clean and severely structural Daily News Building in New York, true product of today—and both for the same corporate interests!

Without ignoring or belittling much sound, honest and inspiring building in America since Colonial days, it is possible to claim that Machine Age America has finally evoked at least the broad outlines of a native solution to its native architectural problems—has evoked the solution, as Sullivan predicted, out of the problem itself. And thereby, American architecture stands ready today to assume the responsibility of Great Interpreter.

Before we inquire into the scope and potentiality of architecture as an interpreting and prophetic art, let us pause for a moment to see just what is involved in the theory of structural form as opposed to that of abstract form. In structural form, the mass, the façade and the internal arrangement are all postulated on use. Not on a lazy or inefficient understanding of use. Rather, on an understanding as boldly imaginative, as all-inclusive, as rigorously honest and as minutely calculating as that of the cost-accountant or the research scientist. There need be no fear that mere considerations of utility will result in something esthetically dissatisfying or even ugly, for in a strange way the genuinely useful carries with it not only the sense of fitness, an esthetic quality in itself, but a simplicity, a directness and an honesty which are strongly akin to beauty. It will probably be natural for the architect who is faithful to structural form to exaggerate simplicity and severity in the beginning, as Hood and Howells have done in the Daily News Building. But ultimately, when he is sure that he is on the right track, there is nothing in the history of art in general or of architecture in particular to prevent the development of structurally significant ornament. In fact, Wright has already taken that next step in several of his California residences.

The theory of abstract form, on the other hand, conceives of a building as a picture—a façade in two dimensions; and sometimes, though not always, a mass in three, although the third dimension, when taken into consideration at all, is almost invariably conceived in connection with the exterior alone. The result is a bank or a church or a library or an automobile sales agency housed alike and indiscriminately in a Greek temple or a Gothic chapel. To be consistent with the external promise, the teller, the curate, the librarian and the salesman should all go to work in tunic and sandals or in shining armor. The result, too, is an internal problem which the architect turns over to the occupant to solve however and if ever he may. Ninety-nine times out of a hundred the problem is not solved because it is insoluble. After admiring the grace and balance and proportions of the façade, we enter to have our most primitive senses outraged by horizontal and angular shelves and counters and pews juxtaposed to Romanesque windows placed without even a consideration for a practical source of light!

Recognition of the utter inadequacy of the theory of abstract form to our living and working conditions today need not blind us, of course, to the honesty, authenticity and original utility of its expression in buildings which have come down to us from the past and which still deserve all the respect the ages have accorded them. Respect, however, is not the tribute we pay to the gim-crack excrescences and ribald dunce-caps which the more vulgar and extravagant adherents to the theory of abstract form have clapped on the summits of our skyscrapers like the New York Central Building. Even those who accept these rococo encumbrances do so in a spirit far from flattering to the architect's taste and seriousness. "I like your pagodas in the clouds," said Ernst Stern, German architect and foremost of Max Reinhardt's stage designers, on his first visit to New York. "You can take them off and change them whenever you tire of them and thus have a wholly new building." But we don't!

Esthetic honesty is a distinguishing factor between these two theories. Structural form uses its materials to appear to do what they do do—rising, slender columns of steel to support the structure, horizontal stratifications representative of floor upon floor, walls that are mere envelopes held up by the supporting framework, windows placed where needed (and for all that achieving a pattern), and the entire structure simply stopping at the top when it is through. Abstract form, on the contrary, condones the use of heavy masonry or massive columns for appearance's sake, whether they support an ounce of weight or not. It is this honesty, or lack of it, to which Hugh Ferriss, most brilliant of our architectural illustrators, refers in forecasting the verdict of a new generation of architects on our contemporary feats: "The whole custom of employing forms which no longer serve functions—the whole frame of mind which conceives that structural beauty can exist without truth—they will view as decadence; just as they will dismiss, as sentimentality, the notion that architectural beauty was once and for all delivered to the builders of ancient times."

Early in Chapter I, in casting up the totals of those who are art-susceptible and art-involved in America today, I included "the millions of tenants of more or less significant buildings whose lives are molded by the structures they inhabit" and who "are daily influenced by the architect's original dream to the extent to which he has been able to realize it." When I wrote those lines I was not yet acquainted with Ferriss's enlargement upon the same fact. "It is well known and generally admitted," he writes in "The Metropolis of Tomorrow," "that a few people are especially sensitive to the element of design; but a more serious and equally indubitable fact is that the character of the architectural forms and spaces which all people habitually encounter are powerful agencies in determining the nature of their thoughts, their emotions, and their actions, however unconscious of this they may be. . . . Certainly no one, however unused to religious emotion, can stand in certain of these designed spaces (the early Gothic cathedrals) without receiving intimations of a life, other, and greater, than his own. It would seem in fact that Architecture was here consciously employed for no less an object than the elevation and evolution of Man. . . . Would it not be surprising if the sense of large actualities, which is often lacking in the words of both contemporary scientists and churchmen, should be brought to us in the wordless device of an architect!"

In other words, architecture can not escape the role of interpreter and prophet. Whether it is a false prophet or a Great Interpreter depends upon its vision and its integrity. Regardless of the high mortality of buildings in the Machine Age city, architecture is an enduring prophet, for the best buildings tend to remain to extend their influence on future generations. It is for that reason, of course, that architecture must ponder seriously its comparatively substantial and permanent output, in order to make sure that it is fulfilling not merely its utilitarian obligations but also its esthetic, sociological and spiritual opportunities.

To compare his concrete obligations and opportunities in a single structure with those of his entire profession in an entire community must dwarf and humble if it does not inspire the individual architect. City-wide control under a single guiding genius is probably impractical, however conceivable it may be in theory. What happens is accident, happy in spots or not. The city of the Machine Age, in Ferriss's words, is "not designed at all . . . not the work of conscious design." Through the apprehended need for such control, the idea of regional and city planning has come into being; and, while the results thus far are pitifully small, the idea has back of it the assent and approval of the new spirit in modern industry, in modern engineering, in modern science and in modern sociology, capitalistic or proletarian. The Regional Plan of New York and its Environs and the five-year plan of economic development of the Soviet Government's State Planning Commission possess a powerful though hidden trait in common, despite their contrasting aspects—the agreed desirability for men to cooperate in a large unselfish way for the communal good.

Toward this goal various forces which have not been accustomed to working together must jointly contribute. The architect's most valuable allies will be the social sciences, from which he must accept guidance, though on occasion he can reciprocate with imaginative experiment; the engineer, who has sometimes mistakenly thought he could dispense with the architect or hire him as a mere underling; and, as we have discovered in the preceding section, the painter and sculptor.

Everyone who is a party to this thrilling prospective adventure in cooperation will have to keep his mind and his imagination free to receive and react upon strange and at first perplexing stimuli and suggestions. Within his own field, new building materials, new metallic compounds and new combinations of materials will tempt the architect to stray from his single faith in structural form, while some of them will justify their acceptance. No dilettante can be entrusted with these and a score of other baffling responsibilities. But if we ever throw off that handicap—and I believe we will—it is even possible that the architect, knowing his own tools and profiting by his increasing acquaintance with other vital factors in communal life through the necessity of their using him as a common clearing house for their ideas, may reach a position of undreamed prophetic power comparable to, but far more significant than, Gordon Craig's protean artist of the theatre.

D. The Craft Arts

It is high time we quit distinguishing in a petty, fussy and precious way between "commercial" art and "fine" art, between "design" and "applied design." That there is a legitimate distinction can not be denied, for so-called commercial art trails off by imperceptible and incalculable degrees into industry so far that we would strain our flexible definition of art to the breaking point to cover the most remote cases. It is much better, however, to err on the side of too broad a boundary than to confine it too strictly. For the farther art and the principles and standards of good art penetrate into industry, the more humanely industry will serve us and the more surely it will dignify itself.

My quarrel is, rather, with those who use this natural and inevitable distinction as a cloak for emasculating art and keeping it servile and idle in an Ivory Tower for strictly private appreciation. If the so-called fine arts are willing to be thus coddled and kept in luxury, they may as well renounce all thought of a prophetic mission or even of natural health and longevity. But they are not willing. Aching and longing for a breath of air, they escape into the market place to elbow life in its raw vigor, drawing from it new energy and inspiration. Show me an artist who is supercilious toward the public, whose senses are too refined for contact with life, and I will show you a pervert.

But the dilettante will not admit defeat in the face of these secessions from his exclusive patronage. Forthwith he coins the word "commercial," and by giving it connotations of opprobrium he intimidates other artists whose instinct is for flight.

I have another quarrel with those who really do commercialize art in the derogatory sense, who lure the honest artist into the invigorating precincts of the market place and then work upon his vanity, his ambition, or his covetousness to cheapen his product and falsify his profession.

In between is the broad field of life unconstrained either by intimidation or temptation. The cynic will tell you that it is not so very broad. But it has been broad enough for man to achieve everything he has achieved which has value. The cynic will tell you, too, that it is narrower today than it has ever been before, that the machine and the pace on which it puts a premium have multiplied the temptations and reduced the resistance to them. But it should be clear by now that I do not impute to the machine the blame for what has happened. Instead, it seems plain to me that the fault lies with the artist who has feared to descend into the market place, the factory and the machine shop.

It is in this field of market place, factory and machine shop that the craft arts lie, the arts which bestow design—"applied" design, if you like—on the things we wear, the things with which we furnish our homes and our offices, the things which afford us transportation, the tools and accessories of our daily life.

To pursue the craft arts into all of their ramifications would require a book in itself. What is important to recognize here is that function and significant form are more important here, if possible, than in architecture, that fitness is obviously a primary consideration, and that fitness carries with it the corollary of beauty. We must remember that the machine can give us fitness to a superlative degree if an artist collaborates with the machine. We must recognize the fact that the retail merchant has awakened to the honestly commercial appeal and value of good design. Nor should we forget that the curse of art as something pretentious, something beyond the range of appreciation and understanding of the average man, is rapidly losing its potency.

For the "fine" artist to descend at will into the market place was as natural in past ages as for him to partake of food and drink. Cellini managed a ring, or a medal or a sword without contaminating his artistic integrity. "Commercial" art, indeed! Is not all life commerce? Commerce of thought and of ideal as well as of stuff and commodity?

It was not in that spirit that Morris and Ruskin undertook to revive the craft arts. Rather, they created an Ivory Tower of their own, helpless to halt the march of civilization and the conquest of the machine.

But it is in that spirit, the spirit of Cellini, that Norman Bel Geddes and Hermann Rosse have taken occasional vacations from scenic design in the theatre and the cinema and Rockwell Kent from the easel drawing and the mural painting, to feed the machine with design which justifies the craft arts as interpreting arts. Whither their example will lead, no man can tell!

6. The Process of Revolution

Having demonstrated in detail the proposition of the arts as potential collaborators with science in the attempt to interpret human destiny, we are now ready to examine the second of the two main implications of revolt in order to acquire another at least tentatively-fixed point of reference in surrounding chaos. This second implication, it will be recalled, "concerns the steps we must take if we wish to preserve for ourselves and posterity the full values of the arts against the inroads of the self-same Machine Age which has called our attention to those values." Let me repeat here the theoretic statement of that implication:

Realizing that the Machine Age has destructive as well as constructive potentialities, such as the displacement of personally-performed art by its mechanical reproduction, and that the clock of progress can not be turned backward, I propose that "machine-made" art should subsidize "hand-made" art, both for the intrinsic value of the latter and for its service as an independent laboratory and testing ground.

What we confront, in effect, is a swapping of horses midstream —repairing the motor in flight, to bring the simile up-to-date. Since this is a difficult and dangerous though imperative operation, it will be well, before entering upon its concrete development, to review the normal course of revolution and to ascertain how that course is susceptible to modification by the new spirit which is rife today in the western world, and particularly in America.

The parallel with political revolution, at least with any specific political revolution, could easily become misleading if carried too far or applied too literally, but I believe that it can be made to throw light on our problem.

The theory and process of revolution deserves the exhaustive study and the imaginative definition of someone with personal experience of it and the faculty of vivid generalization like Maurice Hindus, author of "Humanity Uprooted," or Emil Ludwig. It is from a recent article by Ludwig, comparing and contrasting the French and Russian Revolutions, that I have paraphrased the following skeleton structure of revolution, viewed generically:

1. A stubbornly intrenched and reactionary system, characterized by abuse of power, arrogance, intolerance, sloth and ineptitude, courts its own destruction.

2. A primitive human right, conceived by the few, is passionately proclaimed by them to the masses, impelling them to action.

3. The spark is kindled first in the capital cities and then spreads.

4. The action is national; the underlying idea, international— of world scope and significance.

5. The reactionary system is annihilated by popular rebellion.

6. By moral force acting under natural economic laws, a fresh and powerful majority is substituted for an effete and impotent minority.

7. Carrying their program to excess, the forces of revolt stimulate the reassembly of the forces of counter-revolt, consisting of the sounder elements of the old régime chastened by privation and suffering. Thus challenged, the revolutionists either temper their

excesses to retain their power or, persisting in them, find themselves in turn displaced. Sometimes the pendulum makes several lessening swings forward and backward before stability is reached. In any case, a generous infusion of new blood, new ideas, remains to justify bloodshed and the destruction of capital values.

As a general corollary to this skeleton structure of revolution, it is safe to conclude that no revolution is inevitable if the causes underlying it are recognized and corrected in time. Likewise, it is safe to conclude that no revolution, once in full swing, stops short of self-destructive extremes unless heroically intelligent expedients are adopted to curb its excesses and to substitute a broadly realistic point of view for a narrow and bigoted fanaticism. Both the avoidance and the mitigation of unrestrained revolution are difficult—but possible.

If, with this skeleton structure of revolution and its corollaries in mind, we seek for an analogy between revolt in the arts and political revolt, the correspondences would work out about like this:

Political revolt, on the physical plane, has at its heart, as its essence, economic and social revolt. Often, usually in the long run, the latter proves to be more far-reaching, than the former. The revolt of the machines against the tyrannical tediousness, drudgery and inhumanity of exclusively hand labor, likewise on the physical or material plane, has at its heart, as its dynamic interpreter and vindicator, the revolt of the arts—the arts galvanized by the machine and the spirit of the Machine Age and bent on bursting esoteric and in-breeding bonds and on carrying their message, whether banal or prophetic, to the masses. The time may come—I say it may, for there is no certainty that it will—

when the unprecedented expansion of the arts and their assumption and fulfillment of the prophetic function will be acknowledged as the greatest glory of the Machine Age.

In the same manner, political counter-revolt against the excesses of a revolutionary regime has its economic and social connotations. As we have seen, there is never a complete return to the status which prevailed before the revolt. Whatever was sound and worthy of endurance in the revolt remains or is recaptured by degrees. So, to, if we ever have a physical counter-revolt against the machine, it will be accompanied by a corresponding counter-revolt of the arts, may even be incited and energized by such counter-revolt. Again, it is unthinkable that the manifest and manifold benefits of the machine and Machine Age art, its superiority of distribution and its enormously expanded appreciation if not yet its greater interpretive and prophetic power, should be lost in counter-revolt.

But I am not at all sure that there will be counter-revolt. Certainly nothing seriously resembling it immediately impends. It behooves us, nevertheless, to consider soberly the fact that it would probably be catastrophic if man, goaded by the machine's brutal indifference to human instincts, were to rise up and smash it and all its works.

It behooves us much more directly to consider the spiritual efficiency of the machine and Machine Age art, as contrasted with its dazzling material achievements, not so much to preclude the dire consequences of determined counter-revolt as to humanize the revolt itself and to guarantee for ourselves and our children a free field for the arts to develop their latent potentiality as Great Interpreters.

In past ages, and even in our own in the case of Russia, where primitive conditions effectually provided an archaic setting, the revolutionist has been an upstart, bitter, defiant, fanatical, ruthless, cruel. Meeting obstinate, cynical and equally defiant and ruthless opposition, all his destructive instincts became intensified. It was futile for his farther-seeing leaders to caution him that his ax and brand and bullet might destroy *value,* human and spiritual as well as material value—people and traditions and physical goods which he might turn to his own use and which, once gone, could never be replaced. Such an attempt to dissuade him merely induced suspicion of his leaders, and so he was usually let go to wreak his blind fury on everything in sight. The natural harvest of this sorry seed was a White Terror to match the Red or the swing of the pendulum to counter-revolution.

But a new spirit is discernible in America today, a spirit born of foresight, of taking thought, even if only of taking selfish thought, a spirit which I firmly believe would radically recolor political or social revolt if it came to us and which can almost certainly be depended on to humanize a bloodless revolt in the arts.

7. *A New Spirit Today*

The vital and distinctive aspects of this new spirit are the ability to see beyond the present moment and the salutary modification of the traditional stiff-necked insistence upon one's rights. We still have the die-hard-in-the-last-ditch in politics, in industrial management, in labor administration. But no "Public-Be-Damned" Vanderbilt heads a major American railroad system today. And when our Senators babble in scorn about "the sons of wild jackasses," we laugh at their folly instead of burning up in fear and resentment.

On the positive side of the ledger, the iron law of wages and the conception of labor as a commodity have gone by the board, replaced by the theory of paying the highest possible wages, for the sake of increasing public buying power, and the theory of the shortest possible working hours, for the sake of leaving ample leisure in which the public can spend. Ford increases wages before he is asked to do so, and his example is contagious throughout American industry.

In discussing "The New Age and the New Man" in "Toward Civilization," Ralph E. Flanders, vice-president of the American Society of Mechanical Engineers, attributes this new spirit to a growing "responsibility for humane policies and esthetic treatment in industrial enterprises," sees "the effective pressure of conscience" at work on our "methods of accumulation and of benevolent spending" and contends that "the principal concern of the capitalist of the immediate future must be to so order his affairs that *the very earning of his money will be in itself a social service,* irrespective of the use he later makes of it."

Whatever truth there may be in that sentimental and emotional explanation, I would prefer to trace the roots of this new spirit to rationally economic motives, for a reasoned policy is more secure and permanent than one dictated by the feelings. No matter how selfish it may sound, I would rather repose my confidence in such an admission on the part of the industrial leader as this: "If we must adjust to inevitable demands and changes, let us not wait until they are forced upon us. Let us anticipate them, yield gracefully before the demand is formulated and get the credit for giving what we will have to give anyhow!" Into the making of such a pragmatic philosophy has gone, I believe, not only our Anglo-Saxon heritage with its extraordinary record of bloodless revolutions but also the realistic Jewish philosophy of meeting each issue as it arises, so that a complexity of issues never accrues.

In any case, whatever the source of this spirit, its product is plain. Instead of moving back and forth through a destructive arc of mutual hatred and suspicion, antagonism and retaliation, civilization moves ever onward, forward. By foresight and selfish unselfishness we advance peacefully to that same new ground to which revolt and counter-revolt would take us through a sea of blood and a desert of ashes. It would not surprise me, if human demands should outrun their anticipatory fulfillment and if overt revolution should appear in the offing, to see American industrial leaders relinquish control without a shot, in the firm faith that, as in Russia, their technical knowledge and executive skill would be drafted immediately in service to the new regime. In that sense, as I indicated in Chapter I, revolution becomes simply the speeding up of evolutionary processes at such a rate as to justify the term "revolutionary."

It is to be expected that many will oppose this analysis and interpretation of what I have chosen to call a new spirit in American life and industry. Convinced believers in economic determinism, whether capitalist or communist, will not admit that man by taking thought can control vast and apparently impersonal forces. Those whose livelihood depends on preserving the concept of an inevitable, grim and ruthless class struggle, soluble only by bloody revolution, will scoff, honestly or hypocritically, at the suggestion of a peaceful solution, just as admirals and generals sneer at disarmament. And those who are bored with life will refuse to believe, because revolution at a distance sounds like a "good show."

But the human will is still a power, especially when coupled with the human imagination. The professional busybody and trouble-maker are finding it increasingly difficult to command credulity. And the world, even the American Croesus, is not so wealthy that it embarks on a "good show" without counting the cost!

8. *The Possible Co-Existence of Intimate and Mass-Production Art*

It is in the light of this new social and industrial spirit in America and its extraordinary suggestion for a means of escape from the terror and waste of overt political and social revolution and counter-revolution that I wish to study the revolt in the arts of the Machine Age in order to see how we can temper the logical consequences of revolt and salvage the true values of the old regime while accepting the substantial usufructs of the new. If this spirit prevails in political and social strata, there seems to be no good reason why it should not apply to the process of creation, distribution and appreciation of the arts.

Ignoring for the moment all of those subsidiary revolts, whereby the various arts are seeking a fuller, richer and freer opportunity for expression, and centering our attention on the major revolt of the arts, in association with the revolt of the machine, against a narrow and dilletante service to a privileged minority in favor of widespread service to the masses, we see that the general direction of this revolt is to rob the hand to feed the machine, and that the aim of counter-revolt would be to "junk" the machine and restore the hand to power.

In looking at the subject thus broadly, we must understand the hand, in contrast to the machine, as the artist creating and performing in person in the presence of his audience or in direct contact with them without the mediation of mechanical reproduction. Carried to its logical conclusion, the Machine Age, if left to its own resources, tends to the minimization and ultimate obliteration of the individual artist in intimate relationship to his audience and to the enthronement of endlessly repetitious and intensively standardized reproduction of the artist's achievement. Quite naturally, the self-respecting creative artist resents this wholesale duplication, packaging and ticketing of his work, especially if he is thereby isolated from that natural, personal, human contact with his audience to which he has been accustomed. Quite naturally, there will be two contradictory reactions in the field of appreciation—resentment, indifference or scorn in the part of intelligent connoisseurs; avid delight on the part of those millions to whom a new world has opened as if by magic. Quite naturally, the distributor, who is "not in business for his health," hails the machine as a ready means of pyramiding his profits on a small original investment.

It would seem, then, that only the creative artist and the discerning minority among the public are averse to the rapid and universal completion of the machine program, that revolt has little to fear from counter-revolt and can therefore ride high and mighty. But such an inference fails to take into account two factors: In the first place, the creative artist can strike. He can refuse to provide for the machine the original pattern which the machine reproduces indefinitely and without which it is helpless. In the second place, the discerning minority may find itself recruited overnight into an overwhelming majority whose suffrage means the life or death of an art. Numerous observers report that, just prior to the arrival of the sound film, the silent film was in such a predicament from a buyers' strike unexpectedly declared by a hitherto satisfied clientele.

It is just as important in the arts, therefore, as in the political, social and industrial field, to forestall demands before they are formulated, to give with selfish unselfishness more than is received. By so doing, the masters of the machine will obtain a sobering perspective on their own purposes and program, will recognize the primary, initiatory and indispensable function of the hand and its several analogues as the machine's own source of nourishment, and, while proceeding with their own program, will protect that source from damage and contamination and even foster its independent growth, instead of trampling it out of existence. Approached in this spirit and with these motives, even if they be frankly and honestly selfish, the creative artist can afford to accept the proffered assistance and support, even in return lending his judgment and imagination to the guidance of the machine. He can afford to do so with dignity unimpaired, for he has been beholden in the past to more ignoble patrons.

I am indebted to the contemporary revival of interest in the subject of handcraftsmanship in industry for the hint that this duality of hand and machine may have analogous counterparts in many if not all of the arts. That revival in turn traces back to the critical extent of unemployment in America during the past year. Federal Government, state, city, and industry and labor themselves have undertaken singly or jointly to devise means to avoid the debilitating dole whereby Great Britain has sought to ameliorate her unemployment crisis since the war. Among the expedients which have been tried are: spreading production over the year instead of concentrating it in seasonal peaks; developing side lines and training workers to man them temporarily; installing part time work to avoid total lay-off; stimulating demand by simplifying styles of product to encourage buying in off seasons; establishing unemployment insurance by means of reserve funds to which industry, municipality and employee contribute jointly; opening of employment bureaus and exchanges; "staggering" activity in the several plants of the same industry or company; undertaking of public works ultimately needed, etc., etc.

Effective as these expedients have been to mitigate the suffering and the derangement of the industrial structure which usually accompanies a period of financial depression, they have failed utterly to solve the problems created by technical unemployment. They have failed because technical unemployment is not a temporary affair. By technical unemployment the economist means all of those hands thrown out of work by the steady increase in the efficiency of the machine. According to the figures of James J. Davis, Secretary of Labor, our railroads do more work than they did years ago with a quarter of a million less men; one cotton weaver operates a score of automatic looms in place of twenty; one needle inspector with a machine replaces nine girls who formerly worked by hand. Technical unemployment stalks even in times of prosperity, although it is not so evident then, since workers replaced by machines can shift their occupations and carry on.

Confronted by this stubborn specter which shows no sign of relinquishing its onward march, the imaginative minds in industry are turning their attention to the revival of handcraft in order to reabsorb those workers whom the machine has discharged. Cheaply and speedily and perfectly as the machine can produce, there is a certain quality about its product which betrays the absence of the human hand in its making. In many articles and commodities that quality is not missed, or, if it is, its absence is advantageous. In others, though, the individuality, the personal touch, of hand manufacture has been surrendered reluctantly and at an esthetic loss.

Why not, therefore, say these physicians of industry, give back to the hand that which it can do supremely well, leaving to the machine whatever it has proved it can do better than the hand? Probably no one can say, without experiment, which is which. Certain processes of the textile, ceramic and interior furnishing industries would undoubtedly yield readily to this program. The consumer, of course, would have to be reeducated. Compounded by nature of the contradictory traits of wishing to be different and of fearing to be unlike his fellows, the average citizen of the Machine Age had to be trained by the use of mass psychology to heed his fear and stifle his wish. In order to insure the success of the proposed revival of handcraft, mass psychology would probably have to be used again to bring the consumer back to a normal balance between wish and fear. But, since such a campaign would be working with nature instead of against it, there ought to be no question of the outcome. Neither should there be any difficulty in keeping the hand-made article within reach of the average income. For, in control of industrial experts, who, of course, would have to respect the creative whims of the craftsman to get the best work out of him, the work could be performed with far less waste than is customary in the sporadic handcraft colonies in existence today, while ready outlets through department stores would not only insure a quick turn-over and a reduction in price but also a removal of such goods from the specious category of snobbish demand to that of normal enjoyment and appreciation.

Such a program has nothing in common with the proposals of

Borsodi in "This Ugly Civilization," for, in his hatred of the factory and the modern city, he argues for a semi-rural dispersal of population and the installation of a veritable microcosm of the Machine Age in each domestic unit, with miniature machines to do everything for their owner except eat and sleep and make love for him!

Neither is there any vital parallel between the present program for a rebirth of the handcrafts and the brave but Quixotic ventures of William Morris and John Ruskin in the last century. Theirs was an unqualified defiance of modern industrialism, doomed to sterility from the start as far as altering the course of civilization was concerned. They would have turned the hands of the clock backward. The industrial sponsors of the handcrafts today would *keep those clock hands moving forward,* moving in unison and mutual understanding, the speedier minute hand symbolic of the machine and the deliberate hour hand of the handcrafts. It is the failure of Frank Jewett Mather, Jr., in "Humanism and America," to imagine any other recourse except that of Morris and Ruskin which nullifies his unrelieved pessimism regarding the present and future of both craftsmanship and art.

Before I attempt to prove specifically why I believe that the analogy of "machine-made" and "hand-made" in industry, co-existent and cooperative, can be made to apply to the individual arts, it seems wise to linger a little longer with the machine, get a little better acquainted with it and mollify, if possible, the prevalent suspicion that the machine and all of its reputed progeny— mass production, standardization, monotony, ugliness—are unfit associates for true art, pariahs whose slightest touch will soil.

That this suspicion is false, at least without considerable qualification, is beginning to dawn on artist and connoisseur, economist and social worker, while the engineer is awakening to the duty and the privilege of interpreting the machine and defending it from its detractors. All of these diverse witnesses seem to agree that, whatever the machine can be developed to accomplish, the hand of man, directed by his mind and his imagination, will be required to tell it what to do, and when and where and why to do it.

We are beginning to have a new respect for machine skills. Instead of looking upon the machine as "a puffing thing of cogs and racket," to use Richard F. Bach's phraseology of our former conception of it, we are ready to heed Dr. Dexter S. Kimball, dean of engineering at Cornell University, when he says that "the skill necessary on the part of those who build the primary tools of industry is so far in advance of the old hand worker as to put them in a new class of workers." We stop to reconsider and recheck our habitual opinions, especially when a visitor from abroad like M. Dubreuil, Secretary of the French Federation of Labor, brings perspective to a long sojourn as an ordinary worker in our factories and reports: "I saw with emotion that in spite of the instruments invented by modern mechanical ingenuity, the human hand still has the last word, belying all the somber predictions recklessly made on the disappearance of the traditional trades and the gradual transformation of the entire working class into 'automatons.' In reality, in proportion to the progress of mechanization, the tool grows increasingly intricate and complicated. It constantly requires more work and skill, with the result that manual dexterity, formerly expended on the products, has simply been directed toward the tools which today manufacture these objects in great masses."

Roused to a new appreciation of function and significant form in art, we are ready with Ralph E. Flanders to "search for fitness of line, mass, and coloring, based on structure and use," rather than for mere beauty—fitness, to continue with Flanders, "of the integral, organic sort in which the engineering sense is the determining factor, whether designed by the engineer, or by the despised 'commercial' artist inbred with the modern world, or by that rarer phenomenon, the real artist with the new vision."

In fact, our understanding of the machine has reached the point where we can calmly agree with Lewis Mumford: "To deny that the machine can produce art is a fallacy; to believe that everything the machine produces is excellent art is also a romantic fallacy. To curb the machine and limit art to handicraft is a denial of opportunity. To extend the machine into provinces where it has no function to perform is likewise a denial of opportunity."

If the machine, then, needs the artist, is only partially efficient without him, and if "machine-made" and "hand-made" can co-exist and cooperate in industry—not only can but must co-exist and cooperate—there is only one thing for the machine to do, the machine in its all-inclusive sense of mass-production and mass-distribution. And that one thing is to pay the price which the artist exacts—the price, not only in money but, far more important, in working conditions congenial to him.

That the artist is not to be had without a price, the mass-producer and the mass-distributor know. In fact, it is one of their pet cynicisms that every man, the artist included, has his price. But they are not yet fully convinced that this price can not always or even often be stated in dollars and cents alone. If the artist demands that intimate, personal contact with his public to which he has been accustomed and which the Machine Age has been confining within ever narrower limits, his wish must be their law. Personal performance is the artist's life-blood. Without it, enormous fortunes would be spent on him in vain.

And he must not have to beg for conditions congenial to him. Nor render an accounting.

The sooner the masters of the machine realize that they must accord the artist the same inviolable independence and provide for him the same superbly equipped laboratory, built to his own specifications, as they have already bestowed upon the research scientist, the sooner the arts will be able to fulfill their destiny as Great Interpreters of life, shoulder to shoulder with science.

9. *"Machine-Made" as Sponsor of "Hand-Made" in the Visual and Auditory Arts*

As we examine the several arts for analogies with the apparently contradictory but really complementary attributes of "machine-made" and "hand-made" in industry, one point must be kept clear, a point which I have tried to use as a guide throughout this volume. I have neither aim nor ambition to prophesy. Interpretation and prophecy are the function of the creative artist. My motive has been to point out, on the basis of past and present evidence, what we *can* have, if we desire it earnestly enough, and under what conditions we can have it. If certain goals have seemed to me eminently desirable, and certain others to be avoided at all costs, I have felt it a duty to say so quite frankly, with emphasis commensurate with conviction. For, while I do not expect anyone to agree with me on all issues, I see no reason to infer that I am not generally representative of a large and growing cross-section of mentally sentient and emotionally responsive America.

The effort, therefore, to show that intimate and personally-performed art can co-exist and cooperate with mass-production art, the former subsidized, if necessary, by the latter, is not a prediction but merely a recognition of a possible and, I think, a desirable solution of a difficult problem. It is not a prediction, for there is no assurance that it will come to pass. But if it does not, I see no other hope for the preservation of the personal fountain-head of creative art in the Machine Age except its death and ultimate rebirth out of the deepest needs of the human race.

A. The Theatre

In the theatre, fortunately, we have a practical pattern, a well-thought-out structure and a tested mechanism for the application of this theorem. Strangely enough, both the pattern and the structure were developed to a high degree of perfection years before the dawn of the Machine Age. In one European country or another for several hundred years the endowed theatre has existed under the wing of court, state, municipality or wealthy patron. It attained its most prevalent and its most elaborately-housed if not its most artistically brilliant estate in the quarter of a century before the Great War.

This, then, is the pattern. I maintain that it is a practical pattern, for experience has proved that endowment is not necessarily enervating, that it does not necessarily result in keeping a theatre open to empty seats and that it does not necessarily confine the independent expression of the artist.

The structure under which this pattern-theatre operated was marked invariably by the repertory presentation of plays at the hands of a permanent acting company, administration and technical staff. Other structural characteristics might vary from city to city, from country to country and from age to age, but these two prevailed and survived.

The tested mechanism alone is the product of our own time and circumstance—the Little Theatre. It doesn't matter under how many other names it has operated—"Civic," "Community," "Municipal," "Neighborhood," "Experimental," "Laboratory," "Workshop." Nor does it matter how many scores and hundreds of so-called Little Theatres have been mere society fads and playthings, completely alien to what I have in mind. Still less does it matter that the Little, Intimate and Chamber Theatres of Europe preceded the American Little Theatre. Their motive was rarely, if ever, the same. The European Little Theatre was little because it wished to be, for the sake of intimate presentation of certain types of plays. The American Little Theatre was little because it had to be—at least in the beginning. In its authentic instances it was the spontaneous, irrepressible expression of the urge to keep the art of the theatre free, independent, healthy and significant. The personal, "hand-made" art of the theatre. In contrast to the negative protests of editorial pages, lecture platforms and various Leagues, it was a positive protest against the theatre as made on Broadway and "mailed" to an ever-shrinking list of towns and cities across the continent. If the mountain wouldn't come as desired to Mohammed, Mohammed would make his own mountain. Kenneth Macgowan has recorded the epic of this movement with thoroughness, skill, sympathy and imagination in "Footlights Across America." Out of that record, though developed far beyond the rudimentary form of the Little Theatre and bearing slight resemblance to it any longer, Eva Le Gallienne's Civic Repertory Theatre, Frederic McConnell's Cleveland Play House and Gilmor Brown's Pasadena Community Playhouse stand out as unmistakable justifications and stimulating examples of the movement which the established theatre at first scorned, then feared and latterly has courted as ally. Although all three of these institutions subsist on subsidy, or the assurance of it in case of deficit, and house permanent acting companies, only Miss Le Gallienne's operates yet on a true repertory basis.

But the theatre as a personally-performed art needs more than these three way-stations across the continent. How can they be multiplied?

Now, any art, and particularly that of the theatre, can attempt to subsist in any one of three ways—as an art, as a game of chance or as a business. There is small chance of resultant theatrical art if the gambler's path is chosen; many chances but small certainty if the course of business is elected. To subsist as an art, without thought of profit except as an occasional fortunate addition to endowment, requires the application of the primary tenets of good business, as I pointed out in the second section of Chapter II. To subsist as an art, the theatre usually requires subsidy, although the Theatre Guild has managed to balance its budget for eleven years by practicing the art of the theatre with one eye cautiously on its ledger, risking a "Goat Song" often enough to keep its soul alive, capitalizing its popular successes, receiving a form of endowment in the willingness of actors to accept less than their open-market salaries and latterly organizing subscription seasons in other cities.

If, to subsist as an art, the theatre usually requires subsidy, to whom is it to look for that aid? Not yet to state or municipal funds, although the European theatre is thus served and although the arts of literature, painting and sculpture are thus reinforced in America in the form of libraries, galleries and museums.

Occasionally to the private patron, although that source of aid is far less general or dependable than in the case of music.

What hope of assistance is there, then, from within the theatre itself? A theatre soundly organized as a business might conceivably be willing to endow the theatre as an art, sagaciously suspecting that such a theatre could and would discover and develop talents of acting, of playwriting, of designing and of directing with which it could recruit and fortify its own personnel and which it could use to advantage in mass-production and mass-distribution. But the American theatre is not organized as a business, either soundly or unsteadily. That conclusion is inevitable from the charges against it which I listed on an earlier page. The American theatre is a real estate business, perhaps, short-sightedly managed, but, with a few lone and helpless exceptions, it is a game of chance in every other department.

And gamblers don't subsidize art or anything. They need subsidy themselves!

Is the case, then, so desperate? I think not. It seems to me that we have overlooked one promising and legitimate source of aid in preserving the theatre as an art of personal performance against the inroads of all of its competitors and other obstacles of the Machine Age. I am fully prepared for my suggestion to be suspected as Greeks bearing gifts, and I am aware of its dangers, but I am willing to take the risk. That suggestion is nothing less than that the cinema, heartiest and most opulent of the artistic progeny of the Machine Age, should undertake and maintain the subsidy of the theatre as an art, at least until the established American theatre becomes a business instead of a game of chance.

There can be no question that the cinema is financially equal to the task. There should be no question of the rewards it might reap. Concrete rewards in the form of a steady stream of players, writers, designers, directors and technicians, plucked from the broad stream of the young and inexperienced and trained to skill and mastery. Such a source of supply is indispensable to the cinema, especially since the coming of the sound film. Then, too, there would be the intangible advantage of a free and healthy theatre as incentive and stimulant to a free and healthy cinema, not forgetting the elimination of all bitter disdain of the cinema which is natural to those lovers of the true theatre who today suspect it of being, deliberately or not, the deadly rival of that theatre.

One word of caution is gravely needed: The cinema must not offer and the theatre dare not accept subsidy with a string tied to it. Fair arrangements can be made whereby the film reaps the logical and legitimate fruits of its vision and generosity. But, as I proclaimed in the previous section, for it to dictate or even to suggest, unasked or undesired, should be as unthinkable as it is to the captain of industry who maintains the research scientist in inviolate independence.

B. The Cinema

If the cinema is the present logical "machine-made" sponsor for the "hand-made" theatre, that fact does not relieve it from the corresponding responsibility within its own ranks. Charity may begin at home, but investment is often more alluring abroad. And if the cinema ever subsidizes the theatre as an art, it will do so as an investment. But if the cinema does not undertake the development, encouragement and protection of its own intimate child, the artistic film made for a selective audience rather than for the masses, no one is likely to do so.

Born and evolved as an independent art, if it is that even yet, within the memory of nine tenths of its present audience, the cinema has no traditions and only a crowded decade and a half of history and experience. It has been too busy branching out and taking advantage of the incredible opportunities which opened up before it to bother its head much about the subtler distinctions. Just how fine a film could be made if the box office were forgotten? Just how closely could the film come to grips with life and undertake a truly interpretive and prophetic rôle without the fear of that same box office and of the even more engulfing shadow of the censor? How much of an audience is there for the "hand-made" film? Can that audience be organized? What would such a film cost to make and distribute? How little could it cost without impairing its full power of expression? What is the difference between that cost and the presumptive income? In other words, how much of a subsidy would the "machine-made" cinema have to provide in order to create and maintain a "hand-made" cinema?

If any exhaustive study of these questions has been made in America, I am not aware of it. These questions and others related to them have been asked and discussed casually, and several laudable attempts have been made to establish intimate cinema theatres after the example of such theatres and clubs in Europe: the Film Guild Cinema, the Fifth Avenue Playhouse, the Little Carnegie Playhouse, the Fifty-Fifth Street Playhouse and others. The chief if not almost the exclusive source of supply of films measuring up to the announced standards of these ventures has been France, Germany and Russia. Among the films which gave encouragement to the idea were: "The Life and Death of a Hollywood Extra," "The Last Moment," "Potyomkin," "The Fall of St. Petersburg," "Secrets of the Soul," "Siegfried" and "The Passion of Joan of Arc."

But such a movement is sterile unless it controls the supply at the same time that it fosters the demand. It is effort wasted unless it is undertaken boldly and intensively by those with enough courage and sufficient resources to give it a thorough trial and even to continue it if it rallies an interested audience but still fails to pay for itself.

It does not require an extraordinary imagination to visualize what such a cinema might become. Eliminating the sentimentality, the mawkishness, the false moral standards, the prudery, the compulsion to be obvious, and all of the other banalities of the "machine-made" film, this "hand-made" cinema could strike clean to the heart of life and utilize all of those infinitely flexible and sensitive capacities, which have been permitted to lie dormant and which, released, could easily lift the film to a high rank among the greatly interpretive and prophetic arts.

Modest as American efforts to create a "Little" Cinema have been, interest in them was on the increase when the intrusion of sound turned that interest in another direction and left their programs passe over night. Almost the sole refuge now for the silent film, with its remarkable library of achievement considering its brief life tenure, it would be possible for the gigantic "machine-made" film industry to subsidize them as a hermitage for the silent film until time proves whether it will ever return to public favor, meanwhile conducting the survey suggested by the barrage of questions in the second paragraph of this section and taking steps toward the creation of an intimate and adult sister to the motion picture of the masses.

C. The Dance

The necessity of endowment for the art of the dance is such a foregone conclusion that it seems irrelevant here to repeat the reasons, several of which I touched upon in scanning the dance for its possibilities as a Great Interpreter. Whence this subsidy is to come is a perplexing question, but it is not so pressing as it is in the other arts. In the first place, mass-production and mass-distribution have not yet seriously threatened the art of the dance as personal performance. And, even if they had, that art is still so rudimentary with us that there is little to subsidize.

It is possible, nevertheless, as I have pointed out before, that our scattered native resources in legend, folk music and individual dancing talents will be suddenly coordinated and crystallized at the behest of another Diaghileff, another Isadora Duncan. It is possible, too, that the sound film will awaken one of these days to the universal human appeal of great dancing. With that discovery, of course, the machine will become either portentous or auspicious—portentous if it sucks dry the creative reserves without regard for the perennial inspiration which the artist draws from personal performance in the presence of an audience; auspicious if, in the absence of a private Maecenas, it undertakes the endowment of the dance and assures the artist of the only conditions under which he can satisfy both himself and the voracious appetite of the machine.

D. Music

In music we encounter for the first time an art which has become highly mechanized, which has learned that the protection of the individual performer is not only possible but desirable and which has not had to go outside its own ranks for the underwriting of that protection. On the whole, it seems to me that music is meeting the situation frankly and resourcefully, and that, while a great deal remains to be done, it already provides substantial evidence in favor of my contention that intimate art can co-exist with mass-production art.

More than any of the other arts except the cinema, music has proved susceptible to the inroads of the machine in its capacities of reproduction and distribution. We have seen how first the phonograph and the player-piano and latterly the radio have been at least a potential blessing to millions of people in decentralizing music and thus in making it universally available. But they have not been an unmixed blessing. While reaching out to a daily audience of millions, as compared with one of thousands thirty years ago, music has accomplished this miraculous feat with an actual reduction of performing musicians. Technical unemployment, which we noted as one of the most baffling problems of industry in the eighth section of this chapter, has become more prevalent in music than in all of the other arts put together.

Although still thriving in New York, the concert field across the country has been sharply restricted as a result of the sudden falling off of attendance figures. Dance orchestras which used to thrive at private and public gatherings are eking out a bare existence in broadcasting studios or have disbanded altogether. Theatre orchestras reporting for work have found their post filled without warning by any one of several forms of "canned" music.

It is no wonder that the American Federation of Musicians, with 140,000 members in this country and Canada, has become panic-stricken and in desperation has resorted to a public appeal by paid advertising in the leading periodicals. In rehearsing their plight, these union musicians have been wise enough to forego a bid for sympathy and have concentrated on attempting to show the public how it has been cheated with substitutes and half-way measures. Success in enlisting over three million members in the Music Defense League has been claimed for this unique campaign, but it is not yet evident just how these "members" can do anything about the lock-out of the musicians.

Meanwhile our music schools, our private instructors and similar institutions all over Europe are turning out, as candidates for the professional market, thousands of eager young performers annually to swell the lists of the unemployed and disheartened.

It seems to me extremely fortunate, under the circumstances, that in recent years music has been developed in America as a business on a large scale. Compared with the gambler's den of the theatre, music has been as carefully organized on commercial lines as an automobile factory or a bank. Concerts are booked, season subscriptions are sold for a series of concerts, vocal, instrumental or orchestral, and performing artists are efficiently routed— all long enough in advance to insure the maximum of public response. It seems to be the fashion in certain circles to deplore the so-called "commercialization" of music, in the belief that music as an art recedes to the extent that it becomes a business. To me, such an attitude ignores the enormous administrative responsibilities entailed by the task of providing music for a hundred and twenty million people scattered over a territory nearly twice the size of Western and Central Europe. Wealthy patrons will foot deficits only if this task is efficiently managed.

The wisdom and value of a sound business administration for an art of the vast proportions of music in an age of readjustment and revolutionary reconstruction was apparent during the first wave of mechanization twenty to thirty years ago which put a phonograph in millions of homes and widely popularized the player-piano. Feared at first as a dangerous rival by the performing musician, these extensions of the hands and voice of music soon won him as a collaborator and friendly ally. They were dependent on him for something to say. He profited in the end, after conquering his misgivings, both by the new form of employment which they offered and by the broader currency of the hearing and appreciation of music which they induced.

To the musicians who have been thrown out of work by the latter-day wave of mechanization—the radio, the sound film and the electric phonograph—the wisdom and value of an efficient business administration in music may still seem dubious. Both the mechanization and the business itself come in for their share of recrimination. But it is too soon yet to cast ledger balances. It seems reasonable to me to assume, however, that the confusion would have been infinitely worse, that the performer would have had less consideration and more uncertainty and the public far less satisfaction, if the music business had been as irresponsible as that of the theatre. Only a soundly organized business could have enabled the phonograph to stand up against its own later mechanical rival, the radio, boldly revolutionize its technique by the aid of electrical reproduction, recapture a dwindling public interest, make common cause with the radio, employ the ablest living artists, and successfully take the risk of manufacturing and selling records of the world's greatest music—music, in many cases, seldom heard from the actual concert platform. Only a soundly organized business could arrange for and maintain the nation-wide broadcasts of the greater symphony orchestra concerts. Only a soundly organized business could command the confidence and the respect of Dr. Damrosch for his weekly radio programs for school children. Only a soundly organized business could conduct nation-wide contests and auditions among beginners and establish rewards for the winners, like that sponsored by Atwater Kent. Leaving the field of radio broadcasting for that of general music, only a soundly organized business could have repaired in action the ravaged structure of the personally-performed concert and carry on at a restricted pace until, if ever, the public returns to the concert halls in anything like its old numbers. Only a soundly organized business can afford the Music Defense League any hope through the tendency of business to keep its ear to the ground and sense the direction of public demand.

But this business of music, a machine in itself as all soundly organized business is, has many more obligations to fulfill. Thus far its mechanized processes of reproduction and distribution have subsisted largely on the trained reserves of the old-time personally-performed concert, on musicians professionally acquainted with and attuned to an audience in the flesh. Success in the latter field does not necessarily insure success in the new realm of records and radio, and perhaps mechanized music will have to train its own performers. But those performers will lack something price-lessly valuable, which is taken for granted in the old-school performer, unless the business of music subsidizes the intimate concert-in-person—"hand-made" music, let us call it—to give these recruits that flexibility of expression, that professional assurance, that psychological accord, which come only through personal experience in the presence of an audience. Perhaps one of the answers is a chain of Little Concert-Halls, after the analogy of the Little Theatre, as suggested by Atwood C. Bellamy in the June, 1930, *American Mercury*. These chamber music groups, Bellamy believes, could operate in almost any locality at a minimum cost, to the enduring satisfaction of performer and audience, but what I see in his suggestion is a unique opportunity for "machine-made" music to subsidize "hand-made" music, *both for the intrinsic value of the latter and for its service as an independent laboratory and testing ground.*

I see only one means of escape, however, from the cul-de-sac into which technical unemployment has herded vast thousands of professional musicians. Mechanized music has probably robbed many of them forever of a means of livelihood, just as the machine has ruthlessly discarded untold millions of handworkers in the past century and bade them find something else to do. Apart from personal suffering and damaged pride, which can be deplored without sentimentality, I can not convince myself that the art of music will be seriously affected, for many of these performers were artisans, day-laborers, rather than artists. With a courage which the Machine Age respects more highly than most of the traditional virtues, let these stranded musicians, who would never have advanced beyond mediocrity in the art of music, take their violins and clarinets home for personal solace and turn their hands to another craft. The true artists among them will survive as artists, strengthened, as music itself will be, by an inexorable winnowing.

E. *Television*

With the wireless transmission of synchronized sound and sight experimentally established but still in a laboratory stage as far as general and practical use is concerned, it is purely hypothetical to attempt to visualize what effect television will have on performer and audience in the event of its ultimate achievement. The only evidences we have are the widely attested workings of mass psychology and the influence of radio which is still in course of revealing its hand.

In general it may be assumed that, since television is the extension of the facilities of radio broadcasting to include sight as well as sound and since engineers promise that existing radio receiving sets will merely have to be supplemented by additional apparatus, the coming of television will intensify the decentralization of music and aggravate the technical unemployment which the radio has begun. From the standpoint of the audience, it seems possible that not only music but the theatre may be decentralized— the theatre inclusively rather than specifically speaking—as nothing has dispersed it since the birth of the motion picture. In both music and the theatre, contrary to the sanguine view of certain experts in television, the inevitable concomitant of this enormous expansion of the audience and the provision of service to that audience by a few centrally located performers would be the release of still more hordes of idle artists, musical and dramatic, to recruit the already ominous army of the jobless.

Those who minimize these considerations are fond of contending that the concert and the dramatic performance brought to the home will only whet the curiosity to attend these performances in person. Released prematurely, before the process is perfected to satisfy the eye which is more exacting than the ear, the directly opposite reaction might be expected. But such premature release is not likely, for the experts in distribution learned a lesson from the radio which had to live down a bad name won by the crude performance of the early amateur-built receiving sets. While this home manufacture was ungovernable, even encouraged for a while, the intricacy of television equipment seems likely to keep its control in responsible hands.

Withheld until perfected, television might make audiences, as the phonograph, the radio and the sound film are tending to make audiences, for the concert auditorium, the opera house and the theatre. The thrill of hearing music and seeing a play in company with a crowd of fellow-humans is not to be conveyed by any imaginable mechanism. But it must be recalled that television proposes to satisfy the longing of radio devotees to "see" the performer in action. And whoever sits at home in his own private theatre can not be present on that evening, at least, in recital hall or playhouse.

Television, then, seems destined to carry on the process of technical unemployment from the point where radio and the sound film leave off. I can only repeat, therefore, the warning I have already stressed in the other arts: Once rooted and growing as a new and independent art, television will have to subsidize personal performance, both musical and dramatic, for its intrinsic value and for its service as indispensable laboratory and testing-ground.

10. "Machine-Made" as Sponsor of "Hand-Made" in the Graphic and Plastic Arts

A. Literature

The publisher and bookseller, as we have seen, have squandered their opportunity to remain supreme masters in their own house. By permitting alert and enterprising outsiders to incur the initial risks and reap the ultimate profits of the book clubs, the lending libraries and the weekly and monthly periodicals—all of them legitimate subsidiaries of the process of distribution in the art of letters—they have forfeited the income of the most remunerative side-lines of their profession and all but lost control of that profession.

It ought to be possible at this stage of our survey to visualize by comparison with the other arts what literature in Machine Age America might have been if its distributors had kept on their toes, had grown with the times and had protected their patrimony. Reinforced by the profits of mass production and mass distribution, the publisher could have encouraged and subsidized the writing of important but unprofitable works. He could have incurred the risks or even the certain loss of their publication. He could have conducted exhaustive surveys for unknown or unsuspected talent instead of waiting for it to emerge by chance. He could have organized the comprehensive introduction to us of the significant works of foreign languages in translation instead of leaving that task to personal whims. He could have financed the translation of the outstanding achievements of American writers and their world-wide distribution to the enhancement of America's international reputation in the arts. He could have endowed the education of the American public in the habit of reading books and owning books so that we would not be humiliated by the fact that, according to R. L. Duffus, we buy only two books per capita per annum. And finally, by thus increasing the demand for even books of limited appeal, he could have reduced their cost of manufacture to bring them within the price range of the average purse.

In other words, "machine-made" could have handsomely subsidized "hand-made"—hand-made, of course, not in the literal sense but as signifying that which is intended for a selective rather than a general audience. How far the "book trade" has fallen short of such a goal I have already depicted in exposing its panic-stricken preoccupation with the problem of mere existence. Whether it will solve that problem of mere existence, by realistic adjustment to the times, by mergers of publishing firms and of retail sales outlets, or by the ruthless operation of the law of the survival of the fittest; whether, having assured its continuity, the book trade will have the vision and ingenuity to make common cause with its extramural rivals, trading shrewdly its prestige with the author for a share in the commercial advantages of club, lending library and magazine, and thus recover a portion of the power which it has supinely abdicated—only time will tell.

Apart from the general lethargy of publisher and bookseller, two specific aspects of their practice have been largely responsible for the economic dilemma in which they, the author and the reading public are jointly involved. The first of these unfortunate aspects is the perennial jealousy which has prevented publishers from agreeing upon any radical departure from traditional practice—a lone-wolf attitude which has its counterpart only among the theatrical producers. Akin to this first aspect with its perverse emphasis on individualism, is the second which consists in the pride of both publisher and bookseller that his business is no ordinary commercial enterprise and that he has cultural responsibilities to both creative artist and reading public which mark him off from the manufacturers and dispensers of shoes, shirts and shellac.

Let us examine the latter of these two aspects first. A little over a year ago, when the tri-partite controversy among book club, bookseller and publisher was at its height, two schools of thought emerged on the subject of books as merchandise. One of them, with Roger W. Babson as its disinterested spokesman, insisted that publisher and bookseller were playing the rôle of King Canute in trying to ignore the need and the consequences of mass-production and mass-sales in literature. The other school of thought, upheld by John Macrae, Sr., head of E. P. Dutton and Company, and other publishers, booksellers and scholarly students of the problem, contended that books could not be pigeon-holed with breakfast foods and tooth pastes, that they were a class rather than a mass product, and that to yield to the obvious lure of the Machine Age would be to standardize literature, to destroy its jealously-guarded independence and to reduce it at once to the mediocrity of the contemporary cinema.

I was strongly inclined at the time to hold with the latter school of thought, but I have come to realize in the meantime that the truth probably lies somewhere midway between these two antithetical points of view, that it partakes of both of them. Without doubt there is a type of literature and a certain stage in the life of certain books which are readily and legitimately amenable to the methods of mass-manufacture and high-pressure salesmanship. Equally without doubt, there are certain other books which it would be folly to handle in this way. In suggesting that modern merchandising methods be applied to all books indiscriminately, Babson ignored the fact that, while standardization appears to be the direction in which commodities generally recognized as necessities are moving, there is an equally strong incentive, on a minor scale, it is true, toward the individual, the different. It is well to recall here from a recent page the average citizen's contradictory traits of wishing to be different and fearing to be unlike his fellows, the need of our new age to nourish the wish and allay the fear, and the responsibility of publisher and bookseller for keeping standardization in their own field within legitimate bounds.

There is nothing new in this recognition of a dual and paradoxical trend in the distribution of literature. Individual publishers have not only observed it and practiced it but also frequently capitalized it in line with the theory of "machine-made" supporting "hand-made." Ibáñez's "The Four Horsemen of the Apocalypse" enabled Duttons to spend without stint to bring many worthier books to public attention. Hendrik Van Loon's "The Story of Mankind," Rose Macaulay's "Potterism" and Francis Hackett's "Henry the Eighth" were only three of the periodic lucky "breaks" which have permitted Horace Liveright to indulge in chance-taking with unusual works and unknown authors. Lewis's "Main Street" and Keynes' "The Economic Consequences of the Peace" underwrote the new firm of Harcourt, Brace and Company. Prosper Buranelli's Cross-Word-Puzzle books staked Simon and Schuster in the publication of Schnitzler, Werfel, Zweig and Powys and in the effective introduction of their works to the American public.

These are only a handful of literature's counterparts for the theatre's legends of "Ben Hur," "Turn to the Right," "Lightnin'," "Abie's Irish Rose," "Journey's End." With few exceptions, however, publishers have used the profits of mass distribution more worthily than theatrical producers. As a matter of fact, they do not wait for extraordinary popular successes to indulge their predilection for publishing dignified, enduring books, books which are so unlikely to pay for their actual cost of manufacture that they are known in trade parlance as "prestige books." Economically unwarranted indulgence of this kind has driven more than one publisher to the wall, while scores of booksellers, actuated by similar motives, carry thousands of such volumes on their shelves as dead merchandise. Paradoxical as it may seem in an age when narrowly commercial instincts and practices have crowded out the more ideal impulses in many other professions, the publisher and bookseller have not been sufficiently businesslike for the good of the art they serve.

The question, then, is not so much what kind of books the publisher undertakes to issue as it is what he does for them and their authors and their prospective public after publication. Until very recently, the publisher felt that he had fulfilled his obligation in serving as a filter for the manuscripts which reached his editorial desk and in advertising his products formally in traditionally accepted channels. The bookseller expected little more until, beset by supplantive competition, by the successful rivalry of other and more exciting pastimes than reading, he discovered the need of assistance beyond his local power to provide. It is this assistance in all of its manifold guises, some of which, clearly conceived and understood, I have listed in the second paragraph above, that the bookseller demands of the publisher. The author, too, should demand it. And the reading public has a right to expect it.

But practically all of these suggested expansions of the publisher's function are beyond the reach of any single publisher, no matter how many "best-sellers" he has or how strongly he is financed. Dependent on profession-wide cooperation for their successful application, they encounter first the individualistic pride of the publisher, admirable as it is in some respects, next the inordinate jealousy among publishers and finally the impecunious state of the profession as a whole. Clearly as we may discern the applicability to literature of the theory of "machine-made" and "hand-made," co-existent and mutually helpful, its realization in practice seems discouragingly remote.

B. Painting and Sculpture

Since the distributive economics of the arts of painting and sculpture is still in almost as rudimentary a state as that of the dance, it is purely speculative to try to find in it an analogy with industry's dualism of "machine-made" and "hand-made." That such an analogy will take shape in time and bring along with it the usual consequences is more than likely, for it is not characteristic of the Machine Age to forego any opportunity it can find or create to introduce and spur the methods of mass-production in the expectation of the profits of mass-distribution. I hardly think, however, we need fear intrusion in the form suggested by Maurice Sterne, painter and sculptor, in a recent letter: "I doubt if the Machine Age has had any more effect upon our sculpture than the sculpture upon the machine. When there will be developed a sort of Ford plant for the reproduction of sculpture, we might speak of its influence."

Meanwhile, there are several aspects of the problem of distribution in these arts which claim our attention and which, if satis-

factorily solved, should fortify us against the dangers of an unexpected encounter with mechanization.

In the first place, we must always bear in mind the fact that
there is no inherent and essential sanctity in the hand and its
handiwork. The fallacious belief in such an intrinsic value held
sway with us through the latter part of the Nineteenth Century,
as a distant and perverted reverberation of the doctrines and practices of Ruskin and Morris. In its wake it left on our parlor walls
tens of thousands of banal daubs in oil and water color, as well as
a hideous assortment of hand-painted china on our pantry shelves
and a mélange of badly-designed and uncomfortable hand-made
furniture throughout the house. We know somewhat better today. Or perhaps we behave somewhat better through compulsion,
for the shrunken modern apartment has relegated to the ash-can
most of this cluttering pseudo-art. In its place, the machine is beginning to refurnish our homes with greater esthetic satisfaction,
for the masters of the machine, surprised to find that natural man
uninfluenced by bad tradition responds eagerly to good design, are
employing artists to tell the machine what to do.

Latterly, however, to all intents and purposes as far as the
American home is concerned, the painter and the sculptor have
ceased to exist. For one thing, there is no room for their work as
architects build today. And for another, the cult of the hand has
waned to the extent of eliminating home-made fruit and fish still-
lifes and family portraits from our remnants of wall, without,
however, leading to the renascence of the print or the reproduction
of great paintings, classic or modern.

If mass-production ever confronts the painter it seems likely
that it will come in the form of reproduction of his work by one
of the numerous processes of color printing which have been de-

veloped recently to a high degree of technical efficiency and accuracy. Except for commercial purposes, these processes lie dormant, awaiting evidence of demand sufficient to justify the high cost of the first replica of the original canvas. I see no reason why the painter should not welcome the initiation and widespread development of the reproductive procedure, for acquaintance with his work in particular and with the esthetic motives of modern painting in general could only redound to greater respect for him and his art and greater demand for his original product. I can not help thinking that the tardy understanding and appreciation of modern art is traceable at least in part to the inability of crude black-and-white reproductions to do justice to the originals with their organic and emotionally exciting color values and to the slight opportunity we have had to get really acquainted with true representatives of modern painting in flying trips to Europe and in visits to meager loan exhibitions in this country. Extension of the idea of loan exhibitions in the spirit of Francis P. Garvan's recent bequest to Yale University, or even the inauguration of the custom of renting paintings to private individuals, proposed several years ago by Lee Simonson, might mitigate our deplorable ignorance of modern painting. But if the appreciation of painting is ever to achieve the dissemination and decentralization already attained by the theatre, the cinema, music and literature, it must depend chiefly on the machine in the guise of the color press.

That the machine in this form carries any threat to the hand is too improbable or at least too remote to cause concern. Concern arises, rather, as to what to do with the thousands of so-called and self-convinced painters and sculptors with mediocre talent or less who infest New York or drift back starved from Paris. No machine has displaced them by the process of technical unemployment. There is no one who has grown wealthy by the mass-reproduction and the mass-distribution of their work and who, if he had, might be induced to subsidize their continuing experiments. They have entered an overcrowded profession with open eyes, and the worst of them must take the consequences of the survival of the fittest while the best of them must swallow their false pride and accept the invitation of industry and the crafts to design for the machine.

But even if there is no intramural aid to be discerned, no machine sponsorship of the hand within the art of painting and sculpture themselves, that fact does not necessarily preclude such endowment from the outside. Remember that I have nominated the "machine-made" cinema as at least temporary patron of the "hand-made" theatre. That the painter and sculptor of the Machine Age need and deserve such recognition, incentive and assistance should require no proof. And it seems to me that it is logically at hand in the recently rediscovered commonwealth of interest involving architect, painter and sculptor, with the builder over all as the incarnation of the spirit of the machine—the builder, either as private citizen or public official, who is able to commission both painter and sculptor in collaboration with the architect to spread their interpretive message on walls organically allocated to their independent responsibility.

C. Architecture

It is this same builder, of course, to whom we shall have to look for the stimulating employment, if not the endowment, of the architect. In its very nature, architecture is so intricately, so inevitably, bound up with the machine that the hand analogy is almost inconceivable. Architecture is, or can be, the art par excellence of the Machine Age. In no other art is the machine utilized on such a scale. In no other art, especially if we extend the bounds of architecture to include regional and city planning, does the perfection and increasing power of the machine hurl such a challenge to the artist. In no other art is the vision of the individual artist more needed to guide the machine, to tell it what to do.

Just there, if anywhere, lies the greatest danger to architecture today. Tempted to cut costs, already so prohibitive, the builder may decide to trust to the engineer alone in prescribing to the machine its tasks. But by the very nature of their interlocking and enormous responsibilities, the architect and the engineer of the future may become one and the same person. If this synthetic creature can also be empowered by Government to be the future's builder as well, the Machine Age will have richly justified its tendency toward the concentration of power in ever more compact seats of authority.

D. The Craft Arts

If architecture is least amenable of the arts to the analogy with industry of "machine-made" and "hand-made," the craft arts most readily and most naturally of all fit into that pattern and partake of its consequences. To whatever extent the products of machine and of hand can and must co-exist in industry, to whatever extent the former is able and obligated to preserve the latter in health, dignity and independence, to that same extent do these judgments hold true in the craft arts. For the craft arts are the epitome, the staple essence, of industry. It would probably be more accurate today to denote them as the industrial arts. Ranging from ashtrays to Pullman cars, wherever design may be dictated by the artist to the machine or be imposed directly on the raw material by the hand, the abstract discussion of the subject as applied to industry in general in the eighth section of this chapter applies concretely, point for point, to the craft arts. It seems futile to retrace that ground at this point, but in conclusion I should like to add one clarifying thought, a thought which suggests reverberations back through all of the arts to which we have been examining the pertinence of this theory:

The merchant of today—and we can take him generically as representative of the middleman, the distributor, in all of the arts, whether he be theatrical or cinema producer, concert manager or publisher—the merchant of today is torn between the two horns of a dilemma. Shall he heed the demands of those who desire something just like what everybody else has? Or shall he listen to the still small voice of those few who demand something different, something their own? Shall he take the trouble to detect the wish for something different, still unexpressed and stifled under the fear to be unlike the mass, and nourish it until it attains the courage of conviction? If he decides to answer all three questions with assent, how can he adjust demand and supply? Can he make demand for the "like" pay for providing the "different" until it earns its own way?

On the solutions of these fundamental and universal problems depends the future of the arts in America. Not upon the creative artist wholly, nor upon the appreciative public, does the question of the arts as Great Interpreters rest. For the Machine Age has conferred on the master of their distribution the grave responsibility and the inspiring privilege of the deciding vote!

PART TWO

A Field Survey

Training the Playwright of the Machine Age

By George Pierce Baker

Just as in all of the other arts, the material of the theatre has been affected thoroughly by modern scientific thinking. It has been influenced by all the "ologies and isms"—neurology, psychology, pathology—by free, independent, daring thinking. It has had to yield to readjustment, by thought, of man to all the old ideas accepted in the past as sound and right because of tradition. This new thinking, this readjustment, has called for new methods and technique—experimentation of all kinds. As contrasted with my youth, I find today not "life adjusted to the theatre" which led to melodrama and unreality, but the theatre inventively, imaginatively re-made to meet the demands of accurate representation of life. All this has come with our insistent dramatic realism as compared with romanticized history or imaginative treatment of life.

What can be taught is method in the light of historical and recent practice; how drama has been done in the past, remote and recent; the relation of a dramatist to an audience in trying to interest it in subjects interesting to him and to the extent, emotionally, that he is interested. A feeling must be inborn for what is emotionally significant, especially for people in general, in human conduct, and a deep, relentless desire so to express what is discerned that other men can be made to see it and feel it to the extent desired. Mere interest in character and skill in dialogue are not enough for the embryo dramatist. Discerning the emotional clearly, he must feel

175

about it so strongly as to devote every effort to make others see and feel with him. He must steadily develop power of emotional illustration, a steadily wider and deeper understanding of the persuasion of dramatic art. That "persuasion" can be taught. My experience is that the "born" dramatist is rare. His speed in attaining his goal can be quickened, his labors lightened. But most young Americans mistake an interest in, and some gift for, characterization and dialogue for sure signs of dramatic promise. These persons may better study for the novel and the short story.

Keeping abreast of the revolutionary? This is really very simple. First of all, any study of dramatic technique shows that a few fundamental principles in the relation of dramatist to public have held good from Aeschylus to the most mechanistic modern Russian. Cling to these in instruction. Let all that is of a period or a man go. Secondly, don't stress rules, precepts; help the would-be dramatist to find self-expression. Don't bother him with rules while he is working. After all, the teacher here is more the midwife than the diagnostician. That is, don't worry the student with type, method, rules; help him to bring forth that which is creating in his mind and heart. After it is all over, he may be surprised to find that a process which seemed unique for him is singularly like processes known before—with, of course, individual differences. I cannot supply the dramatic instinct. I do not wish, am not willing, to supply central, creative ideas. I am desirous of helping an individual man or woman to express that which is emotionally absorbing him.

The sound film has had very little effect on me as yet. I am forced to recognize what the film—silent or sound—can do better than the theatre—space, landscape values, atmosphere to some extent, the usefulness of its devices like the "throw-back," etc., to replace soliloquy. I am forced to wonder whether, when the sound film has attained a much more perfect development, its necessarily compacted dialogue may not affect drama dialogue for the better, making it more richly connotative. At present, however, unless one attempts to teach writing scenarios for sound films, I think the teaching of playwriting but little affected. After all, so far as this kind of film aims at being drama, it must share in the use of time-honored fundamentals.

Of course, we have had much of mechanical contrivance—revolving stages, cupola horizons, the mechanical contrivances of the Meyerhold stage, etc., but he who writes for the country at large cannot count on these mechanistic aids; therefore, except in a few special theatres, they have been little considered by our authors. To the mechanistic devices of the recent Russian stage our public seems not to take; therefore, our young authors turn to them only in an early, imitative stage of their career.

But I take it most devices, most mechanisms, come from the desire to express what it is difficult to present by older methods. That means thought on the old attitudes or interest in new attitudes or ways of thinking—as in Russia. In thought our college-trained young dramatist is usually too young to have his own slant on life, to have done much careful, independent thinking. He is consciously or unconsciously the immature product of his teachers or of the men he has read. That is why I want to deal, preferably, much preferably, with graduate students. I am coming to feel that I should like to work only with people between twenty-eight to thirty and forty-five. Before twenty-eight, young people rarely have "found themselves"; after forty-five, I have found that people write plays strongly influenced by the plays the writers saw in the impressionable years between seventeen and twenty-seven. My students have made, particularly the more mature, much effort to find forms adequate to their needs—three, four, five acts, scenes for acts, prologues, epilogues, etc. They have responded keenly to all the experiments in method of O'Neill. But in thought, I have felt less influence of a mechanistic period.

I might add that I encourage all experimentation if I feel it grows out of the demands of the material and is not experimentation just for the sake of being different and with no core of exigent thought and meaning.

The outstanding quality of American playwriting seems to me to be a relentless facing of human conduct for a better, because truer, presentation of it, a willingness to try experimentation in form to meet the needs created by this purpose; and a great interest in understanding more delicately the subtler manifestations—comic and tragic—of human thought and conduct.

We insist at Yale that all would-be dramatists must know something—what a general course of a year can give—of the theory and the practice in all the arts of the theatre; producing plays, lighting, costuming, scenic design, even stage carpentry and back-stage control during performances. At first, young dramatists do not always take to this. But later, one and all admit its value. For myself I can see decided results in a simplification of demands made on each department by a play, an ability to get desired results more surely and wisely. Our course, Drama 9, required of each student in his first year, gives the fundamental theory and opportunities for practice on the crews which work on each of our productions, large and small. We have usually five productions, on the main stage, of long plays, original with us or hitherto unproduced in the United States. We have two bills of original one-acts and almost constant production of short original or well-known one-acts in the class-room for two of the producing courses.

As yet the sound film is so new that generalization seems to me very unsafe. Undoubtedly the theatre and the film can learn from each other. But one fundamental difference may make subsidy of the theatre by the film very dangerous. The sound film, if it is to appeal as widely as the silent film, must reach millions—but can it? The fundamental difference is here: No dramatist expects any such vast audience as is expected for the films. He can, therefore, choose subjects of less wide acceptance, treat them with more freedom than can the film. The new code of Will Hays with its "dont's" would have made impossible nearly all that is best in the great drama of the past and all the daring thinking of the newer drama. If the drama is subsidized by film-producers, must they not quite naturally ask for subject and treatment which will readily go over into the silent or sound film?

On the other hand, I do not doubt that in another twenty years, so responsive, so flexible a something as drama will be somewhat different from what it is today if the sound film is given the fullest possible development artistically.

Some Notes on the Playwright in Revolt

By Paul Green

I

THE playwright like other artists is always in revolt, that is, more or less. Not only is this true of artists, but likewise of people and things.

The word is a difficult one, and if a metaphysic for it were sought it could be found in the old dualism of changing permanence which received statement in Greece some twenty-five hundred years ago.

It is the nature of that which exists—including the living and the dead—to make use of antagonisms and differences in the assertion of itself. In fact, such is the nature of that assertion.

Revolt then is but another term for development or growth—development which is universally contemporaneous in every phase of existence, going on at any instant of time and in any part of space. In this sense all things are in continuous revolt, that is, all things are alive, with the constant qualification of more or less.

Thus any production is the production of something new from the old. Nor is this new ever the same as the old, for there can be no repetition either in nature, art or things, only similarity. In mechanics where the case might demand sameness there is constant wear and tear and response to varying taste and needs and inner upheavals, and there is no abiding in iteration.

The term development is more in keeping with a certain way of the world than revolt. The former means fulfillment of and the latter denial of. And it would appear that life forever absorbs denial in its growth in so far as life is spiritual, if one may use a word so heavily suspect.

II

Since the present then is always in revolt or developing, it is in that consequence the best of all possible times. It could not be otherwise, for in its development it contains the past, the present, and the future, inasmuch as they are significant to us the living—the past which has shaped us to the present, the past and the present upon which it feeds, and the present and future which is its fruitfulness.

This is truest of what might be called the spiritual nature of man and not of the process and wastage of physical nature and things. Accordingly the ancient statement that "now is the accepted time" is always true for man. Errors, mistakes, failures, and tragedies do not alter this, for negative and positive matters alike are one for him.

The recent preachment that the present is a time of cultural waste and decay has found widespread concurrence of witnesses among the confused, the tired and discouraged, who have been overpowered by the vast richness and variety of life and mistakenly apprehended these as antagonistic to art when in reality they are the food of art.

Pessimism therefore is a partiality, and at any present time there is no cause for it. The weak keepers may tremble but the light suffers no diminution; it ever increases. And Everyman ever grows stronger in his service to it. He neither revolts nor despairs, nor has ears for the phrases coming out of the distance that all is hopeless. These are ejaculations cast up in the heat of battle by the weak of arm and frail of will who fall afoul of themselves in the darkness near the edge of light.

And by that light Everyman writes in his book. He is the artist.

III

And as artist he is full of present great possibilities never before dreamed of and which he encompasses in his increasing wisdom.

With the canons of novelty and entertainment some would purvey him into their darkness, but confusion cannot dismay him nor can it interest him. For him beauty still flames upon the earth as in the days of Helen, or Eve or any Thais. Nor is the whole story told therein, for he will have his say.

And as artist he is stronger and freer in the living present. Like the rumor of old he has increased by continuing, grown great by what he feeds upon. And his food is the multitudinous and ever-outpouring matter for art which fertile life in all her forms provides.

And his spirit is freer than before in this province which is the all—the all that exists, all that can be thought or experienced. Nothing for him is tabooed or set apart or forbidden. All is native to his need. All that is mechanical, all that is vital with which the world is overflowing, these are his.

IV

And as dramatist these are the inventions and the arts, the facts and deeds and events to be combined and transformed with infinite variety into his dream made manifest—such as history,

poetry, music, painting, dancing, sculpture, architecture, pantomime; the sciences and all knowledge, and all the machinery of
the modern world.

And from these he is creating the great art, the great drama,
which is his new religion, his new mystery and philosophy.

v

And in the process the two ancient enemies are falling before
him—morality which would bind him in its creeds and commerce
which would use him to its purpose, the former confusing beauty
with ethics, the latter vision with gain. He knows there can be no
immoral art, no immoral drama. There can be bad art, bad drama.
And morality with its censorship must give way to esthetic criticism, not to the enforcement of law.

For to consider, if art corrupts it will corrupt the judges of its
corruption, and therefore the judges should be protected, since if
they are corrupted their judgment is false and they are no longer
judges—and so on to absurdity. Law cannot in any way deal with
the matter. Only intelligence can.

And if art, the drama, to consider once more, is beholden to
gain, commercial enterprises and rents, gambling and exchanges,
whims and fancies of its upholders, it is no longer art but a symbol of barter and vanity, in which beauty becomes a figment on
an expedient currency.

All of these things the artist knows and will show to others.

vi

And the dramatist writes the great drama for the theatre envisioned in the present. This theatre is the home of his art with
schools and training grounds, rooms, laboratories and workshops

for experiment in all the arts—for all the arts will cooperate with the drama as it appears complete upon the stage of either a studio, an auditorium, an amphitheatre, or a large outdoor stadium.

For these are the great theatre with its director, its playwrights, its actors, artists, artisans, and inventors—all parts of the greater whole, to which they give existence and from which they draw inspiration.

VII

And this too will suffer revolt and develop into something new and different.

The Eternal Theatre

By Arthur Hopkins

So long as the theatre abandons itself to an expression of feeling and action which requires no explanation, which is not even rational, it remains an art. True art gives no reasons. Art has nothing to do with understanding. It is pure feeling. It is release of the artist's unconscious treasure—that treasure which I believe to be shared by all men but accessible to only a few. These are the excavators of the common treasure—the treasure which all men possess but can only recognize when brought to view by the artist who through some favoritism of nature has an approach which is denied his equally rich brothers.

The ideal theatre is a gathering place for starved people who seek some contact with their own inner richness, who seek new affirmation of their rightful place in their Father's house.

If people entering a theatre with great anticipation emerge disappointed and angry, are we to censure them because the theatre's effort was worthy? Not if we are wise. The theatre has thrown these people back upon their own emaciated self-contact—this hateful, unbearable contact. Their anger is just!

Who is to cope with this insatiable yearning? Where are the dramatists, actors, scene designers, directors? There is only one answer. There never will be many—never enough. The golden approval is given to too few people. Is there a way for people to

185

find it? Perhaps. Perhaps some day people sensing their treasure will pray to it and find it.

That means a sense of values that will have no accord with the appraisals of our Machine Age. It means a turning away from those highly megaphoned paths to which modern complacency and compromise beckon—hopeful, trustful youth.

Is there any discernible aspiration in the movies that threatens the ideal theatre? The very essence of movies is conscious and objective. It is confined solely to assault. Knock the spectators dead. Kill him with this effect. Bean him with this pie. It has nothing to do with self-revelation. It has no lure for the persons seeking new understanding of himself. Why should the artist go into the movies? They have nothing to offer but money. Artists will ultimately have their way and make occasional movies not for money, and in all probability theirs will be the profitable pictures of the future.

Wherever artists are there will be life, whether it be in a theatre, a movie studio or a blacksmith shop—for these are the people who live. These are the people who find occasional confirmation of the eternal truth that the kingdom of God is within.

The Theatre—Art and Instinct

By David Belasco

The art of the theatre is more than an art—it is one of the earliest of human emotional instincts.

Likewise it is a composite of ALL of the arts; literature, music, the dance, painting, sculpture—even architecture, for it is three-dimensional.

It may seem radical to describe an art as an early basic human instinct, but I believe there is justification for the statement as well as for the further declaration that it is an integral part of the makeup of every human.

What was it, other than the instinctive urge of the *mime* that sent the Stone Age warrior clambering to a ledge above the camp-fire of his own social group—there to reenact his victory of the day, whether in the hunt or on field of battle? What was it that kept his audience breathless with suspense? The process of each picturing himself in the role of the warrior—victorious in the end. *Homo Sapiens* was developing another instinct.

The creation of music, of inspired paintings, of sculpturings likewise cannot be other than the result of instinct—the genius-gift. Love of and appreciation for beauty and rhythm in the arts is the privilege of those lacking the ability to produce these wonders. The instinct is the same; all, failing to create, still revel in the creation of others while imagining themselves as the creators.

187

It is my contention that all of the arts are interrelated, even as the art of the theatre is a composite of all of the others.

All, in their final analyses, are basic emotional urges because they are expressed in terms of God-given talent. Being so closely allied, it follows that they affect one another.

Music, dancing, painting, sculpture, in their changing modes also bring with them changes in the mode of the stage. Inversely, the producer whose acumen permits him to anticipate the changing public interest, and to meet the change in his productions, will have his part in creating the newer trend.

It has been my lifelong faith and contention that the theatre is, in itself, an art—and more; that it is not and never can be a commercial industry, a thing of dollar values and credit and debit balances.

The American theatre today in its finer aspects and achievements, stands recognized as one of the arts: this despite its grossly commercial aspects brought about by strong, well-intrenched interests which seek to keep the theatre in commercial bondage. It goes without saying that these, by their grasping, money-mad methods, are defeating their own purpose.

These I call commercial art-reactionaries—"racketeers" in the language of the street. They are identifiable always by their reckless, hasty, hit-or-miss methods. Compare their offerings with those of any true devotee of the theatre. It will be apparent at once what a vast difference there is between the sham and the real.

In this age of reconstruction when there is so much to be achieved for the theatre, it is regrettable that there is this tendency toward haste and carelessness, this slipshod gambling with chance.

Unfortunately this attitude is mirroring itself in the work of some of the younger artists, who otherwise are sound and fine basically. Further, it is a fault that is having its ramifications throughout the theatre—in the work of the playwright, the producer, the director, the actor: even the critic.

Because of it, many are losing their perspective: the sense of dignity and poise which goes with the privilege of being an exponent of one of the arts.

It is this haste and carelessness that is responsible, more than any other one factor, for the high prices of theatre tickets. Such a course invariably multiplies failures. There can be but one result—when the "dollar" producer finally scores one hit out of half a dozen productions, he must depend on that one to recoup his losses.

Were they gamers with dice, one might forgive this frantic appeal to the Goddess of Chance. But the arts and the sciences are exact. There are inexorable rules governing them, the primary one of which is "hard work, application, toil until perfection is had."

There is no smooth pathway to success. It is a hard, thorny trail, rock-strewn and steep. It is not a royal road, a King's Highway for the oversized tires of the Chariot of Luck. One must negotiate it on foot, weary and athirst, struggling ever upward and never counting the backward slips.

These same producers, were they true devotees, with the art of the stage as their guiding urge, would seek to make each production perfect in its artistry, true in line and scene to life and nature. Any artist, capable of producing a really great piece of work, would not offer a daub for showing at a great exhibit.

Hard work, carefully conceived and carried out, is the greatest guarantee of success of the art of the theatre.

I waited years to give the public my version of "The Merchant of Venice" and I spent months and thousands of dollars in advance preparation. Again with "Deburau," and more recently with "Mima," the same conditions applied. The 'scripts were in my vaults, my property, for months while I waited for the opportune moment, the availability of casts—the right public thought. Then more months went into construction of scenery, costuming and the final direction and rehearsal.

These, like many other of my productions, represented an original investment and subsequent maintenance costs that eliminated any chance of profit, yet I was happy in the thought that in their production I had given something toward the art of the theatre.

Because I believe the theatre is both an art and an applied science I apply the rules of science to my productions. Nothing is left to chance. Having no one to say me "Yea" or "Nay," I count time and effort as nothing as against perfection of detail.

I have said that the arts and the sciences are closely related. Granting this, then let us all give of our time and talents so that the theatre may point the way for the other arts in the struggle for the true perfection. Anything less will be unworthy of the task the Supreme Intelligence has given into our hands for the doing.

The Actor as Artist

By Alfred Lunt

Of course I am surprised to see the actor drawn into any argument about the theatre. Generally the fate of this ancient institution is settled by nearly everyone else. Therefore, it is pleasant to participate, for the actor has listened to ten or fifteen years of interminable discussion of his problems but so far has tried out few of the theories advanced in the aid of his artistic well-being, except perhaps the economic one.

The actor is the highest salaried person for services rendered who ever existed. His working hours could scarcely be bettered. But the actor himself—of his own accord—has taken little interest in the renascence of the theatre, for it is the public which has raised the standard of acting . . . if a standard there is. The molded, bombastic, conventionalized quality is slowly going, and its gradual extinction is, I feel, brought about by a too prodigal display of it in cheap movies and equally cheap stage productions. The reaction against excessive flamboyancy can be coupled with the demands made by modern playwrights for a more truthful and understanding interpretation of their work. Since the actor is a much shrewder business man than is suspected, he readily recognizes the trend and falls into line. In divesting his work of staginess, he becomes *naturalistic* because that is the style of acting now in demand.

It is possible to reconcile an actor's ability to shift his style when you recognize the fact that acting is not an independent art, but merely a secondary medium through which the playwright reaches his audience. The actor is but an interpreter and must remain so unless the entire scheme of the theatre is changed back into the *commedia dell'arte* or into God knows what! Even this would come about through the playwright (or his future equivalent) who would probably be a creature combining the qualities of musician, artist, actor, dancer, director and writer—independent of any material assistance—a sort of super Ruth Draper or Noel Coward. (Or a company of them! Fancy!) Then and only then could there be an independent artist in the theatre.

A rather frequent question concerns the lack in our modern theatre of the *commedia dell'arte* spirit. Why has it vanished? I think the reason is simple, for it implies improvisation, whether of words, movement, music or dancing. Under our present scheme the actor is as dependent upon his part as a table is upon its legs. No great actor ever made a poor play great, and no poor part ever produced a great actor. I have seen a great play hold up pretty well with a rather poor interpretation, but you seldom witness the poor play sustained by excellent acting. The play furnishes the actor with his work, and no individual performance can "make" a play unless that individual's part comprises most of the play.

Thus in drama we find the *commedia dell'arte* eliminated, although it flourishes in vaudeville and the revues to a magnificent degree. In those realms of the theatre we have manifestations of the *commedia dell'arte* which were never better—except perhaps in the Weber and Fields heyday. But the modern dramatist does not demand it, does not in any way call for it. Why, then, should we have it to a greater degree?

The present efforts in the theatre to create permanent and repertory companies are, it seems to me, splendid. Since Equity improved the economic status of the actor, these movements have helped improve the artistic side. The disadvantages of an actor in a permanent company are only physical ones! In case of a continuous change of bill the daily grind of rehearsal must necessarily break down an actor's vitality, but even this can be remedied by rehearsal periods stretched over a greater length of time. The maintenance, for instance, of an eight-hour day, divided between actual performances and rehearsal time, would take care of such a situation. The opportunity to play continuously with the same group in a permanent company brings much harmony into a performance. A fine ensemble can be developed which will heighten the play's values and the author's intention. It also eliminates, I think, the necessity which so many actors feel—that they must act their parts not for the good of the play, but for the good of themselves. Under the system by which actors cast about for engagement after engagement, they may instinctively work with the idea of making themselves conspicuous in order to obtain another part at the termination of the present play. Under the permanent company plan, with its attendant economic security, an actor can afford to act his part for the good of the play. Best of all, however, is the point that playing a variety of roles an actor must, of necessity, broaden, mature and purify whatever talent he may possess.

Despite these movements for the establishment of permanent companies and repertory troupes, a great part of the theatre proceeds on the basis of taking actors for individual engagements and casting them to type. Once in a great while it is perhaps obligatory to cast for type alone—in the case of a giant or a dwarf—but any fine actor, if he so desires, can play a girl or an old woman, an old

man or a boy. But it is often easier for the producer to cast for
type, and although the person selected may make a great success
in the part, it is often the end. The next play or the next are unlikely to have the same type, and there you are!

Personally, I think the audience enjoys an actor "play acting,"
for it appreciates not only the evidences of skill and ability which
may be entailed, but "play acting" is, after all, the fun of the
theatre. An audience enjoys seeing an actor play a part that is
physically and utterly unlike himself—they enjoy the cleverness
of an "interpretation." The actor who plays one part, Himself,
must have a shorter professional life than the actor who has truly
learned his trade and can step from one character into another,
for in the case of the man who offers variations on the personal
theme, I feel that . . . "Time must wither and custom surely
stale."

True repertory nurtures and encourages budding talent. It offers
opportunities and a perpetual freshness which your young player
will never find under the long-run system. It keeps a freshness
to its performances, for although it isn't really necessary that a
performance should go stale, they often do. You can't say a rosary
over seventy times every night for seventy weeks and have it sound
the same as it did the first time. Another great point in favor of
a repertory company is that it acquaints players with many major
items of dramatic literature. It brings them into a dazzling succession of new contacts and new roles, and if they are able and
receptive, it is superb development. And since plays are carefully
and completely rehearsed before they are put into a repertory, the
players have the advantage of what should be careful training.
In stock, of course, an actor gets many opportunities at many new
roles, but he is quickly rehearsed and, more often than not, the

play has run its brief course before he has had an opportunity to settle into the role. That is not true under the repertory system.

In the sound films the modern actor has a new outlet. Many seem to feel that working under the peculiar rules of this new medium will hurt an actor for the stage, but I think this is not true. With the skilled actor this work, lacking in the continuity of expression maintained in stage presentation, becomes a utilization of the by-product of his ability, and cannot harm his acting any more than a manufacturer can harm his principal merchandise by using its by-products. There are, of course, things to learn about sound films, and actors entering that medium would do well to learn them, but the details, such as staying within camera range, observing certain vocal tones, etc., are details to be incorporated into an actor's general knowledge and equipment.

In a sound picture, the "honesty" of emotion demanded by the camera and microphone should tend to make one a better, truer performer. Bad acting in the talkies seems bad acting—good acting good. There is no difference, for good actors appear just as good and bad actors just as bad—but you get a little less of each, the films being fairly short. Which is fair enough.

We shall close on the problem of the oncoming generation of actors.

I am asked what can be done to induce the young, talented actor of today to resist the temptation to rise too rapidly in his profession without obtaining a broad, general foundation and training. I answer that nothing can be done save the possession of an inward desire to *be* better; that, or the lawful realization that one is being offered fewer and fewer engagements. One observes about New York the young players who grab at large salaries offered them because they are the "type," and more hopefully one sees those young players who play on Broadway during the season and hie themselves away to summer companies during what should be vacation time. Some young actors are wise and intelligent and they are preparing themselves for what should be the heyday of their careers, while others, impressed by the excellent salaries and the ease of long-run engagements, pursue the immediate future. I don't feel that anything is to be done about this, human nature being what it is.

The Wasted Gifts of the Scene Designer

By Hermann Rosse

Apparently the stage designer made his bow before the public when men, such as Herkomer, Ricketts and others, started designing for the theatre in England during the last ten years of the Nineteenth Century.

These men, however, were primarily painters. The first entrance of the real designer in the theatre in modern days was with Henry Wilson and his fellow-members of the Art Worker's Guild in London toward the end of the last Century, soon followed by Gordon Craig, who, through his integrity as an artist and his perseverance as a leader, still exerts a great influence on stage designing in this country, as well as abroad.

The importance attached in Germany, Holland and other Continental countries to the English example in the so-called decorative arts, put these countries in a very receptive mood toward the new theory of the English designers in the theatre.

Although obscured, from time to time, by the insistence of painters in the theatre on certain mannerisms of school etiquette, the clarity of purpose of these early designers to this day is astounding. The theatre as theatre, honest architecture of the stage, the theatre as a new reality, such were the battle-cries resulting in canvases hung as textiles, in masterly-designed jewelry, costumes and properties, a world of lights, measuring compositions in space, of steps and rostrums, of screens and hangings, forming masterful arrangements, all wrought out of the action of the drama, emphasizing and illuminating the elusive esoteric beauty hidden in its flow of scenes. The Gothic honesty of the industrial artist, his regard for the essential properties of the materials in which he works, the feeling of fitness for the purpose of his products, swept, as a fresh wind, through the stuffy atmosphere of the fin-de-siècle theatre, and when one looks back to the faith and almost religious ecstasy of the earlier workers of the theatre and the clarity of their purpose, one involuntarily begins to wonder if the American theatre has sufficiently profited by their example.

The designer in the American theatre never was invited among its leaders, as in Germany, for instance, but through sheer persistence has won himself a place, and therefore it is natural that the plays in which he shows his real self are few. For one writer whose tendency is in harmony with what most of the designers set as their ideal, there are dozens of playwrights whose plays get mounted with the aid of designers, plays which sometimes even suffer through this introduction of the strong mind of a different schooling from that of the author or director.

The most notable achievements of the designer in the theatre have consequently been in the revival of antique dramas, written in a technique more adaptable to the treatment they wish to give these plays, and in the opera and the ballet.

It is true that the standards of the setting of most plays today is higher than some twenty years ago. The introduction of the total creative energy of the American designers, and their foreign guests, into the American theatre could hardly be expected to go by unnoticed. But the point remains that, instead of building up a great new theatre, vital, strong and glorious, the designer in the American theatre is used as a kind of theatrical home-decorator and dressmaker. The resentment of his insistence on the importance of his contribution to the plays he illuminates usually grows in proportion to his lack of perspicuity regarding the fitness of the introduction of any theory of design, which differs in essence from the spirit in which the drama is written.

Why, then, it may be asked, does not the designer create his own theatre? If the designers, as a group, have so much creative energy, why don't they create drama?

The answer to this is that the country does not want that kind of drama any more than it wants the modern arts, or architecture, which are an outflow of the same tendency in the arts. When a new art and a new architecture will have become part and parcel of the mind of the every-day public, when not the ephemeral imitation of certain external forms, but the creation of new forms according to standards of honesty and fitness, modified by inventiveness and creative beauty, shall have become the object equally of the author, the director, the actor, the designer, and everyone connected with theatrical production, then, and not before, shall the designer have found his real place in the theatre.

The only reason that comparatively so much has been accomplished by the designers in the theatre in so little time is that the work required of them is so easy. The designer is rarely asked to demonstrate his real strength, as designer, but is usually asked to perform a far easier task. And his usurpation of any authority, by attempting to utilize his creative faculties, is usually resented.

It is useless to blame the theatre in general, or Broadway in particular, for not making better use of the designer in the theatre. When the public is ready to pay money for a different kind of theatrical art than that provided for it at present, the designers, playwrights, actors, directors and musicians will have an opportunity to try their mettle.

Until then, all the designer can do is to help to educate the public, either by means of his work in the theatre on all those occasions that are offered to him, through his writing, his painting, or designing of objects of daily use, or whatever way he finds at hand.

The designer's tendency to assume another role in the theatre, either as dramatist or as director or whatever it may be, though entirely harmless, is of no great purpose, because the public's mind changes only slowly, and in the present state only few attempts have any real chance of success.

To the layman, who may read these lines, all this may seem belittling to the designer. He has seen fat volumes on the art of Bakst; he has bought the illustrated souvenir programs, with portraits of the designers among the theatrical élite, but he forgets that most of the men, well known in that way, are really painters. The public knows better what a painter is and bothers very little whether the art which he professes would be better applied as such on paper, on canvas, than as a part of a different art—that of the theatre. The art of the architect with which he is slightly familiar, or of the interior decorator, or of the lighting engineer, are all allied to the art of the theatre, as well as painting and sculpture. But the architecture of the stage answers to the fantastic requirements of the play and the sight conditions of the audience. The interior decoration of the stage applies itself to stage proportions, to stage lighting, to stage visibility, to stage living, where comfort is negligible compared with the necessity of preventing pieces of furniture from blocking vision or light, while the lighting problems of the stage apply to the interpretation of natural lighting effects as much as to the lighting of the actors as objects in a gigantic show window—problems entirely different from those which are offered to the illuminating engineer in real life.

The immediate future of the stage designer seems to offer little variation from the present; the ultimate future is a marvelous one, that of helping our poets and philosophers to create a world more fit to live in.

We are part of a well-fed and impatient nation. And the question naturally arises how all this can be speeded up, how we can give to all of these noble and aspiring stage designers a chance to express themselves in terms of pure theatre. The answer to this is the same as in the case of doctors, economists, etc., in their arts or sciences, namely, by enabling them to experiment before a public which they might educate to their viewpoint. Endowments of certain theatrical groups, performing before audiences, would seem a surer way of getting quick results than isolated workshops which would leave the audiences uninfluenced.

What is true of the theatre is true in aggravated form of the motion pictures. The cinema needs new plays, new audiences, new everything. It is about as hopeless to expect great cinematic art spontaneously to sprout under existing conditions as it is to expect great furniture to come suddenly on the market by way of Grand Rapids.

We need a new public which will demand the new and vital in the arts of the theatre. The men engaged in creative work in the cinema should be protected and fostered, as the experimental workers in all other arts. They should be protected, not with the idea of training them to earn greater dividends for existing commercial organizations, but with the idea of bringing one step nearer some kind of art which at one time fulfills the hopes of the individual creative artist and the needs of the masses.

The Light Musical Stage at the Cross Roads

By Arthur Hammerstein

One of the most persistent questions during the theatrical season of 1929–30 was, "What will the sound film do to the American light musical stage?" Most of those who asked the question did so in a tone of voice which indicated their hope or fear that it would do a great deal and that the result to the latter would be disastrous. Instead, and so swiftly that everyone concerned is still rubbing his eyes, disaster has befallen the musical sound film. By its almost catastrophic failure, the musical picture has only served to advertise the musical stage production.

Anyone equally acquainted with the technique of the two arts should have been able to predict just such an outcome. The American musical comedy, corresponding in a general way to European *opera comique,* has a notable record, a rich tradition, and a fund of experience which protects it from everything but the most perfectly equipped rival. From the latter decades of the Nineteenth Century down to our own day, American composers and librettists have held their own in competition with the best that Europe sent us. "Erminie" was soundly American. "Robin Hood" was an American product. Many of my father's productions helped to develop and continue the tradition. Victor Herbert did not lack appreciation in his own day, but he would probably be amazed at the vital interest in his scores which persists today in the face of an age supposedly devoted solely to jazz. To go further in naming names would be unfair to those who have kept the tradition alive, for the roster would require pages and even then someone might be left out.

The failure of the musical picture has been due simply to the fact that its producers tried to make it in the same manner as the silent pictures, jumping from place to place and breaking the continuity of the story. If they had followed the methods of the musical stage, the result might have been very different.

Even if musical pictures are ultimately entrusted to Broadway producers, I have no fear for the musical play personally performed. It is impossible to replace the human being on the stage. No machine can serve as a substitute. Whatever the machine records, is repeated night after night. Will Rogers on the sound film never varies a hair's breadth throughout the life of the film. Will Rogers in person alters his lines from performance to performance, keeping an intimate contact with the audience of the evening and the events of the day. The musical sound film can be made to serve as an excellent substitute for distant localities, but it will always be a substitute. You are alone when you look at a machine!

Much of my father's efforts and all of my own have been devoted to an attempt to bridge the gap between the ordinary musical comedy or revue on the one hand and grand opera on the other. *Opera comique* bridges that gap in Europe. We wish to do it in our own way. And I am convinced that it will come by the steady improvement of musical comedy rather than by the popularization of grand opera. There is no essential reason why this goal could not be reached from both directions, except that the American public has lost interest in grand opera and faith in its power to meet their needs. The masses are not interested in listening to twenty-minute arias. The opera impresarios think that, because

Puccini is dead, there is no one to write new operas. They are blind to a host of composers and a wealth of interesting and significant subject matter.

The American light musical stage has been saved from the bogey of the musical sound film through no virtue of its own. It is still in just as much danger as it ever was of cutting its own throat by extravagant expenditure. The public does not care how much money is spent; it wishes to be entertained. No amount of scenery and costumes ever makes up for the lack of a good book and score.

Another supposed rival of the light musical stage in America is the revue. That supposition, too, is false. The only logical point of view from which to consider the revue is as a testing ground from which, just as from vaudeville, the musical comedy draws its talented recruits.

Standing at the cross roads, the American light musical stage holds its destiny in its own hands. If it spends wisely, sets its aim high, looks upon the revue as a collaborator rather than a rival and persistently refuses to take fright from the threat of the sound film, there is nothing to prevent the maintenance of its admirable tradition.

Suggesting a Dramatic Declaration of Independence

By Maurice Browne

As co-director during the seven years of its existence and as co-founder with Ellen Van Volkenburg of the Chicago Little Theatre (which is frequently spoken of as the parent theatre of American Little Theatres), I have been asked by Oliver Sayler to represent, and express my opinion on, the Little Theatre. He states (confound him!) that it is my right—and my duty—so to represent the subject. Rights—and duties—are singularly disagreeable things, of which, fortunately, I have little experience; but inclination, a safer guide, is sufficient motive.

The Chicago Little Theatre was started in 1912, with unqualified enthusiasm, unqualified faith, and a corresponding lack of experience or cash. Today its unruly grandson, the New York Theatre Guild, posthumous child (on a doubtful side of the sheets) of the Washington Square Players, is the most powerful theatrical organization in the English-speaking world. There have been many births, deaths and miscarriages in the intervening period; the family is a prolific one, even if the offspring are not invariably legitimate. Their progenitor regards his own fertility with amazement, and may perhaps be forgiven for feeling that such vitality is not far from being its own justification.

During the first two decades of the Twentieth Century there began the current revolt (in America) against Victorianism in the arts—a revolt against old forms and old contents (not because they were old, but because they were sterile) on behalf of authenticity and vitality of form and content alike. In that revolt the Little Theatres were, in two senses of the phrase, dramatic pioneers.

Those two decades showed that this revolt against what in New York is known as "Broadway" and in London as the "West-End" was able directly to produce in the professional theatre richer standards of play-writing, producing, acting, staging, costuming and lighting, and indirectly, in the semi-professional and amateur theatre, to stimulate to an extent immeasurable at present laboratory work alike for the artist and for the audience. Eugene O'Neill, Frederic McConnell, Robert Edmond Jones—a dramatist, a producer and a designer who are direct products of the Little Theatres—are household names in America today. Any versed reader can add to these three names a dozen others of equal or almost equal, of perhaps even greater, significance. The Little Theatre movement has produced such men as these because it has given them, despite its economic limitations, more esthetic and spiritual incentive to create authentically than the old "Broadway" gave. Their influence on the American theatre may be measured by the new "Broadway": the New York Theatre Guild has today a coordinated and articulate audience in New York alone of approximately thirty thousand persons, and Gilbert Miller said to me the other day: "It is the New York Theatre Guild which created the audience for 'Journey's End.'"

On the other hand, it is noteworthy and should be recognized that this "new Broadway" is readier to accept Molnar or Sherriff than it is to accept its own dramatists, unless, like O'Neill, they have already become popular heroes. The great failure of the Chicago Little Theatre, and of the Little Theatre movement generally in America, is the fact that it took and is taking its values from Europe instead of creating its own theatric forms and dramatic literature. An analogous failure is common to all the arts—except architecture—in America today. Yet your United States are not a suburb of London, Paris or Budapest. Is it not time that you recognized the fact?

The Provincetown Players recognized it, and, despite inadequate producing and acting, gave birth to significant dramatists. The New York Theatre Guild has shown itself a master of finance, organization and stagecraft, but presents a play by myself (an Englishman—who, incidentally, is profoundly and anomalously grateful), when it would better be presenting a play by one of its own members. The Pasadena Community Playhouse, the most distinguished example of community drama in America, has not added one distinguished play to the world's dramatic literature; nor has the Cleveland Play House, the most distinguished example of the esthetic theatre; nor, for the matter of that, did the Chicago Little Theatre: the tarbrush in the parent has colored the children. Nor have any of these or the others created new theatric forms— though the Chicago Little Theatre at least came near to pointing the way. And the Goodman Theatre in Chicago, built with American money, on American soil, for American ideals, culminates—after more than a decade—in an Englishman and an Irishman, not to mention two Americans, simultaneously resigning from it, because what "the best people" think rather than what "the people" feel is the standard of its activities; in other words, because its standards are parochial European, not autochthonous.

Why does America continually look to us foreigners for enlightenment and guidance? Our history hardly points to our being fit to lead your blindness anywhere other than into the ditch. Let the Directors of the Art Institute of Chicago, Mr. Otto Kahn and the other "patrons" of the American theatre realize that the best thing which could happen to their institutions would be for every head of a department and every scrubwoman to stand on his or her head in Michigan Avenue or Times Square and waggle irreverent legs in the air—provided always that the legs waggled were the legs of American and not of European irreverence. No industry can survive healthily unless it is continually refertilized by the finger at the nose and the tongue in the cheek of greatly mocking, because greatly dreaming and desiring, youth.

America boasts its eternal youthfulness. That boast begins to grow tiresome in its middle age—after all, you are a considerably older country than Germany—unless it is made by Americans who are themselves young. The young men and women of America today have, as individuals, a unique vitality and the power to create authentic beauty. They lack and need collective opportunity to bring these qualities to fruition.

We colonized you a few hundred years ago. Two or three decades ago I—it is said—in a certain sense colonized your theatre. And I beg you to throw your theatrical tea chests into a new Boston Bay and to issue a Declaration of Dramatic Independence. The statue of Abraham Lincoln faces Westminster Abbey. When Phil Moeller, Jimmy Light, Dan Reed, Gilmor Brown, Irving Pichel and Eva Le Gallienne (that daughter of an Englishman) have fired a bomb under Maurice Browne and all that he and his stand for, they will have a clear space of ground on which to build a monument to themselves as the liberators of the American theatre. *Then,* by all means, if they wish, let them build it in Piccadilly Circus. It will not be needed. Monuments never are, when the

208

work which they commemorate is good. And the only theatrical work good enough not to need a monument—for it will automatically create its own: authentically American Drama will be, when at last it comes, the authentically American Theatre.

The Repertory Theatre

BY EVA LE GALLIENNE

In speaking of the age of Pericles, Mr. Lane Cooper of Cornell University says of the Drama, "And in modern times this art receives virtually no support from the State. In the age of Pericles, all the arts received public encouragement. Painting, sculpture, architecture, flourished with all the rest, BUT DRAMA ABOVE ALL OTHERS. The efforts of the poets were directly favored by the government and by wealthy citizens. In particular the cost of staging the play, and of supplying and training the chorus, was borne by a private citizen who, unless he volunteered for the service, was chosen by lot and obliged to serve as 'choregus.'"

The important thing in the above statement seems to lie in "But drama above all others." In this age, when the general public in our country is so intimately influenced by such usually inferior entertainment, as that offered by the radio and talking picture, it seems a pity that the true art of the Drama is not made more easily accessible.

In all ages since the days of Aeschylus (the father of the Drama) this art has been one of the greatest influences in the cultural life of the community. It originated from the profoundest need of the people—Religion. It is true that, at several abbreviated periods, it was dogmatic religion that tried to interfere with its further development. But these periods for all art and all beauty were arid and unproductive. The Drama in spite of all obstacles in the past, and all obstacles to come (whether dogmas or mechanical contrivances) has continued to thrive and will continue to thrive, as long as man has imagination, and the desire to see his everyday problems transmuted beyond photography.

Machinery can never take the place of human magic. Under present economic conditions, it is well nigh impossible to undertake lengthy tours of the spoken drama, superlatively performed. The obvious solution for this problem in this country (the keeping alive of the drama) is a number of centers, sponsoring *popular priced* repertory theatres, functioning within a given area.

Let us be quite clear on what is meant by a Repertory Theatre. It is not a Stock Company. It is not a Little Theatre.

It is not a Little Theatre because the people actively concerned in a Little Theatre, notwithstanding their sometimes excellent work, do not (as Monsieur Jourdain says in Molière's "Le Bourgeois Gentilhomme") "give their whole time to it." In other words they are not professionals. "Amateurs," or those who follow a calling through love of it, are sometimes less reliable than those who follow it through a combination of love and necessity.

It is not a Stock Company, because a Stock Company, no matter how fine in its intentions, is always hampered artistically by the time limit of the stock system: it is impossible to produce a sensitive and finely balanced performance of a great play in a rehearsal period of one or at most two weeks. Here lies the greatest contrast between Stock and Repertory. The Stock Company produces a new play every week. The actors, after inadequate rehearsal, have the chance of playing the play only one week or at most two. It is then completely discarded. The public is given a half-baked production; the actor, if by some lucky chance (in an enlightened stock company) he should happen to work on a great and sensitive play, has no time to reach the depths or the heights of his potential understanding. It is probably for this reason that most plays produced in Stock Companies, are bad replicas of insignificant, though possibly successful, Broadway productions.

The Repertory Theatre, on the other hand, can be best compared to a library. A library of living plays, representing the world's greatest dramatic literature. Books not growing dusty on their shelves, but ever newly imbued with life, through the public's demand and through the increasing development of the actors as human beings and as craftsmen in their art.

If you spent one evening with Plato, you probably would not have the audacity to say that you understood Plato completely, or if you had any intelligence you would not dismiss him as a person of no importance. At some other time you might want to take him down from the shelf again, and, having grown yourself in mental stature and understanding, you might find great enjoyment in finding yourself closer to his human wisdom.

Over the proscenium arch of the Royal Theatre in Copenhagen is the inscription *"Ej blot til lyst"* which means not *only* for amusement. I underline the "only" for naturally the Repertory Theatre should be catholic in its presentations (presenting comedy as well as serious plays) but its great function should be to *stimulate* the mind and not send it to sleep in a miasma of stupidity. What the public calls "highbrow" is not of necessity dull. Recreation means after all re-creation and the act of creation is never static.

If you see Ibsen's "The Master Builder" you may not understand it the first time, just as, if I had played it in a stock company after a week's rehearsal, and for one week only, I could never have hoped to reach its inner meaning, but if you don't understand it the first time, or even the second or the third, that is not Ibsen's fault, but *yours*. On the other hand, if you saw it three times in the same week with my same ineffectual performance, you would be no richer; but by the Repertory Theatre system, which would enable me and all the other actors concerned, to grow in depth of interpretation and enjoyment of understanding, you could come back year after year as you yourself grew in the richness of cultural living, and discover and enjoy the life work of the great man and artist Ibsen undeniably was. This is the essential good of the repertory system. It is like a perennial in your garden instead of an annual. It grows, it expands, nothing is lost, nothing is thrown away.

The theatres of the world that have carried the greatest weight, both from the point of view of actor, author, and public, have been under the repertory system. Shakespeare, Molière and his "Comédie Française" which he created, the Moscow Art Theatre, Reinhardt's Theatres in Germany, the Royal Theatre of Copenhagen, the Manchester and the Birmingham Theatres in England, and innumerable other theatres of the same type all the world over. Our Symphony-Orchestras and our Opera-Companies in this country are all pure repertory, and these are of course subsidized and sponsored, at great financial loss yearly, by our magnificent philanthropists and patrons of art. Why is it that the art of the drama alone, the art closest to the people, and most intimately influencing them, should be the only one neglected? To live up to its fullest and truest function, the People's Repertory Theatre should be made as easily accessible to the public as the art museums, the libraries, the educational institutions, not to speak of the movies and the radio. If in every great community-center of the United States, as for instance Boston, Philadelphia, Pittsburgh, Cleveland, Chicago, St. Louis, Kansas City, San

Francisco, etc., etc., there could exist either through private capital or State and Government interest, or through popular community cooperation, a net-work of *popular priced* Repertory Theatres, directed by directors of professional ability and high ideals, employing a company of competent *professional* actors, with a love for the theatre, pledged to present to the people a program of great plays, perpetually rotating, perpetually alive in the *true* repertory system, one center interchanging with the other and radiating into the smaller towns surrounding these centers, I think the problem of keeping the better drama alive in this country would be solved.

The important ingredients in this proposed work are of course *Talent*—Energy, Faith, Vision—and above all the most scrupulous *Integrity,* in dealing with the public especially; our poor American public, who has been fooled so often, but who does so *want* to believe.

In connection with these centers and theatres, *Free Schools,* accepting a minimum of *non-paying* students, with possibly a system of scholarships, but always discarding the incompetent, and developing gradually into first studios, such as that sponsored by the Moscow Art Theatre, would be beneficial in keeping the true Theatre alive, and in carrying on through America the tradition of the art of the drama, as we have inherited it, among so many other things, from our mother countries in Europe, and in giving it the benefit of what, with our youth, our vigor and our energy, should constitute a *higher vision.*

Art on a Manufacturing Basis

By Jesse L. Lasky

THE greatest problem of the motion picture today: Box Office Successes—and how to get them.

We are all trying to be as esthetic as possible without interfering with the economic side of motion picture production. Every producer who hopes to remain in the business, and be an important factor in it, is trying to do better things—finer, more realistic, more intelligent things—for two reasons. First, to justify his faith in himself and in the craft with which he has cast his lot, and second, to keep pace with the public in its continually rising appreciation, and its more and more insistent demand for stories which reflect the infinite variety and splendor of real life rather than the faded situations and boresome cliches of mawkish fiction.

The greatest task of the motion picture executive today—and tomorrow—is teaming Pegasus with a plow horse. Or, to come out of mythology, to successfully establish Art on a Manufacturing basis. The obvious answer to this appalling statement, of course, is—it can't be done! But it has been done, to a certain extent, and must be done more and more if the motion picture is to remain the world's premier entertainment. A man may write a book in a year, or two, or three; a theatrical producer may stage one play in a season; a composer may spend half a lifetime on a symphony. But the motion picture, which costs a great deal of money, depends for its very life upon a complicated tie-up with a vast theatre and distribution system which depend for their revenue upon a more or less constant stream of standard product. He who hesitates in picture production misses his release, and he who misses too many releases, is lost. These are not ideal conditions, but they *are* the conditions, and we can only do the thing we want to do by trying to make the thing we *must* do worth while. How to reduce these material hamperings, or at least to get them where they do not interfere with giving all necessary creative thought, directorial artifice and acting finish to our screen productions, is perhaps the greatest executive problem.

The sound film is as definite an advance in screen entertainment as the railroad was in transportation. And it will be as permanent. There are doubters for years after every great step forward in the arts or sciences. When the railway was firmly established in England, conservatives were still trying to legislate against the destructive, dangerous, fire-breathing locomotives. After electric lighting was installed in New York, anxious men sent letters to *The Times* arguing that these charged wires would burn down the city, or at least shock many of the inhabitants to death.

The only improvements possible in sound lie in the direction of perfection—and of course there is plenty of room. There will be for many years. Naturalness of voice, lifelike reproduction of all other sounds, more perfect sound perspective—these are some of the problems upon which our engineers feel that they have only begun.

Color has a definite value on the screen, but it has suffered two misfortunes. Perfect color reproduction has not yet reached a commercial stage. Yet, certain producers, utilizing the admittedly imperfect color devices we now have, have seemed to feel that the mere presence of color atoned for all other lacks in screen entertainment, and have overworked it until at the moment color has lost at least a portion of its appeal. It will regain it. And it will be better, year by year.

There is a grave acoustic problem in cinema theatres throughout the country, just now. Hundreds of theatre owners, rushing in with sound equipment, fitted their theatres with the first sound machines—as good as there were, at the time, but now definitely dated. Nevertheless, in all but the finest city theatres, the managers cannot afford to junk all this equipment so soon after its installation. Consequently, the average theatre is much behind the studio in sound, and in addition, the complicated mechanism is too much for the average theatre crew to keep in perfect order. These conditions are being remedied slowly—as fast as the managers are financially able. The poor business conditions of the past nine months have not helped the theatres in this regard.

As for the third dimension: it will come. The first inventor to patent a device which is really practical and commercial will make a great fortune, and it will be incorporated in all the producing units of the world. But the third dimension is a future luxury—not a present necessity. Earnest engineering research is going on—has been going on for more than ten years—and every once in awhile the newspapers carry a flamboyant story saying that screen depth and space have arrived. So they have—but in extravagant, clumsy and costly devices which cannot be used in public entertainment. The fact that we do have it, although in impractical form, makes me confident that the practical solution is only a matter of time.

The coming of sound has ameliorated the censorship problem everywhere. I feel that this is largely due to the fact that it has

made real and audible *everything* which is said on the screen, and
—but by no means secondarily—because it has brought better
plays, and the intelligent creations of the best authors to the screen
in unmutilated form. The censorial reaction, I think, is largely
psychological. When a man is looking for incendiary conversation
and can hear none of it—except occasional printed excerpts which
he is allowed to read—he is apt to interpolate, by his own imagination, many censorial implications not at all intended.

The relationship of theatre and cinema would merit a very
lengthy chapter in itself. There is vast argument on both sides.
Every day some stage producer says that the screen has ruined the
theatre—and side by side with those dismal pronunciamentos is
chronicled the news of another celebrated managerial defection
to Hollywood. I think I can speak as authoritatively as any of
them, for I know both sides of the picture. I am, primarily, a
theatre man. I came from the theatre, and I shall never cease to
love it and believe in it as a splendid and eternal mirror of human
conflict. Sound has made possible a practical and immediate co-
adjutorship of the two arts. Screen and stage are beginning—even
now—to go forward hand in hand, and to help each other. We
have not "stolen" the great artists of the footlights. We have merely
given them another medium, and it is to our advantage henceforth to have our Chattertons and our Hustons and our Colberts
and all our comedians alternate between camera and proscenium,
projecting their personalities for part of the year in fine new plays,
and for the rest, fixing and perpetuating those creations upon the
lamplit canvas. Space is limited, and without permitting myself to
indulge in many paragraphs of comparison and argument, I will
say that this teaming of theatre and screen is already established
generally, and cannot but lead to splendid results, not only for the

masses of the screen, but as well for the classes of the playhouse.

The necessary, commercial restrictions of motion picture production have never encouraged the making of limited productions for the restricted class which was once described by that badly overdone word "intelligentsia." More seriously, censorial and legislative restrictions have absolutely banned the frank, earnest and realistic drama for us. However, it is impossible to conceive of motion pictures as going on indefinitely without making some provision for the purely mature and sophisticated audience. As a matter of fact, the whole general tone of production is, I think, rising to a more and more mature level. We are not only coming up, but we are taking our audiences with us. Also, every company of size is now releasing, each year, productions of special and limited appeal—either in drama, or in travel, or educational spheres, or in the historical field of actual human achievement.

Royalty payment for great works has definitely arrived. In fact, the whole writing situation is definitely in a process of change. No longer do we consider it good policy to shackle real creative brains to a desk contract for fifty-two weeks in the year. Once the industry bought creation by the term—or it thought it did. Now we want what a man has done or what he proposes to do—not his hours. That of course concerns the men who have proved themselves, not the students, or the men and women who are learning the business. On smaller stories, on unknown originals, a definite, stated sum is the only fair basis for both parties. But it is inevitable that the screen, like the theatre, should make the really worthy author a partner in its ventures. It works well for both sides.

Since the motion picture is after all America's major contribution to the arts, American enterprise and invention are meeting, in a surprisingly effective way, the problems raised abroad by sound. Formerly, this country supplied the world with pictures with very little difficulty; the silent titles were merely translated into the various languages and the subject was as thoroughly effective in Spain as in Illinois. But with the coming of sound, prophecies of foreign failure were heard on every hand. There were no more titles, English was spoken, it was quickly found that speech could not be successfully "dubbed"—as the process of substituting another voice for the original is called—and there were many who believed that American-made pictures would henceforth be good only for this country and the British Empire. But since this menace showed itself so plainly, it has, in our own case, proved a blessing in disguise. As a first step in solving this problem, Paramount imported artists from France and from several Spanish-speaking countries, and—in Hollywood—produced several pictures in those languages which have been enthusiastically received by all countries speaking these tongues. The Hollywood studio is continuing to produce such pictures. Meanwhile, we have established a studio near Paris in which we are already manufacturing foreign-language pictures on a major scale. Already, pictures are being made in this studio in ten different languages: French, Spanish, Italian, Portuguese, Swedish, Hungarian, Czecho-Slovakian, German, Polish and Jugo-Slavian. With these ten languages the company will effect distribution in a majority of all countries where motion pictures are shown. Spanish pictures, for instance, suffice not only for Spain, but for South and Central American countries, and Mexico. Swedish versions are shown in all the Scandinavian countries, and Portuguese not only in Portugal, but throughout Brazil. And back in Hollywood, we have already made a few short subjects in Japanese. On the face of it, this would seem to be a very expensive process. As a matter of fact, all ten language productions are now being made in our Paris studio at a cost only 20% greater than that of the original American negative! The American film is shipped to France with the original scenario, and various specifications for sets, scenes, costumes and so on. When a particular set has been finished, the American replica of the scene is shown on the screen for the guidance of the foreign actors, directors and technicians. Then the scene is filmed, and if it is to be done in all ten languages, the various players follow each other in succession, so that with as much economy of time, space and labor as is possible, ten different versions of the same episode have been screened. Native celebrities are imported to play the various roles, so that the picture is assured of an enthusiastic reception in countries where these stars or featured players are favorites. As to the popular reception of these pictures, our latest figures show that the foreign revenue from several recent films has been from 400 to 500% greater than from similar productions in the old days of the silent screen.

Television? Practical television is still far, far away. Its eventualities are, so far, pure speculation. And your speculation is as good as mine.

Sound Stimulates Story

By J. L. Warner

AFTER more than two years of the Vitaphone film's universal life we who are responsible for its birth know that it is here to stay. The reason for this, beyond the natural deduction from its proven success, seems to me to be in the "bedtime story" theory of the films. It has been said in the past that the silent film success was due to that art form's natural, easy and universal satisfying of mankind's desire for bedtime story, as evidenced by the habits of children who ask that they be told a story to put them to sleep, and by adults who read in bed. What the Vitaphone has done is to make this story better and more clear. It has compelled the author to write the kind of story in which backgrounds—once paramount in importance in the films—have become secondary and story values have forged to the front. This absorbing kind of story helps the audience to give itself whole-heartedly to the enjoyment of the picture.

There are still doubters who predict the return of the motion picture industry to the silent films. These doubters are mistaken. The only return to the silent film has already been accomplished in the new technique of the talking picture. The theatre has always been a mixture of spoken lines and of pantomime. So the sound film has become a blending of silence and speech, depending upon the dramatic effectiveness of the particular situation, scene, sequence or entire story.

The Vitaphone has a distinct advantage over the theatre. It need not confine itself to a limited space, nor to the convention of the footlights. It requires less imaginative effort from the audience for it does not display papier-mâché scenery, nor does it describe, through the words spoken on the stage by the actors, portions of the story which, though indispensable, are left to the imagining because of the space-time, progressive-continuity limitation of the theatre.

The theatre on the other hand has the advantage over the cinema in its human relation that passes from actor to audience and back across the footlights. It can depend upon the personality of the player. It is concerned with a human reality rather than a shadow. It is tangible while the film is intangible.

Because of this, from the purely esthetic point of view, it is much more difficult to produce in the film than it is in the theatre. To this difficulty of production the film owes the question: "Is the sound film an independent art?" It is, beyond all shadow of a doubt. Why? Because the ideal theatre as described by noted esthetes throughout the ages is a blending of all the arts. The Vitaphone is a more complete blending of these fundamental arts, and the modern spirit is ever present, since the blending is accomplished by purely scientific means. Consequently, the sound film is that new art in which meet pure beauty, as old as the world, and pure science, as newly discovered as this morning's sun. In comparison with other arts the film has no limitation. It is not hampered by lack of time nor space nor color. To make it the greatest of all arts it is necessary only to find its master. Writers, directors, producers must be endowed with the infinite of human imagination. Such masters are now arising with the realization of the possibilities of this art which will release what has been held in check due to a lack of media.

The Vitaphone is indebted to the theatre for a great many of its performing artists, because the theatre, thousands of years old, has supplied tradition and experience and training to actors. We find that stage actors trained in the modern school of acting have been successful in pictures, while the declamatory actor of yesterday's theatre has been unsuccessful. The majority of silent picture actors who had not come from the theatre to the screen a decade ago, have failed to approach even the popularity which had been theirs in silent days.

The motion picture industry must and will foster a healthy theatre. The theatre can be the training school, the laboratory for the picture player. This form of training, because of the comparative costs of production in the theatre and the film, is economically more sound than would be the assumption of the motion picture industry of the same function.

The cost of talking picture production is from 35% to 50% higher than was the cost of the production of the silent film. Some of this increased cost of production has been met by the increased attendance at picture theatres, giving increased receipts.

But while the silent film was a truly international form of expression, the talking picture has become a national art, due to the introduction of language with thought and theme implications. To the American imperialist the realization of this fact is a hard blow, for it means the loss of a worldwide supremacy—of American-made motion pictures.

On Behalf of the Silent Film

By Lillian Gish

I may as well be very frank and admit at the outset that I do not believe in the sound film. Something very right, very true, very precious, was cut short on the verge of its ultimate and certain perfection by the intrusion of spoken dialogue and by the consequent throw-back of the cinema toward the theatre. The silent film was slowly coming into its own as an independent art which had nothing to do with the theatre, an art closely allied with music, dependent on music, an art which visualized music, creating independently to a certain point and completed thereafter by music.

In order to determine the specific qualities of the silent film, it is necessary to relate it to the art of pantomime. Now, pantomime in the theatre is something wholly apart from pantomime in the cinema. In the silent film, it was a case of pantomime without letting anyone catch you at it.

Perhaps we had better trace the subject from the birth and use of pantomime in the theatre. Pantomime as such is an obvious and florid affair characterized by exaggerated gestures and crudely superficial expression. In pantomime you stress details by the pointed finger, by the grimace. These obvious methods are toned down perceptibly when pantomime becomes a component part of the expressive media of the ballet. They are minimized still further when we enter the traditional theatre and utilize

225

gesture as a means of underscoring the spoken lines. When the cinema broke away from the theatre, really broke away from it to follow its own path, there was need to salvage the subdued pantomime of the traditional theatre and enrich it in such a way as to replace the missing spoken lines of the theatre. At first this was done broadly. But little by little we learned how to express emotion, to convey story, by the subtlest means. We mastered this modified pantomime for use in restricted planes. At a distance, the entire body was the expressive medium. A little closer, what we had to say was said with the upper portion of the body and arms only. Still closer to the camera, the face and shoulders bore the burden. Closer yet, the face alone appeared on the screen, sustaining the narrative responsibility without other aid. And finally this task was entrusted solely to the eyes while the rest of the face remained passive.

All, or nearly all, of this skill and of this technique was nullified when the cinema annexed speech in the talking picture. Oddly enough, the talking picture has served to call to our attention the most obvious flaw of the silent film. That flaw consisted in the fact that, even though our words were not heard or registered, we thought we had to speak lines while we were acting for the silent screen, lines at least generally associated with the action, even if they were not actually written or rehearsed. Just by exaggerating this custom and making words audible in the talking film, we have unexpectedly come to realize that words had nothing essentially to do with the silent film. If the silent film ever returns, it will owe this realization to the sound film. If it ever returns, it will salvage from the sound film the elements of incidental music as counterpoint to the action, the sound effects of nature, and mass sounds and tones such as chants. But

226

there will be no words—no words written or spoken, no words in the form of captions.

The problem of the actor on the screen differs from that of the actor on the stage much more widely, of course, in the case of the silent film than in that of the sound film. In the theatre the actor is both restricted and assisted simultaneously as compared with the actor in the cinema. He is restricted in that he is tied down to exact speeches written for him, speeches which he cannot alter, speeches written perhaps before he was born, speeches which on occasion have become laden with tradition by the interpretation by actors who preceded him in the role. Of course, this restriction is helpful in a sense, for it leaves nothing for the player to guess at. In the silent film, the actor relied on his own creative powers as a pantomimist. The scenario provided hardly more guidance to him than the plots of the *commedia dell'arte*. The scenario told us what to convey, but the task of working out the means of conveying rested upon the mind and imagination and technical skill of the player.

I have yet to experience anything resembling aid or stimulus from an audience just because it is present while I am playing before it. The perfect audience to me is that which permits me to forget its presence. I cannot understand, therefore, those who, like Pirandello in his novel "Shoot," insist that the player in the film is at a necessary disadvantage as compared with the actor on the stage. On the contrary, I have always believed that the actor in the cinema has a marked advantage over the player on the stage. In the first place, he can see the result of his work in the projection room and retake a scene until he is satisfied with what he has done. He has an opportunity, therefore, to be strictly objective in reference to his work. He is his own critic. In the theatre, on the contrary, the player's work disappears as fast as it is created, giving him no opportunity to stand off and judge himself. I used to wonder why the actor on the stage seemed so often to be self-centered and egotistical. But I finally realized that in most cases it was not a question of actual egotism but simply an effort to find out what his work was like, to create through the impressions of others an objective realization which was beyond his own power to achieve. The objective opportunity of the player in the cinema often extends further. Not only can he watch and check his own work, but, without the preoccupation of creating a role, he can sit in the audience and peer into the faces of those who have come to see his work and learn from their reactions to it how he can improve it.

Although the sound film still permits the objective opportunity of checking one's own work, it has surrendered the freedom from specified words and speeches which the silent film enjoyed. Thus far, at least, these lines and speeches, while equally restrictive as in the theatre are infinitely inferior in value to those of the theatre. Furthermore, as compared with the theatre, the fine shading of the voice is impossible yet in the sound film. The microphone, as thus far developed, seems to limit the voice to a narrow range of tonality, analogous to the limited range of colors which are thus far available in making the colored film.

I do not believe that any definite conclusions can be drawn from the current widespread exchange of players between the cinema and the theatre. Ever since the cinema was born, we have had actors crossing the line in cycles from one to the other —first in one direction and then in reverse. In the long run, I am convinced that the sound film will have to develop its own character interpreters just as the silent film did. So far as censorship is concerned, I can see little difference between the silent and the sound film. It is perhaps simpler to obtain a definite decision from boards of censorship as to what they will pass when you have definite dialogue to submit to them, but the problem of censorship is a problem of politics rather than one of esthetic or moral standards or technical media. As long as political leaders are able to place their friends and supporters in these powerful and remunerative positions, we shall not be able to free the cinema from this ridiculous and stultifying control.

It goes without saying that the silent film was one of the greatest factors in the international success of American motion pictures and that the introduction of the sound film has been a serious if not fatal blow at our international film outlet. To this same source may be traced the lapse of most of the notable efforts to create and develop motion pictures of interest to a selective audience alongside those made for a vast general public. The excuse that such films are economically unsound because they cannot be produced at a cost appreciably less than those made for mass distribution, was and still is groundless. Some of the greatest films ever made, films fully measuring up to the standards of a selective audience, were made by individual artists, carrying their cameras into the jungle, into the frozen north or into the southern mountains, backed by no wealthy corporation and operating with a minimum of technical equipment—such films as Karl Brown's "Stark Love," Robert J. Flaherty's "Nanook of the North" and "Moana of the South Seas" and Merian C. Cooper's and Ernest Schoedsack's "Chang" and "Grass." Other cinema productions which appealed to such an audience and which were made inexpensively although in studio suroundings included Victor Seastrom's "The Stroke of Midnight," "He Who

Gets Slapped," "Wind" and "The Scarlet Letter"; Murnau's "The Last Laugh," and L. B. Dupont's "Variety." To this same class, too, belong the Russian films "Potyomkin," "The Fall of St. Petersburg," and others.

In films like these the cinema proved its right to be considered as an independent and important art. In the nature of the case the silent film is far better equipped to achieve these results than the sound film—better equipped, at any rate, than the sound film imitating the theatre with exact dialogue. Until the cinema returns from its prodigal excursion into sound it cannot expect to resume its logical development as an independent art.

Directing Sound Pictures

By Monta Bell

In sound pictures I should say that direction differs particularly, because today we are more dependent on the actor, who must carry through without assistance as the director must remain silent during the actual taking of a scene for a talking picture.

Sound films frighten me, and I must say I prefer the silent medium. I do not believe sound pictures will be a passing fad, but their treatment during the past two years is a passing fad. There is too much dialogue. I believe that economy in the use of dialogue will give sound its greatest possible power, heightening effects that we could never attain with the silent picture.

I certainly believe in the close-up, and whether it originated through accident or design, it has enabled us to do something the stage could never approach. If a playwright could find it possible to take his audience up on the stage and look into the faces of actors playing some climactic moment, his task would be much easier. Again, I like the idea of showing the face of one player, while the voice of another is heard. In such an instance, we are able to attain both cause and effect. Hearing one player giving everything he has in his voice and showing the attitude of the listening player, with his reactions to the voice of the other player, gives us a two-ply effect.

I do not believe that there will be any noticeable shake-up among the silent film stars. They have become favorites through personality developed in a tried medium. Most of them have voices of average caliber and most of the stories demand just such voices. As pictures are shot in a series of short scenes, it is perfectly simple to direct and coach even an amateur to a point where he can play a scene of two or three minutes' length. I do not mean by this to say that we will not obtain many recruits from the theatre. We will, because we need actors of such experience, but the influx from the stage, is rapidly narrowing down, and in the survival of the fittest there remain but a few stage personalities who have undoubtedly made good and will continue in the motion pictures.

During two years as a producer at the Paramount Studios, Long Island, I tried out many theatrical people. Of those whom I gave their first opportunity to appear in motion pictures, the following have more than made good and many are destined to stardom: Walter Huston, Claudette Colbert, Charles Ruggles, O. P. Heggie, Kay Francis, Edward Robinson, Betty Lawford, Lillian Roth, Ginger Rogers.

Producing pictures in New York, I naturally had the advantage over Hollywood producers in this direction, as I was near the seat of the theatre. I saw every play that was produced, and the outstanding actors were immediately given an opportunity to appear in one of the pictures I was making. It is very agreeable to note that all of those I have listed as starting on their picture careers are now in Hollywood, having stepped up many rungs on the ladder of screen success.

To my mind, the greatest mistake made in sound pictures, was the sheep-like hysteria with which the producers rushed into it. They have long since learned the folly of this, but I am afraid it has done great damage. Music has failed in sound pictures, so much so, that today there is a thumbs-down attitude toward musical pictures. This is unfortunate because music undoubtedly belongs in sound pictures. No one has yet, however, found the proper method with which to use it. The producers in their excitement are also in a fair way to lose their foreign market, practically handing it to Europe on a silver platter, because, despite the importations of foreign actors to Hollywood, we could never approach pictures made in their natural locale, with native actors. With the elimination of this huge market, established stars will slip from their international standing back to where they are simply national artists, known only in English-speaking countries. Charlie Chaplin, the lone survivor of the silent pictures, is finishing his picture, "City Lights." It has no spoken dialogue and therefore can be shown all over the world. I believe its reception will prove that there is still a most extraordinary market for silent pictures and that other producers will find that their goose with its all-talk diet is laying much smaller golden eggs.

The Player in the Films

By Ruth Chatterton

THERE is a much greater difference, I feel, between the acting technique demanded of the screen player and that of the stage actor than most people making the transition are ready to accept. The screen, it is very obvious, is a medium for intimacy, and at the same time one of great scope. Both in catching minute emotions and in playing them against limitless backgrounds, the screen has a tremendous advantage over the stage. A story written for the screen uses different technique; entrances and exits are minimized by the use of "cuts" and "dissolves" and "fades." In the same way, because of this difference in method of telling stories, the camera must depend on an entirely different group of emotions from the actor, in telling his story.

The camera follows the successive action and thoughts of a character, and tells its story through the various "shots"—close-up, medium shot, long shot and revealing camera angles. It is obvious, then, that, instead of an actor telling his story in general, very definite wide strokes, he must, for the camera's eye, do his scene with painstaking care—with minute, fine use of the eyes, the body, the face. He doesn't have to tell his story to the back of the house—the microphone and the camera lens are his audience. Mechanism can project his voice and his personality as far as the back walls of the cinema theatre. It is the difference between paint-

234

ing colors on canvas and painting pastel shades on ivory. For the cinema, the detail must be more evident than the flair.

I should say that there is absolutely nothing to replace for the cinema actress the joy of feeling an audience in the theatre. Certainly the $5.00 or $11.00 Hollywood première, with its ermine coats and air of Babylonian splendor and with the subsequent paeans of praise from the Hollywood press, is a doubtful substitution—even for the actor's ego. The cinema actor must be sufficient unto himself. He gets his only inspiration from his fellow players. There is no outside force, no audience with whom there is communion. Certainly, this factor is sorely missed.

Feeling as I do, I agree, of course, with Luigi Pirandello's indictment of the lot of the film actor insofar as the element of missing the audience's reaction is concerned. Also, in a limited way, I agree with his discussion of the disappointment to the actor's ego resulting from the fact that there is no one to applaud him when he has finished his scene for the films. Although it may not sound quite genuine coming from one who, at best, is one of the cinema's stepchildren, it must be obvious that to an artist a job well done is a job well done. The cinema certainly cannot immediately pander to the actor's ego. Any applause that comes in the theatre certainly comes to a shadow. But, to speak a little naively, God must take the place of the audience to the cinema actor. Probably the fact that motion picture "gods" are in bad repute these days might make this just a bit unsatisfactory.

It is impossible for a film actor to make up for the readjustments and improvements that occur during the run of a play. But, on the other hand, the cinema actor has one tremendous advantage over the stage actor. It is possible for him to see his role grow in front of his eyes. During one day, probably four or five scenes will be taken. The next day, the actor can see his "rushes." You see yourself—your mistakes and your successes. You stand in the place of a critic.

A scene definitely unsatisfactory is reshot, after the actor has discovered what he had done that is wrong. There is not the finality of error that occurs in the theatre. How many plays and careers have been spoiled by a nervous first night? In the film, there is no place for errors. Every scene is usually shot three or four times, and the best "take" chosen as the one that will stand for the completed film. This, obviously, is of invaluable assistance.

Again, the camera catches details which no one, during rehearsals, could detect. It is possible for the actor, seeing thus some detail either particularly good or bad, to reconstruct his entire conception of the part for the better. If there were any way of getting an accurate photograph of a rehearsal in a play, it might often give the actor a key on which to work. But that is out of the question, for, if a photograph were to be taken of an actor using his stage technique, it would seem so false in the film that it would ruin his entire performance. That is a perfect example of the difference between the stage and the photographed performance.

But there is another serious limitation for the screen actor. Scenes are shot in bits. This often, practically always, means that it is impossible to give a sustained performance in a theatrical sense. The film actor must learn to go on from day to day without having forgotten the mood in which he was left during the previous shooting. Sometimes, although not so often these days, the end of the picture may be shot first. What is the actor to do? How is he to know how the character is feeling at the end of a play when he has not yet built up to that point? And yet, he must know. Therefore, he must know and be his character so thoroughly, that he would know what that character would do in any given situation. Acting is often useless—sincerity and sureness of purpose are prime requisites of the actor for the film. He builds his part intellectually—not emotionally. He cannot rely on his emotions. There is no chance of "resting on his emotions," as he does during the course of a play's performance. Every moment is a unity of its own and the actor cannot afford to be sloppy—or even tired for a moment. This, it seems to me, is the most bewildering limitation in films for the theatre-trained person.

Never having been a silent film player, I do not feel capable of discussing the differences between the silent film and the talking picture from the actor's point of view. But I cannot see how the screen can avoid the constant need of the actor from the dramatic stage. The stage-trained actor has so much to bring. His training is so thorough, and he does learn so unforgettably the traditions and the fine points of his craft. Naturally at this moment, the screen realizes its need for stage people and we have seen a great influx of them into the cinema world. Whether this will continue or not has been an open question.

But the screen has definitely realized in the past six months that more than ever audiences are refusing to accept actors of the screen who have no more to bring than their beauty and personality. That goes, of course, for stage-trained actors as well. The use of the voice has made it imperative that actors must understand and know the ins and outs of projecting their parts through words as well as gestures. Although in some future time there may be a training school for talking picture actors, producers are finding that the cheapest and best training school for their players is the stage. They are constantly encouraging their actors to return to the stage—and are calling their youngest recruits in from Broadway and stock companies.

Personally I feel that the element of time is the most important one in teaching the actor the best use of his voice. In the theatre he plays every day, and every day he learns better and better the subtleties of his craft. Teaching is important, too, but he best can teach himself. This, I believe, is the reason why the motion picture will not try to train its own speaking actors. They cannot put actors through the grind of playing day in and day out before an audience until the rough spots are ironed out. After they have a pliable actor, they can better teach him the tricks of the camera craft.

The Pacific Coast is certainly developing a dramatic stage of its own. It is amazingly separate from New York, however, and I believe that it will continue to be so. New York is the financial center of America. People pour in and out of it—bent on business and relaxation. That, with its great group of theatregoers, will make it always *the* center of the theatre. But the coast is building up very consistently a high class theatrical audience whose demands are steadily making Los Angeles and San Francisco theatres sophisticated stage play centers.

As for New York becoming the center of cinema production, that I doubt. Films need large studios. Huge grounds are necessary. Property is far too valuable around New York to make production there financially sound. That is one thing. Then, on top of that, there would be the expense of moving. And the lack of sunshine is really an important factor. The best films are partially made in natural surroundings. The country near Los Angeles is perfect in that respect.

And for the actor—in Hollywood life is so constructed that he can lead a normal, healthy outdoor existence. He has a home and the decent comforts of life. Therefore he is better fitted to stand both the nerve-draining life of a motion picture actor, and is able to keep constantly fit and looking his best—a demand of his audience. He cannot depend on the illusion that exists in the theatre. He is not on a stage at a safe distance from his audience. He is dissected by the camera—cruelly. These are important matters to consider. Eventually, I believe, the actor who wishes to divide his time between the stage and screen can do so, either here, a plan which has been tried with a great deal of success recently, or by going now and then to New York. The change will benefit him both as a stage and motion picture actor. In all, Hollywood is a far more ideal place for a film center than New York could hope to be.

In my humble opinion, I should say that there is not a chance for the silent picture to come back. As for its revival being artistically desirable, I definitely say no. A talking film well done should have the same values pictorially as a silent film—with the added interest of voice. A play with talk is far easier to understand than a play without. It seems to me that in their foundations, silent films were far too involved an art to be really first class. In silent films the use of the voice was substituted for by various extraneous elements. The use of the literary sub-title was always bad dramatically. It interrupted the flow of the picture— just as it does now in talking pictures that attempt to use it. The use of music—the elaborate orchestra and the whining organ— tried to take the place of speech. With the coming of talking pictures, it became obvious how useless they were. A story is told simply with all the elements of life. Truly great art is great simplicity. How logical it is that a complicated way of telling a story is more inartistic than the natural, easy, simple way!

The great argument for silent pictures seems to be that beauty left the cinema with the exit of silent films. But it is probably the present conception of talking pictures that is at fault. They are certainly still very literal; whereas the best silent directors were concerned more with leading an audience up to a point—and then skipping the brutal telling of the point. The finest talking pictures have combined the fineness of silent technique with the skillful use of the spoken word—to great effect and usually big success. There is no reason why we won't have a general return to the beauty that was occasionally realized in the silent picture. We already have cases in point. Such pictures as "All Quiet on the Western Front" possess all the beauty that was so prized in the silent film—and combine it with a heart-tearing eloquence that is unique to the talking picture.

The subject of censorship is a sore one. It is the most signal menace to motion˙ picture˙ art. I am afraid that as long as our present standards of censorship continue, motion pictures will stay in the nursery. Just as a personal reaction, I feel that one wide black line should be drawn through all gangster stories. They are our present very dangerous substitute for the adventurous tales that are so beautifully related in the works of Stevenson, Dumas, Hugo. Gangster stories represent crooks in this grand, adventurous light. Their harm is untold. We must go back for our thrills to the classics. They are grand screen material!

The Cinema Designer Confronts Sound

By Joseph Urban

In the staging of motion pictures much of the clutter, which ten years ago was a universal expression of the motion picture designer's art, has disappeared. Directors have more and more turned their attention to the proper lighting of scenes, to an expressive location of the camera eye in the scene picture and to the development of new beauties in the art of photography. Now a corps of camera men is available skilled in taking pictures from a rapidly moving standpoint, in taking shots upward, downward, and across a scene. Books such as "Urformen der Kunst" bear witness to the artistic interpretation of the subject matter of photography in a degree unknown a few years ago. In the scene painter's province the practicality of photographing action before a miniature setting has opened up enormous possibilities for the creation of fantasy, control of lighting, mechanical manipulation of the scenes and sensitiveness to the will of the designer. Color photography, though still a thinly-watered shadow of what it might be, has improved. The possibility of mass effects, of compelling color and powerful light, seem within grasp, though the probabilities of intricacy in color pattern are still remote.

Aside from the responsibility of handling the added resources of the film, there is a tendency to rely on the designer for effects in setting to supply deficiency in dramatic interest. The tendency on the part of directors to put a picture through a mass production process, whereby plot is done by one specialist and dialogue bolted on to the plot by another group of adepts in the way nuts are attached to an automobile frame, places the responsibility of achieving unity largely on the scenic director. Often it is only a unity of veracious local color. Directors seem increasingly prone to shy at the fantastic and the abstract personal expression. They have tried the idea that "Art" in the movies pays and the attempt has not increased their faith in art. They are more likely to stick to what appears a good plot, dialogue, and the pet locality-formula for the year than to court the risk of producing a novelty.

The sound picture brings with it the possibility of greater simplicity of setting. It assists the scene designer by providing a richness of mood, permitting the designer to simplify his detail since the picture is not called upon to present all of its moods in dumb show. There may be a temporary decline in pantomime as an art and a temporary approach to the technique of the theatre. Nevertheless, the screen possesses resources which the theatre cannot imitate. Any imitation of the theatre on the part of the talking motion picture will only make clear the difference in opportunity and result in a return to expressions more characteristic of the picture.

Some stylization of dialogue must be found for the motion picture. Even if pictures can be developed to give the illusion of depth and the appearance of solidity, the action is still not that of real actors but of their images. Just as good theatre does not copy life in diction and action but gives a non-actual and heightened feeling of life, so the cinema can give limitless scope to our pictures of life, their sound, color, movements in minute detail or in overwhelming mass. The actor and the scene designer can convey the realities of their own interpretations of life as in the theatre, but the spectator is called upon to accept the conventions of the flat pictures and of mechanically controlled sound in connection with the action.

Color may be a means of attaining spacial depth, at least in part. With color and spacial depth added to moving pictures, there will be still no more actuality than in the flat picture, but only a third dimension in which the artist can develop his effects. It will emphasize the difficulties of relation of sound to its supposed source on the screen and create the same problem which the theatre has of locating the spectator in the planes of action. If it seems desirable to bring the action of the theatre out from behind the plane of the proscenium, what a gain in force the motion picture will make, especially if by some means it can take place around, above and among the audience.

And what then of sound? When the novelty of sound with pictures has worn off, as seems already to be the case, it will become necessary for pictures to excel in plot and direction. Possibly the day of the highly individual picture dominated by one creative will is going to arrive. Meanwhile there are the tricks of the animated cartoon to draw upon and the possibilities of creating changing backgrounds by means of mechanically moving shadows and forms like those of the clavilux.

Part of the problem of moving picture scenery is that of the architect. Unlike that of the painted picture, the point of view of the moving picture is flexible, architectural. The cinema can utilize the same property of motion past objects which the observer of architecture experiences. In architecture the point of view is infinite, varying with each step, each turn of the head and movement of the eye. This quality can be approximated in the moving picture and translated into terms of space shown flatly but with unlimited change of viewpoint.

As the resources of the motion picture are brought into more complete use, there will be changes in the motion picture theatre. Already good acoustics is a necessity to the motion picture auditorium. A further development of sound technique may lead to attempts at abolishing the screen behind a proscenium and to making the theatre a part of the environment of the picture as Geddes and Reinhardt did in the Century Theatre for "The Miracle." Until the picture is free to appear in various parts of the building and the audience no longer sits facing in one direction toward a screen, there seems to be little need of providing any source of sound away from the screen. When the conception of the screen passes, there will open out the possibility of a panoramic picture of great size and of flexibility in the projection machine. Until someone builds such a theatre, until pictures are taken and projection machines adapted to a new conception, the motion picture theatre will require only its present forms restudied for the improvement of their acoustics. If pictures ever become truly extra dimensional and sculptural, then some scheme like a vast amphitheatre, with action taking place in the center of the audience on any plane beneath the roof, may become a possibility.

Nature, Teacher of the Dance

By Elizabeth Duncan

WHEN in 1904 Isadora and I founded our first school in Berlin, it was looked upon most critically as an event violating all accepted standards of morality. That we uncovered children's legs and arms and draped their bodies in brief tunics aroused much shocked indignation. It even went so far that the police came to prevent a performance by the children of the school, charging immoral lack of clothing. We were saved only by the fiery enthusiasm of a few friends who used their influence to show the falseness and ridiculousness of such a complaint.

The religion of the beauty of the human body had been forgotten. Only in museums and in books the searching student of beauty and truth could study about it and draw his inspiration, and then, returning into the world, find all laws of nature hopelessly disregarded and the human body covered by and forced into stifling and ugly clothing.

Isadora brought a new freedom of the body and spirit, the wide influence of which is felt in modern life and which has not yet reached the bounds of its fulfillment. Twenty-five years ago the great majority, anchored in the standard conceptions of that time, could not follow but remained looking on nervously or sneered. The small minority, mostly artists who saw in Isadora's idea the dawn of a new human freedom, cheered her as she turned her hopes to the child to be the bearer of her message.

In a perfect school the fundamental idea should be to make a stronger and freer human race. That motive will give the leading light and purpose to all studies artistic and academic. It gives the school the quality of a shelter where in the rhythm of nature the child can grow. This is of essential importance. The delicate and sensitive process of equal development of body and mind can take place only under sensitive guidance and understanding for the wonder in nature, with the simple gesture of taking the child gently by the hand, as it were, instead of imposing an alien force upon it, as in the past, or with too much applied psychology, as the modern trend implies.

There should never be a school teaching only the dance. Isadora and I never meant that. The dance can be the leading art, as it is the most free of all, having the human body as its instrument, but the other arts complete the circle. This brings an unstressed natural understanding and feeling that it all is part of life, giving to it, drawing from it, linking the study of form, line, color, music, the word and movement, so that they are always new sources for one another to draw from and build upon.

It is from the limitation and compression of time and energy in city life that the "dance school" has sprung. Its danger to the growth of the art of the dance lies in this cause. The dance school, by force of circumstance, concentrates on form in the dance and finished product instead of on principle. It must be remembered that not all persons who wish to learn to dance, wish necessarily to become professional dancers or even amateurs, but may desire to dance merely for relaxation, for joy in movement or for some entirely detached interest in the art. To these it is as interesting and valuable as it is necessary to the professional dancer, to learn about

246

the universal connection of the dance with the other arts. It gives the dance an appeal of the greatest width, enabling everyone, whether they qualify as a dancer or not, to enjoy it and find inspiration in it. I have had in my school large numbers of children and grown-ups who have really felt the joy of natural, unforced movement of the body, draped only in thin tunics, lifting themselves upward toward heaven or drooping to the earth or stretching as if to touch the horizon all around. The children in their own way, to some singing instrument such as the flute or violin, or to a simple beautiful poem or folk-song which they sing themselves, or to nothing but the rhythm of the wind. The grown body to older music, to words of greater depth, such as Walt Whitman's or an ancient Greek poet's, to songs or also to the sounds of nature. They learn about great music and folk-song at another time than that designated for the dance. They have great teachers to guide them in the finest expression in painting and drawing. Masters in the theatre give them inspiring moments of great poetry and drama. They study about ideas essential in philosophy and have renowned musicians play to them. All these studies are pursued with separate emphasis, and therefore, when the students come together to dance, they have something all their own to say and express. Not by intellectual manufacture but out of the richness of experience of their inner self.

Folk-dancing cannot be arbitrarily created or forced into existence. The folk-dance originated and grew with time, as did the folk-song. If we wish to bring about a new folk-dance appropriate to our time and equal in strength only to that of ancient Greece by virtue of its absolute unity with nature and truth to it, we may hope to do so only by swaying people to an ecstasy in the dance comparable to that exhilaration which we receive from a great actor or poet or which stirs us to song in great public concerts of beautiful music.

For the gifted student of the dance, and for those who wish to make a profession of it or become teachers, there should be a definite time daily in which they can work to perfect themselves in the art and strive toward new expression.

In my school I use a method of gymnastics that regards the human body foremost and frees it from the restraint of clothes as the dance does. I do not believe everybody is strong enough to dance immediately upon entering the school. While in this system of gymnastics muscle building, straightening and strengthening of the body and physical control are concentrated upon, the exercises for the dance should start with making the body supple and striving for a control much finer than that of pure physical effort. Both are necessary to the human being. In the dance the energy and spirit radiate through the controlled suppleness of the body.

If we follow our greatest teacher, Nature, recognizing her astounding simplicity and always remembering that we are part of her, and if we weave her wonder into our dance, letting it radiate from one central point, swaying like the trees, fluid as water, strong as mountains and warm as the song of a bird, the dance will lead all other arts. It will reconcile the mechanical and technical elements, so strong now in the world, with the magic of the human spirit and be the torchbearer of an international understanding. Therefore our hopes are with that school which can embrace, uphold and help to grow in freedom the precious seed Isadora gave the world.

Seeking an American Art of the Dance

By Martha Graham

INTEREST in the dance as an art of and from America, is new—even to dancers themselves, fettered as they have been, together with the general public, to things European. Recognition of the place the dance is destined to hold in the future of the people has been slow in coming—but to a few of the initiate and the lay, it is already a peculiarly great force, an exciting and glorious vitality, that is gradually assuming a form. Although she may not yet know it, America is cradling an art that is destined to be a ruler, in that its urge is masculine and creative rather than imitative.

Strangely enough the America that produced Isadora Duncan, the greatest individual stimulus to the dance of modern times, has been blinded for so long by the shining glory of an old culture. There crossed this country in majesty and splendor such great dancers and dance forms as were produced by the Russian ballet, justly arousing a great wave of enthusiasm but leaving in its wake an impression imitative of a culture foreign to us rather than an expression creatively from us.

Subject as we are to immigration physically, and sympathetic to it as we are spiritually, these waves of influence almost engulfed us. With what result to the art of the dance? That as an integral art form it did not exist and that the foreign forms were reduced to decadence in this country by the transplanting. This is true of the Russian dance, born in integrity, of fierce climatic and social

249

conditions, impossible to duplicate—the Spanish dance, which in its tradition, its beauty, its cruelty, its pride, its essential nationalism, is impossible to imitate—the Oriental dance, least comprehensible of all, with its hieratic symbolic gesture, impossible of assimilation because of its involved philosophy—and last the German dance, nearest to us of all, dangerously near, the voice of a determined, tired, but forever mentally undefeated people.

As a result we have had a dance of "appearance" rather than a dance of "being"—instead of an art which was the fruit of a people's soul, we had entertainment.

The theatre which has always in its pure form fed from a vital and independent dance, had, in its general decadence, overburdened that art with tremendous paraphernalia, making it a handmaid of music, of drama, even of costumes and stage sets. Great orchestral organizations presented it against stage sets that rendered movement as static as "a painted ship upon a painted ocean."

Fatuous in our adulation of all things European, we gazed longingly at the fruits of a tired culture, while Europe smiled and reached past us to help itself to the wine of our land; its monstrous vital rhythms, crude, glowing colors, dynamic economy of gesture, and that divine awkwardness which is ever a part of what is vital, fresh and masculine in the arts. We were still blind. Our dance performances had become in their misuse of borrowed forms and cultures, not unlike a Roman holiday, equally obscene in their lack of artistic integrity.

Then it was that what is known as the concert dance came to be. Concert is a borrowed term—often awkward and indefinite when applied to the dance—but in the name itself is the key to the state of consciousness that has helped to establish the dance as an art form in this country and of this country. Burdened with the demands for excitement and entertainment, for itself, that the theatre presented, the dancer looked toward the concert stage with its simplicity and concentration as a haven where the dance might regain its integrity as an art and determine its bent as a native cultural form. So the name concert dance has come to mean that performance where dance is the focal point of performance —the reason—where it possesses that integrity and vital integration necessary to any art form. Contrary to the views of the general public, the concert dance has nothing to do with any particular style or type of dancing. It is a question of purpose, an attitude toward itself as an art, rather than exploitation of any given style or form. Whether the form be pure movement, mime, or as in the case of Angna Enters, a combination of the two elements, whether music is employed or whether silence is used, is not important.

Sunday evening concerts were inaugurated. Due to economic conditions, Sunday was the only day on which a theatre was available for single performances. The wave of criticism that a Sunday dance concert was unnatural, came from the conventional theatre-goer, and that it was immoral and sacrilegious from the religionists, "the Sabbath League." That it is immoral need not be discussed, except to dismiss it as an indication of an unhealthy, backward mind. Our only fear has been that it may close the theatres to us on the only day on which they are available. As to the other accusation, "unnatural"—what is unnatural about a necessity? Unusual it may be, in that it marks the dancer's revolt from the "theatrical," confused in the minds of so many with what is "theatre." Do not these same critics realize that the almost fanatical ritualistic simplicity and concentration of these dance concerts is

the life stuff of which theatre has ever been made—that this attitude of mind will produce that art form, that quintessence of life,
the dance, which has ever produced great theatre in past cultures
—and that the healthiest sign of all is that the audience has been
relegated to its true position as collaborator, rather than as dictator?

This movement of revolt from place and forms, has in its youth
and the extremity of its need, demanded that we shun the im-
perialism of the ballet, the sentimentality engulfing the followers
of the great Isadora Duncan, the weakling exoticism of a transplanted orientalism. Time will perhaps bring a balanced use of
old and new forms, but in the intensity of self-penetration, that
condition of ease and sophistication is at present impossible. We
do not deny the intrinsic value of these older forms in and for
themselves, nor their fruits for a general world, but we have found
it necessary to deny their influence over us, and by so doing to
enable us to arrive at the starting point for the American expression, the American gesture. I avoid using the term American ballet. The term has been so exploited commercially, as to be useless
and shabby at present—having no art value. In each instance
where the name American ballet has been used, it has been an
American ballet in veneer only, never in inner substance.

Granted that rhythm be the sum total of one's experience, then
the dance form of America will of necessity differ greatly from
that of any other country. So far the dance derived or transplanted
has retarded our creative growth, in spite of the fact that there are
thousands of ardent dance pupils in this country. It is difficult
to imagine a great ballet dancer emerging from a country in which
the pioneer is one or two generations removed. Necessary to the
ballet, with its crystalline cold technique, its strange disinterested
fire, is patronage, intelligent patronage. Furthermore, the ballet

at its height, in Russia and in Italy, marks that point in a nation's development when decadence has begun. It may be a glorious golden autumn as in the Russias, but decadence it is nevertheless. We must first determine what is for us the Primitive—that expression of its psyche only possible to a supremely cultured and integrated people.

In America the revolt of a few visionaries from European dance culture has not been animated by a spirit of nationalism. It is not to establish something American that we are striving, but to create a form and expression that will have for us integrity and creative force.

It is through the individual that the new must come, the emancipation of the individual, and it is in that state of individualism that the American dance finds itself today. The concerts presented have been largely running commentaries of moods, desires, furies, reflections of the intense individualist, without whom no great movement is possible. There have emerged five or six distinct individuals. As we are a polyglot nation, so the individual dancers present strongly conflicting types, interesting and vital in their dissimilarity—Angna Enters, Doris Humphrey, Tamiris, Charles Weidman and myself.

When the Dance Repertory Theatre was formed in the winter of 1929–1930, by Doris Humphrey, Charles Weidman, Tamiris and myself, there arose intense criticism of the esthetic purpose of the organization. This criticism was made blindly, not in realization of the fact that the very freedom existing, the lack of similarity, and the frank pride in that lack, is its safeguard artistically. The Dance Repertory Theatre was established as a theatre where the dance as an art was the focal point. This organization came as a definite outgrowth of the concert dance.

So far that which has been achieved by what is known as the concert dance, has been definite and sure. It has produced and been produced by five or six individuals distinctly American in type; it has brought about the establishment of the Dance Repertory Theatre; it has stung a public into protest and curiosity—a few artists, musicians and painters, it has intoxicated by its daring and honesty and its potentialities; it has created the need for dance critics on all the leading newspapers; it has fired musical organizations—the Philadelphia Orchestra, the League of Composers, the Cleveland Symphony, to collaborate in a production for stage and orchestra.

As to form, which is the heart, there is manifest an economy of gesture, an intensity and integrity of mood, a simplified external means, and above all a concentration on "the stuff" of the dance, which is—movement divinely significant.

Now the individualism must give place. Already the circles are widening. Groups are beginning to form. The universal is being made manifest through the employment of mass. This is true in the group of Doris Humphrey and in another sense in my own. Further evidence of the concentration of the dance is evidenced by the fact that the best dance compositions of these two organizations have been without music.

We are an essentially dramatic country. We build in mass and are built in mass, spiritually and physically. We have two primitive sources, dangerous and hard to handle in the arts, but of intense psychic significance—the Indian and the Negro. That these influence us is certain—the Negro with his rhythms of disintegration, the Indian by his intense integration, his sense of ritualistic tribal drama. Our greatest dance form will eventually be an orchestration of various physical rhythms and spiritual melodies in mass movement. It is life as seen through our eyes and manifested in our art that is essential and of value to the future of the dance. So the answer to the problem of the American dance on the part of the individualists who point the way is, "Know the land"—its exciting strange contrasts of barrenness and fertility—its great sweep of distances—its monstrous architecture—and the divine machinery of its invention. From it will come the great mass drama that is the American Dance.

Toward an American Ballet

By Robert Edmond Jones

THE assumptions are always the same: that there is no ballet in America and that there ought to be one. Suppose, for a moment, there is one; or, suppose, there is no pressing need for one.

Is there one? Not if we insist on a Russian Ballet like that of Diaghileff. But isn't it possible that the animated cartoon might be the American form? The line of a hundred mice leaping from a motor-car, the staircases that bend and come back into shape, the unreal sounds—abstract sound used where the talkie always tries for realism—may be the counterpart and equivalent of ballet for America.

Why have we no ballet in America? Why do we not all speak Russian? When Isadora and her school danced "Iphigenia" in Craig's settings at the Century, ballet existed for us, in spite of Isadora's contempt for ballet as she knew it. Perhaps she was right.

Perhaps she was even more right than the people who demand a "mechanical ballet" to express the Machine Age. It seems to me that these people are a little too certain about America. What we call the spirit of America has not yet come into being; we know something about its first manifestations, the externals, and these are very well expressed in the typical American dance, on the revue stage, the dance of Ann Pennington or James Barton or Jack Donahue, with another strange impetus from the dance of the negro, from Bill Robinson, which suggests something deeper.

But the machine—rigid, certain, inflexible—does not represent the inner spirit, and if we dance machine-dances, we may satirize, but not express, the spirit of America—I mean the spirit which has a future as well as a present. The present is thwarted, turned in upon itself, uncertain. The machine is not bewildered—the spirit of America is. And whatever confidence, assurance and faith America will have, cannot be expressed in ballets devoted to the machine. We can create a good mechanical ballet with animated cartoons treated in counterpoint—say with a subject in slow motion shown against a related subject, a commentary, in normal speed. Even that would leave us far from the "spirit of America."

For that spirit, people demand folk-lore, tradition, because the ballet of Diaghileff has its sources in folk myth and tradition. For us, that kind of legend does not exist. We have what someone has called "dramatists going antiquing," but we have no body of lore—which means racial wisdom as well as an inheritance of story —to count on.

The ballet cannot be a graft, grown into the American habit of life. So far as it has existed—as a shadow of grand opera—it has been a failure. So far no one has arisen who not only believed in ballet, but saw how to make it relevant to America, to the way we live and think. The material is magnificent—it is full of the strain of American life, of the tension between pioneer and Puritan, the strain of races, native and immigrant. We get something of that magnificence in a few skyscrapers; we get something of it and of the tension of our lives in Norman Bel Geddes' work.

When someone arrives who can own people as Diaghileff did, and own money—not merely borrow and spend it—as he did, we may have the focal point of a ballet. We have miraculous bodies and extraordinary technical control; we have not two generations

of masterful dancers, no great ballet masters, no technical traditions. We have had masters in iron-puddling, designers of dynamos,
even a tradition of good motor-car technique. The discrepancy
shocks artists and lovers of art; but it is perfectly natural. We have
had masters where we wanted to have them; and have neglected
them where they failed our immediate purposes.

It is possible that dancing is as irrelevant to our time as archery
—and we will not throw a bridge over a gap in time by changing
the outward appearance; a ballet about aeroplanes may have less
to say to us than a ballet about Pierrot and Columbine. It is, obviously, the inner content that counts; yet if we are to have Pier-
rots, they had better be genuine and convey their legend, and not
parallels laboriously worked up to prettify a literary legend. The
setting for a folk-ballet of California today is a Ford car in motion—and even that might not be a profound commentary, a significant expression of California's reality.

We shall not approach that reality until someone finds himself unable to say what he is *compelled* to say, in any other form
but the ballet. There are signs that such a person may presently
appear, and the immediate interest, in ballet, must be to provide
this still unknown, perhaps unborn, genius with a framework.
That is what gives the efforts of the League of Composers and
Leopold Stokowski their great importance. Both of them are open
to the suggestion of ballet totally separated, if necessary, from the
old and the Russian traditions. Both seem willing to produce a
Russian ballet as a beginning for a school. In music they have indicated a willingness to hear and to make others listen; in ballet
they would need to re-train the American eye. It is not so difficult a problem if the object presented to the eye has any fundamental relevance to the reality of American experience.

New Ideas in Music Education

By John Erskine

There is no revolution, properly speaking, in music education today, no startling innovations in technique, nor in the method of teaching it. There is, however, a new orientation in the music world. The century or so just passed was dominated by the virtuoso, and music education has aimed at producing artists for the concert stage. The teacher like Leschetizsky is famous for a pupil like Paderewski; Leopold Auer is known to most people as the teacher of Heifetz, Zimbalist, Elman. Until recently the emphasis upon the virtuoso has been so great that we have somewhat forgotten the sterling qualities of Leschetizsky and Auer as musicians, and certainly young students have overlooked the fact that no amount of brilliant teaching can produce a Paderewski, a Heifetz or a Zimbalist unless the pupil is himself by temperament and self-devotion a musician before he is a concert performer.

For various reasons the brilliant virtuoso period seems to have come to an end. The causes usually assigned for this change are the development of mechanical music, as it is called—of devices for reproducing music, as in the phonograph, or for distributing it, as over the radio. I personally believe that these causes are less important than the effect upon the public at large of the magnificent performances the virtuoso artists themselves have given. Twenty years ago we feared that player pianos might take away the average person's wish to master the instrument. Today more people than

259

ever are studying the piano, especially in the United States, and the player piano is rather definitely in the discard. The wide distribution of music from the concert stage and over the radio has roused in vast numbers of people the wish to participate in the art, not as professionals but simply as human beings desiring the privilege of creating beauty.

The demand for an education in music on the part of this large group has been answered in various ways. It would be impossible to compute the number of private teachers who have tried to make pianists or violinists or singers out of the children in the neighborhood. You have only to glance over advertisements in certain magazines to see that on the lowest level there are some teachers or schools which promise quick results with little effort. If you wish to play the piano, the advertisement assures you that your ambition can be reached without the annoyance of long practice. You can be taught to sing almost over night, or to play the saxophone in two hours and the ukelele in fifteen minutes. Tragic or ridiculous as this kind of quackery may be, it witnesses to the wide-spread wish to become a performer in music.

Among conscientious and competent teachers instruction in piano, violin or voice has had reassuring results, according to the ability and the application of the pupils. But such teachers have themselves become somewhat dissatisfied with their contribution to musical education. Just because they are competent and conscientious they know it is first of all important even for the amateur to become a musician. They know also that to become merely a piano player or a violinist without becoming a musician is for the amateur as well as for the professional a tragic failure. To become a musician the pupil must have a thorough knowledge of harmony and composition, an acquaintance with other instruments than the one he plays, and most of all a familiarity with the literature of music as a whole. Very few private teachers are able to provide all these opportunities.

Some progress can easily be recognized in the methods of the best teachers. Twenty-five years ago most music pupils in the United States "took lessons." They went to their teacher's study, played their pieces, were criticized, and then went home to practice until the next lesson. They rarely had an opportunity to hear any other pupil play, and they usually knew no music except the pieces they themselves had worked at. Today every first-rate teacher gathers his pupils from time to time in a general class where they can listen to each other and hear a great deal of music which they themselves may not be playing. A few teachers, very fortunately placed, are able to put their pupils in the way of hearing or of playing chamber music. Some teachers insist on the study of composition; all good teachers would of course advise it.

The theory behind this change is that mere technical skill, however essential it may be to good performance, is not what makes music important to society at large. Technical skill, when it outruns musical talent, is no more entertaining than any other form of acrobatics. What brings us to the study of music is the music itself, the emotional and intellectual substance of the art. An adequate education in this substance of music anyone is entitled to, even though he may not become a proficient performer.

Or to state the theory in other terms, it is now generally believed by educators that some practical proficiency in the arts is advisable for every human being. The geniuses may be few, but almost everyone is potentially a musician. To leave the talent undeveloped is bad for us. To develop it in everyone is to shift the emphasis of musical education from the isolated genius, destined for the concert stage, to the great numbers who, if properly educated, will constitute his sympathetic and understanding audience.

In the conservatories in which the most promising talents are prepared for the concert career there is a growing recognition and a growing respect for this large audience, musically trained. The amateur is no longer thought of as necessarily an incompetent who plays or sings badly. Of course, many amateurs will always play or sing badly, and so will some professionals. But in the past, as we now see, the competent amateur made the audience for the competent professional, and to train the professional without at the same time preparing his audience is to leave him suspended in mid-air.

We are beginning to recognize, therefore, a greater responsibility upon the music profession to teach, and a greater need in all parts of the country for well-equipped schools in which the pupils will find the opportunity to become complete musicians. Concert performers have always done some teaching, but rarely from motives which were cheerful or broad-minded. They taught either because they needed more money than could be earned on the platform, or because they had discovered some talent which they hoped to train into a concert performer like themselves. We begin to recognize that the biggest service the first-rate musician can do for society at large is to inspire and train the love of music in others. His ability as a player will be invaluable to this end, but the end is more important than his playing, no matter how excellent that is.

The consequence of the virtuoso ideal has always been to lure the artist to the great cities of the world, where large and profitable audiences could be found. The present congestion of music in New York City is perhaps the last, as it is certainly the worst, manifestation of this tendency. The result of the new idea of music as an art important socially to the whole country, will be to take young artists out of the large centers into the smaller towns, where they can be leaders of public taste, and where they can build up their careers on a solid foundation of musicianship.

If this tendency develops, the time may come when talented youngsters will find their career in the general region in which they were born. At present they almost always desert the place which produced them.

It may be also that the children now playing in high school orchestras in the United States will continue to play in amateur orchestras after they have left school.

It may be that the choral groups rapidly multiplying in schools and colleges and communities at large will carry the understanding of good music even into areas to which the orchestra cannot reach.

If all these good results arrive, the position of the professional artist will be sounder than ever. The amateur musician will not stay away from a concert because he himself plays; for that very reason he will be eager to attend. But the concert which the professional gives will be less and less an exhibition of personal agility, and more and more an opportunity to convey a musical message to an audience prepared to receive it.

The Composer in the Machine Age

BY GEORGE GERSHWIN

UNQUESTIONABLY modern musical America has been influenced by modern musical Europe. But it seems to me that modern European composers, in turn, have very largely received their stimulus, their rhythms and impulses from Machine Age America. They have a much older tradition of musical technique which has helped them put into musical terms a little more clearly the thoughts that originated here. They can express themselves more glibly.

The Machine Age has influenced practically everything. I do not mean only music but everything from the arts to finance. The machine has not affected our age in form as much as in tempo, speed and sound. It has affected us in sound whenever composers utilize new instruments to imitate its aspects. In my "American in Paris" I used four taxi horns for musical effect. George Antheil has used everything, including aeroplane propellers, door bells, typewriter keys, and so forth. By the use of the old instruments, too, we are able to obtain modern effects. Take a composition like Honegger's "Pacific No. 231," written and dedicated to a steam engine. It reproduces the whole effect of a train stopping and starting and it is all done with familiar instruments.

There is only one important thing in music and that is ideas and feeling. The various tonalities and sounds mean nothing unless they grow out of ideas. Not many composers have ideas. Far more of them know how to use strange instruments which do not require ideas. Whoever has inspired ideas will write the great music of our period. We are plowing the ground for that genius who may be alive or may be born today or tomorrow. If he is alive, he is recognized to a certain degree, although it is impossible for the public at large to assimilate real greatness quickly. Take a composer like Bach. In his lifetime, he was recognized as one of the greatest organists in the world, but he was not acclaimed as one of the greatest composers of his time or of all time until generations after his death.

I do not think there is any such thing as mechanized musical composition without feeling, without emotion. Music is one of the arts which appeals directly through the emotions. Mechanism and feeling will have to go hand in hand, in the same way that a skyscraper is at the same time a triumph of the machine and a tremendous emotional experience, almost breath-taking. Not merely its height but its mass and proportions are the result of an emotion, as well as of calculation.

Any discussion of the distinction between presentation and representation in music resolves itself into an attempt to determine the relative values of abstract music and program music. It is very difficult for anyone to tell where abstract music starts and program music finishes. There must have been a picture of something in the composer's mind. What it was nobody knows, often not even the composer. But music has a marvelous faculty of recording a picture in someone else's mind. In my own case, everybody who has ever listened to "Rhapsody in Blue"—and that embraces thousands of people—has a story for it but myself. "An American in Paris" is obviously a program piece, although I would say half of it or more is abstract music tied together by a few representative themes. Imitation never gets anyone anywhere. Originality is the only thing that counts. But the originator uses material and ideas that occur around him and pass through him. And out of his experience comes this original creation or work of art, unquestionably influenced by his surroundings which include very largely what we call the Machine Age.

It is difficult to determine what enduring values, esthetically, jazz has contributed, because jazz is a word which has been used for at least five or six different types of music. It is really a conglomeration of many things. It has a little bit of ragtime, the blues, classicism and spirituals. Basically, it is a matter of rhythm. After rhythm in importance come intervals, music intervals which are peculiar to the rhythm. After all, there is nothing new in music. I maintained years ago that there is very little difference in the music of different nations. There is just that little individual touch. One country may prefer a peculiar rhythm or a note like the seventh. This it stresses, and it becomes identified with that nation. In America this preferred rhythm is called jazz. Jazz is music; it uses the same notes that Bach used. When jazz is played in another nation, it is called American. When it is played in another country, it sounds false. Jazz is the result of the energy stored up in America. It is a very energetic kind of music, noisy, boisterous and even vulgar. One thing is certain. Jazz has contributed an enduring value to America in the sense that it has expressed ourselves. It is an original American achievement which will endure, not as jazz perhaps, but which will leave its mark on future music in one form or another. The only kinds of music which endure are those which possess form in the universal sense and folk music. All else dies. But unquestionably folk songs are being written and have been written which contain enduring elements of jazz. To be sure, that is only an element; it is not the whole. An entire composition written in jazz could not live.

As for further esthetic developments in musical composition, American composers may in time use quarter notes, but then so will Europe use quarter notes. Eventually our ears will become sensitive to a much finer degree then they were a hundred, fifty or twenty-five years ago. Music deemed ugly then is accepted without question today. It stands to reason, therefore, that composers will continue to alter their language. That might lead to anything. They have been writing already in two keys. There is no reason why they will not go further and ask us to recognize quarter or sixteenth notes. Such notes, whether written or not, are used all the time, only we are not conscious of them. In India they use quarter tones and, I believe, consciously.

Music is a phenomenon that to me has a very marked effect on the emotions. It can have various effects. It has the power of moving people to all of the various moods. Through the emotions, it can have a cleansing effect on the mind, a disturbing effect, a drowsy effect, an exciting effect. I do not know to what extent it can finally become a part of the people. I do not think music as we know it now is indispensable although we have music all around us in some form or other. There is music in the wind. People can live more or less satisfactorily without orchestral music, for instance. And who can tell that we would not be better off if we weren't as civilized as we are, if we lacked many of our emotions? But we have them and we are more or less egotistic about them. We think that they are important and that they make us what we are. We think that we are an improvement over people of other ages who didn't have them. Music has become a very important part of civilization, and one of the main reasons is that one does not need a formal education to appreciate it. Music can be appreciated by a person who can neither read nor write and it can also be appreciated by people who have the highest form of intelligence. For example, Einstein plays the violin and listens to music. People in the underworld, dope fiends and gun men, invariably are music lovers and, if not, they are affected by it. Music is entering into medicine. Music sets up a certain vibration which unquestionably results in a physical reaction. Eventually the proper vibration for every person will be found and utilized. I like to think of music as an emotional science.

Almost every great composer profoundly influences the age in which he lives. Bach, Beethoven, Wagner, Brahms, Debussy, Stravinsky. They have all recreated something of their time so that millions of people could feel it more forcefully and better understand their time.

The composer, in my estimation, has been helped a great deal by the mechanical reproduction of music. Music is written to be heard, and any instrument that tends to help it to be heard more frequently and by greater numbers is advantageous to the person who writes it. Aside from royalties or anything like that, I should think that the theory that music is written to be heard is a good one. To enable millions of people to listen to music by radio or phonograph is helpful to the composer. The composer who writes music for himself and doesn't want it to be heard is generally a bad composer. The first incursion of mechanized reproduction was a stimulus to the composer and the second wave has merely intensified that stimulus. In the past, composers have starved because of lack of performance, lack of being heard. That is impossible today. Schubert could not make any money because he did not have an opportunity through the means of distribution of his day to reach the public. He died at the age of thirty-one and had a certain reputation. If he had lived to be fifty or sixty, unquestionably he would have obtained recognition in his own day. If he were living today, he would be well-off and comfortable.

The radio and the phonograph are harmful to the extent that they bastardize music and give currency to a lot of cheap things. They are not harmful to the composer. The more people listen to music, the more they will be able to criticize it and know when it is good. When we speak of machine-made music, however, we are not speaking of music in the highest sense, because, no matter how much the world becomes a Machine Age, music will have to be created in the same old way. The Machine Age can affect music only in its distribution. Composers must compose in the same way the old composers did. No one has found a new method in which to write music. We still use the old signatures, the old symbols. The composer has to do every bit of his work himself. Hand work can never be replaced in the composition of music. If music ever became machine-made in that sense, it would cease to be an art.

Opera and the Symphony Will Survive

By Albert Coates

In the present period of confusion in the arts, the opera and the symphony orchestra will exist and persist unimpaired. And the reason I believe is this: they remain the best mediums in which the composer can work. Large yet elastic in form, they are adaptable to progressive types of musical expression. Accordingly, there is more vitality in music cast in the orchestral or operatic mold than in music composed for the voice or the individual instrument.

This does not mean that the opera and the symphony will not change but I doubt whether they will ever be discarded. Opera today is not the opera of the last generation. The opera of tomorrow will not be the opera of today. The symphony orchestra of one hundred and ten men as you see and hear it at Carnegie Hall is not the one remembered by your grandparents. Since Mozart scored his works, the proportion of instruments has varied, the number of musicians greatly increased. Both opera and symphony as we know them are the results of a long period of evolution. They are still and always will be in a healthy state of flux and development. But basically both forms will persist.

In opera I find that the modern tendency is to displace the music from its traditional position of first importance. Opera, which dramatically has always been at least a hundred years behind the times, is learning from the modern theatre. The music of present-day opera must be matched by the story and the stage action; sometimes it is even secondary and complementary to the latter. We demand *musical drama* as contrasted with old-style grand opera. In Germany—in Berlin, particularly, the pioneer city in music—I have seen recently the latest productions of contemporary composers—Krenek, Berg, Weinberger, Weill, Milhaud. They can be extraordinarily musical on occasion but the most stimulating part of their work is the interesting way in which they clothe their subject matter musically. To cite an example: in Franz Schreker's "Der Singende Teufel," the "Singing Devil" is the new organ. The time is the middle ages. And the climax of the opera is the scene in the church where the monks in arms are awaiting the attack of the people. Gradually you become aware of some sort of sound rising from outside. Actually it is a big double chorus singing behind the curtains, singing in an entirely different tonality from the organ. And you do not feel that it is anti-musical. It is part and parcel of the opera. You would not expect a mob about to sack a cathedral to sing in tune or to be in harmony with the "devil" which is going to conquer them. Tradition has given way to realism. The libretto has become significant, rather than a peg on which to hang a few arias and duets. Scenery, action, music, all are esthetically unified. It is Wagner's dream of a "mélange des genres" conceived and executed in the tempo and spirit of today. Everything is becoming simplified, stripped to essentials. The result is not always beautiful, not always easy to understand, not "opera" as the subscribers to the Diamond Horseshoe have been taught to know it. But it is the opera of today.

Less obviously touched by the "Zeitgeist" is the symphony. I remember being in Russia when the Revolution broke out. At that time a great number of insurgent composers sprang up and said: "Away with the orchestra of the old regime. We must have a new orchestra. New instruments. Everything must be new. Everything must be scrapped—the violin, the 'cello, the flute, the oboe." It went so far that finally I came out in print and said: 'Gentlemen, your ideas are excellent. Nothing would interest me more than to see new combinations of instruments invented. But first you must write new music for the old instruments. And don't worry about the new ones. Leave them to take care of themselves. Because necessity has always been the mother of invention."

The jazz orchestra is a good example of this. The leader—perhaps Paul Whiteman—needs a new sound effect. Immediately his men find a way to make it! Our serious composers owe much to the jazz-band idiom. Although the saxophone has been used for a long, long time, its possibilities had never been plumbed or exploited until they were discovered on Broadway. Today the modern composer would be as lost without the saxophone as Beethoven would have been without an oboe or clarinet.

Much is being done in the theatre today to revive interest in the classics. "Lysistrata" is turned into a Twentieth Century comedy. "Hamlet" is given with modern clothes. And people ask: "Why cannot we do something similar to stimulate more general interest in good music?" Except through education I am aware of no way in which this can be done. New interpretations of classic music are a silly and dangerous experiment. Played one hundred years ago or one hundred years from now I know of nothing which could be done to alter the interpretation of Beethoven's Fifth Symphony. The best music has a life of its own. It represents a permanent and timeless esthetic experience for the world. Interpreted and performed through the mediums of sympathetic, vital personalities, the composer's message is as contemporaneous and stimulating to an audience of today as it was yesterday and will be to-morrow.

I have little patience with those persons who say that music is being ruined by its present-day mechanization. I feel that the radio and the gramophone are enormously useful both for education and for entertainment, and that they are building up audiences for the concert hall and for the opera house rather than diminishing them. When television comes, this may be less true. People like to listen with their eyes as much as they do with their ears. At present many who should be listening keep right on talking when the gramophone or radio is turned on. Television will be the attention-getter for radio. On the other hand, I feel that nothing will ever take away the thrill of sitting with thousands of others, of sharing an experience with a crowd—a sensation impossible to experience at home.

Of course, it will not do to forget an important drawback of all radio and gramophone reproduction. To me it is still only half developed because nobody as yet has invented a process in which the "sucking up" of the music has been accomplished by two ears. Man listens, normally, with two perfect ears. The orchestra should be listened to with two ears, or microphones, so placed that they correspond to what acoustic engineers call the binaural effect. When we have accomplished this we will have overcome one of the greatest defects of picking up a radio concert or making a record. Not until then will the "canned music" effect be entirely eliminated.

A great responsibility rests with the radio, one which America seems not to have accepted. As the most far-reaching means of touching the average man as yet discovered, the radio could be a tremendous help in musical education. In England, where the radio is under Government auspices, the British Broadcasting Company is doing extraordinarily good work. But in the United States, where the radio program rests largely in the hands of advertising agencies and commercial interests, the potentialities of the radio have not been fully realized. This is rather a dangerous situation, especially when viewed side by side with the fact that home-made music is practically dead, that the average child who formerly was taught to play the piano or the violin now gets its musical knowledge and interest second hand. The best way to appreciate anything of course is to have a shot at it yourself. The next best thing is to be sufficiently educated so that you can be intelligently appreciative.

The radio, too, could be helping to give new music a chance. The average music lover fights shy of works he does not know. Put a new name on a program and he is instinctively prejudiced against it. If the radio, through its infinite resources, could create curiosity in music and help popularize not only new but comparatively unknown works, it would save many great compositions from obscurity. It might even do what England has done with the Ernest Palmer Fund, an institution which is responsible to a great extent for the flourishing school of British music today. The Ernest Palmer Fund, administered by a committee of responsible and broad-minded musicians, provides a full orchestra, with competent conductors, to play before the best critics any music submitted which shows signs of talent. The parts are made without expense to the composer and presented to him after the performance. Through this Fund such well-known works as Vaughan Williams' London Symphony, Holst's Planets, Arnold Bax's First Symphony, etc., all had their first hearings. A composer can sit at a desk for months and write but he will never know what he has done until he actually hears it played. That is why experimental performance is so valuable. If the radio could provide a means of performing such works at regular intervals before an audience representing not only the whole country but the best critics of each city who would be requested to "listen in," the net results would be incalculable.

The sound film is another field which thus far has not realized the untapped resources of musical literature. While the radio carries the great symphonies, chamber music, jazz and so forth to the people, the sound film has the entire world of opera at its disposal. Properly produced, with a full-sized orchestra, a carefully picked cast, a good stage director, and a conductor of vision, opera would make so thrilling a sound film that it would sweep the country.

There is no doubt in my mind that all the mechanical developments of the day—the gramophone, the radio, the sound film, and television when it comes—are definitely advancing the cause of good music. Used as an ally and not as an enemy, they will popularize the classics and break ground for the contemporary composer. In the end music will become not what it is today, the pleasure of the cultured minority, but what it was meant to be, the entertainment and joy of the masses.

And all the mechanical reproduction of music will not compete with music in the concert hall and opera house but will help it. Perhaps the radio and sound film interests may even become the patrons of the future, replacing those generous individuals without whose support the symphony orchestras and opera houses of America today could not exist.

The Challenge of Mechanical Music to the Powers of the Young Artist

By Albert Spalding

The steady and irresistible advance of the mechanical device in the field of musical art has the appearance of a menace to individual artists—especially to those who are on the threshold of their careers. The young post-graduate eager to test his freshly found powers finds himself in an almost impossible situation. There seems to be no door of opportunity that will open to his knocking—only an endless blank wall. How is one to scale it? Public favor, recognition and material success perhaps await him inside the enclosure, but, even so, it is already well populated with established reputations, and scaling ladders are obtainable only at a prohibitive cost: the giving of expensive recitals in such large centers as New York, Boston, Chicago, etc., and a campaign of extensive advertising in the numerous musical publications.

The young artist whose material resources have already been taxed, and perhaps exhausted by the necessary outlay for his education, is thus confronted with the disheartening task of procuring fresh capital before he can attempt to make even a modest start.

The cost of giving these recitals ranges, according to the size of the respective halls, from seven hundred dollars to fifteen hundred dollars each. Now then, this would not be such a hopeless risk to undertake were there a reasonable chance that definite results would occur by the giving of a few such recitals. But such is not the case. The law of averages conspires to make the début recital (and even many following ones) an almost unnoticed affair. Of the hundreds given yearly in our principal cities the few that are conspicuous by more than a brief and perfunctory notice in the daily press can be counted on the fingers of one hand. In other words these exceptions may be said to have been attended by a fortunate accident. But in most of the walks of life the chance of a "fortunate accident" is not an alluring temptation as a material venture. It would be a matter, however, of interesting conjecture to speculate on how many just such chances are blindly undertaken in the field of music prompted by personal enthusiasm and generosity untempered by the cool judgment that would pause or halt the proceedings in any other line of action. A correct tabulation would, I think, make the confirmed gambler or margin speculator on the stock market appear to be a hopeless conservative.

It must be remembered that in presenting the difficulties which await the young artist I am assuming the while that he is endowed with the talent and equipment to justify recognition and public favor. The difficulties I have already mentioned are considerable. But, when, added to these, you have the further ones promoted by the advance of mechanical devices, the beginner's plight has been inestimably aggravated. For, whereas, formerly he had to meet the competition of well-established artists whose activities were restricted to their own personal contact with their more or less limited audiences, time and space were reasonably in his favor. Today, however, this same time and space no longer function for him. He may be thousands of miles distant from a famous and feared competitor, yet a reproducing agency in the form of a phonograph disk, a radio, or a "talkie" is likely to swamp his modest effort toward obtaining public notice. It is all very disheartening and discouraging. And it may well be that new factors —new menaces—will loom large on the horizon with the impending new devices, television, for instance.

In the face of this black picture, is there any way out? Is there any promise in the future for the young artist? At the risk of being thought an incurable optimist I believe that there is. My answer to the question is based on the premise that the mechanical device, the reproducing instrument, is a supplement to, but not a replacement of, individual and spontaneous performance. It will no more replace the individual performance than can a photograph replace an original picture—nor more than can a canned fruit replace a fresh one. Unless this premise, of which I am convinced, can be established, there is, indeed, no hope for the future.

The first key to the solution of the situation lies with the young artist himself. In his present plight we hear the endless complaint against conditions outside himself—how his individual art is stifling under the neglect and lack of recognition by a public sated with mechanism. He seldom stops to ask himself whether his art is really an individual one—whether it, too, has not been infected by mechanism; whether, in acquiring technical efficiency in his studies by the help of the phonograph and the radio, his interpretations have not been obtained by these labor-saving devices, well-cut but ready-made suits of clothes that make a presentable appearance, but which mask rather than grace the substance within. What a mess of potage for which he has bartered his birthright—an individual style.

Today is above all the day of extraordinarily efficient performances. The averagely gifted young débutant presents a program of great difficulty with amazing technical equipment and the outward semblance at least of impelling conviction. The main flaw lies in the fact that what appears to be conviction is in reality imitation. It is spurious and does not bear the test of real examination. Real conviction and a really individual style come from the inner man and are born of a thousand pangs. They represent the sum and total, the true portrait of his character as he stands alone. How big or how small is the extent of his ideals and aspirations is relatively unimportant, provided he has the art and the courage to revolve securely and serenely within his own orbit. His message will have value because it will be true and will reflect himself. For how can the young and unknown pianist hope to compete successfully with a phonograph record or a radio recording of Paderewski if his interpretation is only a parrot-like copy —glibly performed, but spurious?

This then is the valuable challenge which mechanical music makes to the powers of the young artist. In a sense it is a noble challenge if accepted in this way—and it can and should be nobly met.

Radio as an Independent Art

By Major Edward Bowes

To my mind, no one factor in any art, at any time, has created the right kind of revolution so thoroughly and completely as radio. The fact is that it really is an art in itself. True, there remain a few occasional growing pains, but this magnificent child-of-man will continue to blossom forth a true son-of-the-gods, pushing its penetrating rays to whatever nook and corner of the globe where man fancies to hie himself. To this immense responsibility and opportunity, radio broadcasting is very much alive.

The struggle and ability to separate the wheat from the chaff is an important stage in any art. Radio's progress in this respect is gratifying. For a significant study in comparative evolution and revolution, one need only contrast the history of the piano-roll and the phonograph record with that of radio. Remember the early crude results with roll and record, their gradual improvements and refinements, and at last today's finished, yet limited, product. How much more swiftly and thoroughly radio grasped its opportunity, conquered its legitimate field and spread round the world! From the start, its mechanical, commercial and artistic development was considerably swifter, more orderly, more confident.

While records and rolls never became an independent art, radio offers such a possibility. First, because of its universal appeal to its own master—man himself, man in the tens of millions. Secondly, because of its true, living contact, its power of instantaneous response to every manner and walk of life. And thirdly, because of its distinct ability to transfuse warmly such contact and response into living, breathing influences. These characteristics and their far-reaching effects are peculiar to radio alone. Player-piano and phonograph stand in relation to music in much the same way as the printing press to literature, while the radio presents not only music but drama and literature directly to its audience under conditions peculiar to itself by which its component arts assume new and hitherto unsuspected qualities and combinations.

Radio's great speed, adaptability and flexibility make it a powerful contender today for supremacy over the public press—not merely in the matter of news, although such is undeniably the case, but particularly in respect to the fostering and sponsoring of the arts, not even excepting sculpture and painting. For individual or collective instruction, training, understanding and entertainment, it is difficult to conceive of a limit to its ultimate opportunities.

With the air fairly alive with the melodies of composers of all times, the esthetic and economic influence of radio on music personally-performed before an audience should be both deep and immediate. As I conceive it, radio is not altogether a machine, for it is based on the personal performance of the artist, even if not always in the presence of an audience, a personal performance which differs on every occasion and is not recorded for endless routine repetition. For that reason, I do not believe that any radical readjustment of personally-performed music as we have known it in the past is necessary.

The influence of radio in this connection will take the form, rather, of providing for artists, both young and old, the world's greatest testing ground and laboratory. In that lies intrinsic value and importance to all concerned. Here, in the natural order, and hence harmoniously, the individual comes first, at the same time permitting co-existence with the practical advance of civilization and mass-production. With its mammoth support and innumerable contacts, radio in a new and striking sense reflects public taste and serves as an invaluable guide and asset toward immediate benefits in a healthy music and concert field.

It is not easy to exaggerate the warm intimacy and true dignity which radio adds to personally-performed music. Its happy faculty of drawing leaders from almost every field of endeavor is exemplified by the spirit and vision with which those leaders have seized and made use of this opportunity. We can quickly appreciate the resulting benefits to the arts and artists. While such cooperation is almost imperative in this day and age, yet the calibre and character of our leaders persuade us to expect still greater things of radio. Incidentally here is a very definite indication that whatever necessary adjustments the future brings will be marked by intelligence, sympathy and understanding.

The response to my own activities and contributions to radio along such lines over many happy years has been most gratifying, indeed, especially in the light of the fact that we have always been on a strictly non-commercial basis. That, I believe, is a good indication of a fine public taste and attitude toward both the individual and mass-produced art.

This country has been charged time and time again with materialism. What a striking rebuke it is to our adversaries, when one considers the millions upon millions of dollars which America has liberally poured into radio to speed up still further its improvement and refinement! America's attitude, from the topmost leader down, has been "spare no expense and give us the best." There need be no fear of our own future—or that of art among us—when such an attitude is typically native to our people.

While only generally acquainted with television to date, I can not believe that it will bring about any such thing as revolution in the arts. For that matter, it will only be an added complement to radio, for of necessity radio will be the heart and center of it, and its eventual refinement and success will be but the final step in the revolution which radio itself has brought to the arts.

A New Art in Birth-Throes

By David Sarnoff

THE latest child of the electrical arts is still in the birth-throes of development. It will require careful nurturing if it is to grow into a great public service. In the present stage of public interest, it would be easy to cry, "Television is here." It would be easy, and it might be profitable, but it would not advance the day when sight is added to sound in an adequate service to the home.

The problem of television is not merely the problem of making a magic box, through the peep-hole of which one may view diminutive reflections of passing men and events. The fundamental principles are well understood. The greater problems of television are those inherent in the limited channels of transmission presently available through the air, and these are largely bound up in the secrets of space.

But no greater inspiration could move scientific thought. No vaster array of scientific forces has ever been focussed upon a single problem. Nearly every fundamental development in the science of electrical communications bears directly or indirectly upon the problems of sight broadcasting. I am convinced, therefore, that within three to five years we shall be well launched into the dawning of the age of sight transmission by radio.

Clearly, the mission of television is to bring to the home the panorama of life of the great world outside. To a large extent radio has already brought the opera, the concert stage, the theatre to the fireside. Television will complete the picture by bringing to the home the visual spectacle made possible by the stagecraft of the opera and the theatre; the stirring events of life that must be seen as well as heard in order to make their due impression.

In the field of education, television will add the force of demonstration to the exposition made possible by the present-day status of broadcasting. The development of television, the next step in radio progress, will give a new meaning to educational programs by radio. Sight added to sound should create a new educational medium.

Industry, it is not unlikely, will find in television as valuable a means of communication to the home as it has already discovered in the broadcasting of sound. Effective as may be the modern machinery of exploitation, it is the unique promise of television that a new product or a new method, not to mention the standard commodities of industry, may be introduced simultaneously into millions of homes, when the art has sufficiently developed to be placed upon a regular and continuous service basis.

In the meantime radio continues to chart new paths industrially as well as scientifically. We are still largely in the throes of ancient conceptions of the forces that made for or against industrial and commercial growth. Competition is still worshipped as the life of trade, denounced as an uneconomic force, embraced as a balance between buying and selling interest—nursed upon one hand and hated upon the other. More recently, too, there has been raised before us the specter of gigantic competition as between industry and industry, wherein wheat and meat are to struggle for primacy, where coal and oil are to engage in a combat, where coffee and milk are to race for the public cup, wherein cotton and silk are to fight for favor.

Instead of a gory battlefield, the struggle between the giants of industry for the public ear and the public purse, brought to a focus by the "new competition," may well result in a love feast. Aided by present-day machinery of education and exploitation, both wheat and meat, for instance, in their struggle for supremacy, may be found to have forged ahead in public favor.

No better instance of industrial adaptation can be cited than the present situation in the phonograph industry. For the fact of the matter is that while the phonograph of the pre-radio age is thoroughly dead, the modern electrical phonograph is both alive and flourishing. Today the products of both the phonograph and radio industries are housed in the same cabinet, often distributed by the same wholesalers and sold by the same dealers.

Today television is emerging from the laboratory and preparing to enter the home. Progress both in the educational and entertainment arts will be stimulated by the home. There is little in the field of cultural education which cannot be visioned for the home through the new facilities of electrical communication. Every household equipped for reception· may, at certain times, become an art gallery. The Louvre and Metropolitan could then extend their cultural influence to millions of firesides. Just as sound broadcasting has brought a new sense of musical appreciation to millions of people, so could television open a new era of art appreciation.

It will not be possible for the home theatre to approach the exact conditions of the public theatre in the field of complete entertainment. The gregarious instincts of man will always lead him to desire to share his pleasures with his fellow men. Mechanically, artistically, psychologically, the public theatre as a focal point for mass entertainment promises to continue as a permanent factor.

With mass entertainment expressing itself through the public theatre and through the broadcasting stations, and with the vast variety of selective entertainment and educational programs forecast in the home, the field for creative talent becomes ever widening. The inspiration and opportunity for creative talent should be multiplied manifold by the enlarged cultural conception of entertainment which selective programs will make possible. There is no saturation point in the vast public interest in everything that amuses, entertains, informs or instructs. The new age of electrical entertainment which will bring the artist to the public, the lecturer to his audience and the educator to his student body, offers a vast field of opportunity to creative talent.

The Novel in Transition

By Louis Bromfield

I

Within the past ten years the term "revolt" has been tossed about rather loosely in the world of the arts. The tossing began, I think, some time before the War when, in France, a handful of individuals representing various arts grew restless and began plotting a variety of bombs and conflagrations. Few, if any of them were in the true sense artists. They were able, however, to use the experiments of artists as material for their campaigns, for there was at the moment a considerable number of talented and distinguished men engaged in finding new ways to do old things. Being artists, these men were interested in their own problems, working in solitude to achieve ideals known only to themselves. The "revolt" was the product of the excitable young men who issued manifestos, created riots in theatres and launched new revues. It began in·France and spread elsewhere.

Such, in brief, is one history of the Revolt in the Arts 1900–1930. Now that the smoke has begun to clear away, the revolt appears much less serious than we supposed. The Dadaists have passed away having diverted the world for a little while, and all the arts show signs of settling down into a long and rich period of production. Picassos no longer seem odd to the public and even the most conventional of novel readers swallow, unnoticed, new manners and methods, which ten years ago would have choked them. What looked for a time like the end of the world appears, from a decent perspective, to have been only a slight conflagration.

II

We, in America, were the latest and the least affected. How deeply we were affected remains to be seen. In another five years we shall possibly be able to judge more clearly.

In order to analyze the effect of the revolt upon the novel it is, I think, necessary to attack it from two sides. (1) From the point of view of material. (2) From the point of view of manner or method.

If we define material as the content of a novel, the first concerns both public and censor. It has, I think, nothing to do with any revolt but rather with the swinging of the pendulum which makes one thing the fashion in one generation and its opposite fashionable during the succeeding generation. What was scandalous yesterday becomes merely boring today. We flatter ourselves, I think, when we assume that in the present decade we have attained a new peak of frankness. We have still a long way to go before we outdistance the Georgians in grossness of speech or the Restoration in cynical morality. We are, perhaps, more scientific in our novels and our conversations. We happen to know more of physiology, neurasthenia and sanitation. That is all.

The frankness, cynicism and bawdiness of our day is much less the product of any revolt than it is of the times. By 1914 we had already begun to tire of the special prudery and romance of our grandfathers. The War finished those things. A war makes the world frank and bawdy and terrestrial. Otherwise it would be unendurable. And·the young writers who emerged from the War did so with a bad attack of bitterness and disillusionment. It is only now, twelve years after, that they are recovering. The embryo writers were even worse. "We will," they said, "always call a spade worse than a spade." It is only now they are beginning to rediscover the virtues of subtlety.

No revolt taking place among a small group of writers could have altered the principles and the point of view of the whole literate public. It could not have forced frankness down the throat of the man in the street if he had not, himself, been hungry for frankness. We should, I think, have been just as frank in 1930 if there had never been a literary revolt.

As to manner and method, one must accede much to the "revolt." The evidence is all about us. One has only to pick up any novel written before 1914 to see the vast difference between it and the novels written by the important younger and middle-aged novelists during the last decade. Material for novels has remained the same but fashions in writing novels have changed. There are new ways of getting inside the heart and the mind of a character, new ways of setting forth his story, and for these changes we are, beyond dispute, indebted to the handful of experimenters, English and French, who as individuals wearied of old formulas which had been demonstrated to the point of perfection and sought to discover new ways which have not as yet become formulas. Of these, the names of James Joyce, Virginia Woolf, Dorothy Richardson and Gertrude Stein seem the most important. They, and a few less important experimenters, did find new and valuable ways. "Ulysses," "Mrs. Dalloway" and the "History of an American" are, in a sense, textbooks and it may be that they will survive principally as literary curiosities, but they are gold mines of instruction to young writers seeking to broaden and enrich the traditions of the English novel. Imperceptibly, through a process of literary and intellectual filtration, the experiments of this group are being accepted unrecognized as such by the literate public. Less radical writers have consciously or otherwise drawn much profit from them.

III

It is the habit of critical minds to appraise and classify novelists as romantic, realistic, naturalistic, classicist and lately as humanistic with the inference, subtle to be sure, that the novelist will accept the ticket bestowed upon him and rest content. In these ten years and more of transition in all the arts, this labelling process has become increasingly difficult. The younger novelists and some of the older ones have upset the applecart and mixed together all manner of styles, traditions and innovations. They have taken to writing what they want to write in the way they choose to write it, using bits of romanticism, realism and what you will all in one piece of work, striving for an effect by using the best possible means to achieve this end. Such a method does not, perhaps, produce a "pure" and devitalized bit of work, but it does achieve for the novel a new kind of freedom and virility, which in the last analysis is the most important quality of all. That much, if nothing else, the "revolt" has achieved. A writer may solve his problem as he chooses with no critical tickets glued arbitrarily to his artistic baggage. He is free.

The whole revolt is, I think, less planned and deliberate than many critical writers would have us believe. Miss Woolf, Miss Stein and Mr. Joyce did not gird up their loins and set out upon a crusade. They worked as artists to solve the individual problem they set for themselves. Others to be sure, both writers and readers, have profited by their experiments. The rest is accident, unless we are willing to accept as effective the campaigns and the propaganda launched by their satellites.

Schools and traditions in writing, even critical appraisals, are of very little importance to the novel except in an historical sense. A school usually means one fine writer surrounded by a group of satellites with meager talents. Tradition is unescapable. It steals up jogging the writer's elbow when he least expects it. Even Mr. Joyce has not escaped it, but taking the bull by the horns has turned it to his own uses. Critics are valuable to ticket and classify and appraise fifty years after. At the moment the important thing is freedom, and that has been achieved. The novelist who is worth his salt will always write what he wants to write in the way he wants to write it, but it is easier for him today than it has ever been before; his audience having been prepared for experiment is not openly hostile.

The "revolt" (if there was ever such a thing) is nearly over. It was, I think, more a transition than a revolt, and now that the transition is beginning to fade, we may look for magnificent new things which could not have been written, or even conceived, twenty-five years ago. The writing of the latest quarter century will go down, I suspect, as the writing of a transition period, when great things were accomplished and literary curiosities were created. Freedom of manner, of idea, of material is a fact. The censor, I think, must not trouble us too much. He is born of his day and the Puritan censor is quite different from the censor of the Restoration. Any novelist has a distaste for censorship, but we shall never be able to escape it in a world which daily grows more democratic, for censorship is as much a product of democracy as it is of a dictatorship. Even the bureaucracy of Russia accepts it as a necessity. The censorship of taste is the only sound censorship and that should be exercised at the source by the novelist himself. There is no thought—no action, which cannot be recorded without offense, and almost anything can be made offensive by manner or method.

Whether in the process of time, the literature of this transition will assay as pure gold, remains to be seen. It will, I think, possess if nothing else the qualities of intelligence, virility and intellectual curiosity. It will always remain stimulating and even, perhaps, exciting and all of these qualities are fine ones. Certain names will certainly remain as typical of their period if for no other reason— the names of Joyce, Woolf, Stein, Huxley, Hemingway, Cocteau, Giraudoux and a great many others. Proust was the last great illumination of a period that was moribund, and Joyce the first flare of a new epoch. Between comes the transition which may or may not have been a "revolt."

The Anglo-Saxon novel has always been a chronicle and comment of the times. Clearly it has a new branch, and the new branch is a very sturdy limb, almost, indeed, a new tree springing from the roots of the old—a new limb which is the American novel.

For the first time the sense of division is unmistakably clear. The best American novels of the past ten years have been written by Americans of America. They could never have happened in England. The period before us is the one in which we may look for great things and these things will be written without regard for classicism, romanticism, realism and humanism or any other dim-colored labels. They will be written, I think, by novelists as free as Tolstoy and Dostoievsky were free. "War and Peace" has yet to be surpassed. It was written without labels.

Modern Poetry

By Hart Crane

Modern poetry has long since passed the crest of its rebellion against many of the so-called classical strictures. Indeed the primary departures of the early intransigeants were often more in a classic direction, with respect to certain neglected early European traditions, than were many of the Victorian regulations that formed the immediate butt of attack.

Revolution flourishes still, but rather as a contemporary tradition in which the original obstacles to freedom have been, if not always eradicated, at least obscured by floods of later experimentation. Indeed, to the serious artist, revolution as an all-engrossing program no longer exists. It persists at a rapid momentum in certain groups or movements, but often in forms which are more constricting than liberating, in view of a generous choice of subject matter.

The poet's concern must be, as always, self-discipline toward a formal integration of experience. For poetry is an architectural art, based not on Evolution or the idea of progress, but on the articulation of the contemporary human consciousness *sub specie aeternitatis,* and inclusive of all readjustments incident to science and other shifting factors related to that consciousness. The key to the process of free creative activity which Coleridge gave us in his "Lectures on Shakespeare" exposes the responsibilities of every poet, modern or ancient, and cannot be improved upon. "No work of true genius," he says, "dares want its appropriate form, neither indeed is there any danger of this. As it must not, so genius can not, be lawless: for it is even this that constitutes its genius—*the power of acting creatively under laws of its own origination.*"

Poetry has at once a greater intimacy and a wider, more exact scope of implication than painting or any of the other arts. It is therefore more apt to be indicative of impending changes in other media such as painting or music. This is a logical deduction that facts do not always favor, as in the case of some modern composers such as Stravinsky, the full purport of whose inspiration seems to lie beyond the reach of current literary expression. Literature has a more tangible relationship to painting; and it is highly probable that the Symbolist movement in French poetry was a considerable factor in the instigation first, of Impressionism, and later, of Cubism. Both arts have had parallel and somewhat analogous tendencies toward abstract statement and metaphysical representation. In this recent preoccupation it is certain that both media were responding to the shifting emphasis of the Western World away from religion toward science. Analysis and discovery, the two basic concerns of science, became conscious objectives of both painter and poet. A great deal of modern painting is as independent of any representational motive as a mathematical equation; while some of the most intense and eloquent current verse derives sheerly from acute psychological analysis, quite independent of any dramatic motivation.

The function of poetry in a Machine Age is identical to its function in any other age; and its capacities for presenting the most complete synthesis of human values remain essentially immune from any of the so-called inroads of science. The emotional stimulus of machinery is on an entirely different psychic plane from that of poetry. Its only menace lies in its capacities for facile entertainment, so easily accessible as to arrest the development of any but the most negligible esthetic responses. The ultimate influence of machinery in this respect remains to be seen, but its firm entrenchment in our lives has already produced a series of challenging new responsibilities for the poet.

For unless poetry can absorb the machine, i. e., *acclimatize* it as naturally and casually as trees, cattle, galleons, castles and all other human associations of the past, then poetry has failed of its full contemporary function. This process does not infer any program of lyrical pandering to the taste of those obsessed by the importance of machinery; nor does it essentially involve even the specific mention of a single mechanical contrivance. It demands, however, along with the traditional qualifications of the poet, an extraordinary capacity for surrender, at least temporarily, to the sensations of urban life. This presupposes, of course, that the poet possesses sufficient spontaneity and gusto to convert this experience into positive terms. Machinery will tend to lose its sensational glamour and appear in its true subsidiary order in human life as use and continual poetic allusion subdue its novelty. For, contrary to general prejudice, the wonderment experienced in watching nose dives is of less immediate creative promise to poetry than the familiar gesture of a motorist in the modest act of shifting gears. I mean to say that mere romantic speculation on the power and beauty of machinery keeps it at a continual remove; it can not act creatively in our lives until, like the unconscious nervous responses of our bodies, its connotations emanate from within—forming as spontaneous a terminology of poetic reference as the bucolic world of pasture, plow and barn.

The familiar contention that science is inimical to poetry is no more tenable than the kindred notion that theology has been proverbially hostile—with the "Commedia" of Dante to prove the contrary. That "truth" which science pursues is radically different from the metaphorical, extra-logical "truth" of the poet. When Blake wrote that "a tear is an intellectual thing, And a sigh is the sword of an Angel King"—he was not in any logical conflict with the principles of the Newtonian Universe. Similarly, poetic prophecy in the case of the seer, has nothing to do with factual prediction or with futurity. It is a peculiar type of perception, capable of apprehending some absolute and timeless concept of the imagination with astounding clarity and conviction.

That the modern poet can profitably assume the roles of philosopher or theologian is questionable at best. Science, the uncanonized Deity of the times, seems to have automatically displaced the hierarchies of both Academy and Church. It is pertinent to cite the authors of the "Commedia" and "Paradise Lost" as poets whose verse survives the religious dogmas and philosophies of their respective periods, but it is fallacious to assume that either of these poets could have written important religious verse without the fully developed and articulated religious dogmas that each was heir to.

The future of American poetry is too complicated a speculation to be more than approached in this limited space. Involved in it are the host of considerations relative to the comparative influences of science, machinery and other factors which I have merely touched upon;—besides those influential traditions of early English prosody which form points of departure, at least, for any indigenous rhythms and forms which may emerge. The most typical and valid expression of the American *psychosis* seems to me still to be found in Whitman. His faults as a technician, and

his clumsy and indiscriminate enthusiasm are somewhat beside
the point. He, better than any other, was able to coordinate those
forces in America which seem most intractable, fusing them into
a universal vision which takes on additional significance as time
goes on. He was a revolutionist beyond the strict meaning of
Coleridge's definition of genius, but his bequest is still to be
realized in all its implications.

The New Biography

By Gamaliel Bradford

THERE is little that is new, in literature or in anything else. The same instincts, the same tendencies, manifest themselves, repeat themselves, renew themselves, in more or less elaborate developments, then disappear and give way to others. Still, in general it may be said that up to the middle of the Nineteenth Century there were three main motives in the writing of biography. There was first the impulse of plain record, the desire to retain and perpetuate the story of great men's lives, of what they had done and how they had done it. More than this, apparently irresistible and inescapable, was the desire of eulogy. The biographer's first duty was to exalt his subject, to emphasize his virtues and attenuate his weaknesses, to differentiate him from the common mass of mankind and represent him as having achieved things quite out of the reach of the humble rest of us, who travel the dusty round of day to day. Even biographers so sane and so skilful as Boswell and Lockhart did not escape this tendency, and while the minute chronicler of Johnson's career professes to analyze his humanity, he manages to suggest and imply his divinity at every step. The third object and purpose of biography was to set an example. What had great men lived for, if not to teach us how we ought to live, whether we can or not? And with this exemplary ideal there was even more disposition to conceal the defects and emphasize the excellencies. For us in America the typical case of the exemplary biography is the great production of the assiduous Parson Weems in dealing with Washington. But it is not Washington alone, but a host of others, whose lives have been virtuously disfigured and distorted, so that they might serve as useful and effective models for the training of the younger generation.

The spirit of revolt, so characteristic of the Twentieth Century, as of some others, showed itself in nothing more ardently and strenuously than in the rebellion against these somewhat artificial tendencies in biography. Of what use was it to make a record of facts when the facts were altered and colored to suit ulterior purposes? How could eulogy serve any profitable end when it was based on lies? And could there be any real, substantial benefit of example in setting a figure up on a pedestal, so remote and so intangible that the younger generation was not inclined to imitate it, nor capable of the imitation even if it were desired.

Therefore the cry was, give us fact, give us truth, and let the eulogy go. Reduce these historical figures to their true proportions, let us see them as they were, in their actual humanity. If their grandeur, if their exemplary dignity, are somewhat diminished in the process what matter? No grandeur, no dignity can long avail, when it is based on a lie.

No doubt there were baser elements mingled with this ostensible passion for truth. There was the journalistic impulse to produce an immediate sensation. There was the sordid desire to make profit out of vulgar curiosity, to emphasize gossip and scandal, as remote from the truth as the eulogy of an earlier day, and much more damaging. Yet in sane and healthy spirits the protest against the more artificial type of biography was normal and beneficial, and the natural response to this protest at once appeared in the singular popularity which biography has enjoyed for the last ten years. Men like to admire, they like to praise, they like to imitate, but in the end they have a respect for truth, and when they feel that it is being really offered to them, they turn to it with avidity.

But, as always if revolt is to be permanently fruitful, there was here a deeper and constructive tendency and meaning. And the new biography, like almost every other branch of human thought and human action, was showing the influence of the scientific spirit. The great intellectual movement of the middle Nineteenth Century, which is most typified in Darwin, affected not only science, but philosophy and theology, and even politics and economics. It was vitally active in the various forms of literature. The whole treatment of history was modified by the new passion for simple truth in itself. Realism in fiction was merely a manifestation of the same intellectual tendency. And the new biography is preeminently the desire to study facts, to relate them, and to analyze their larger, profounder bearing and significance, precisely as Darwin investigated the facts of natural history.

The supreme name in biography of this type, though even yet the supremacy is not recognized as it should be, is the name of Charles Augustin Sainte-Beuve. Sainte-Beuve was as perfect an embodiment of the scientific spirit as Darwin. He said of himself, "I botanize, I herborize, I am a Naturalist of Souls." He studied human beings for what they were, with the profoundest sympathy for all nobleness and the profoundest understanding for all weakness, because weakness and nobleness alike were human. And the value of Sainte-Beuve's work lies not only in its penetration and in its delicacy, but in its vast extent. He made perhaps seven or eight hundred studies of different human souls. No such collection has ever been made before, or will ever be made again, and it embalms dreamer and doer, lover and hater, man and woman, sinner and saint.

This scientific treatment of biography means the study of human beings as phenomena in the movement of the universe and the development of life. It involves the nice, subtle analysis and discrimination of motives and the delicate tracing of those motives as they evolve in act. It implies the careful investigation of the relation of one human being to others, the profound probing of antecedents and influences, so curious, so inter-related, so far-reaching, so difficult to detect and disentangle. But always, in this obscure and complicated web of relations, the supreme object of biography is the individual, and this distinguishes it alike from history and from psychology, both of which seek to use the individual to illustrate larger movements and principles. To biography the individual is all, is the centre of the universe, and general principles serve only to illustrate the individual soul.

Yet at the same time, under the study of each individual, there is the consciousness of the common, universal humanity, without which the study of the individual would be merely curious. On the surface we may be impressed with the vast diversity of life, and this diversity supplies endless matter for fascinated speculation. But the real, fundamental matter of biography is the human nature that is common to all of us, and the protest of the new biography is precisely founded in the fact that great men are the same as we are and not forever different. If they had not our passions, our aspirations, our hopes, and our despairs, why should we care for them? If they had not something of our weakness, how could we ever possibly achieve their strength?

The secret of biography, the reason it takes hold of mankind and will take hold ever more and more, is that biography is just simply the story of you and me, and that is and always will be the most enthralling story in the world.

Speed and the Essayist

By William Lyon Phelps

During the middle of the Nineteenth Century the essay flourished abundantly in America. Our most versatile man of letters, James Russell Lowell, was magnificently equipped. He was a scholar in ancient and modern languages, he seemed to have read everything, and his wit was as spontaneous as foam on the sea. When he wrote on Chaucer, for example, he wrote out of a rich knowledge of Fourteenth Century life and literature, out of a thorough familiarity with the English language of that period, and out of a natural kinship with Chaucer's boundless sympathy with all manifestations of human nature.

Besides the essays of Lowell, where the art of literary criticism reached its height, there were essayists of a different type, who wrote works of genius, permanent additions to the literature of the world. I refer of course to Emerson and Thoreau.

Lowell himself gave one reason for the decline of the essay; for toward the close of the Nineteenth Century, and during the early years of the Twentieth, the essay as a literary form went into almost total eclipse in America. In speaking of the long, golden days of the Eighteenth Century, a repose of mind symbolized by the roomy armchairs in which men reclined at ease, Lowell said that in those days "responsibility for the universe had not been invented."

The essay in its true form represents culture, and there can be no culture without leisure. The essay is seldom dynamic, as a novel or a play or a poem may well be and so often is. No matter how virile the mind from which the essay comes, it must come from that mind in a state of relaxation.

Now toward the end of the Nineteenth Century, the age of machines began to assume its present domination. The transition from the eighties to the second decade in the Twentieth Century was so swift, so sweeping, and so violent that the period of 1885 seems as remote as the period of Julius Caesar.

Invention followed invention, and the whole manner of living was transformed. Such violent and startling changes were by no means favorable to the production of good essays, whether essays in literary criticism, or "personal" essays.

For nothing is more certain than this: every time-saving device has left us with less time. The one characteristic of our present age is SPEED. The difference between now and a hundred years ago has been well expressed by the man who said that when a stagecoach left Boston every other day for New York, a traveller was not vexed if he missed it; he simply took the next stage, two days later. But now, a man is excited if he misses one leaf in a revolving door.

It is not an uncommon sight to see a man with his hair being cut, his shoes being shined, his nails being manicured, while a secretary takes dictation.

But while Speed is our motto, we are now becoming used to it. It is as natural to travel fifty miles an hour in an automobile, as it used to be to make eight miles an hour with a horse and carriage. But it took time to become used to this acceleration, as it did to various other inventions. Now we look around, take stock of ourselves, and criticism follows naive enjoyment. Hence the recrudescence of the essay in the last few years.

Machines were made for men, and not men for machines. Human nature has not changed, and personality has not been destroyed. Machines will eventually become our servants, not our masters. The essayist will either consciously or unconsciously express this.

Our magazines and newspapers, by accommodating themselves immediately to every new change or advance in customs, manners, and ways of life, have unintentionally acted as a formidable and at least temporarily successful rival to the essay. Just one amusing illustration will suffice. A certain publisher asked a scholar-clergyman to write a brief, vigorous Life of Christ, wherein the style should be adapted to the comprehension of the man in the street. The clergyman did his best to "write down" on this sacred theme. But when the publisher read his manuscript, he said, "Oh, this won't do at all. What I want is a snappy Life of Christ!"

The Tabloid has invaded every field of information.

Europe has suffered from the transition to the machine age although not so sharply as America, because the transition has not been so sudden. Still, today, England has no Matthew Arnold, France has no Sainte-Beuve, Scandinavia has no Brandes. But the roots of European culture go deeper, and a weekly literary review like the *London Times Literary Supplement* is on a higher plane than anything of a similar style in America.

In our machine age, the essayist cannot retire to his Ivory Tower and view the landscape o'er. He must live in and with his times. He must be at the heart of things.

During the last ten years, there has been an enormous increase in America of interest in contemporary literature. I ascribe this partly to the fact above mentioned that we are getting used to our environment—machines are becoming familiar—and also to a heightened alertness of mind, which takes an interest in every form of literary expression. Lotze said that To Be is to be in Relations; the more connections we have with things and ideas the more we are alive. Well, we are living in an age of super-vitality; and the rebirth and increasing vogue of the essay is an inevitable result.

The Newspaper as Literature

By Heywood Broun

THE newspaper can and does serve the cause of literature directly by affording the most fertile field now in existence for the short essay. One might point to the work of the late William Bolitho as a case in point. If Mr. Bolitho had been introduced for the first time to the reading public between covers, he might have attracted very scant attention. The word "Essay" is forbidding. It suggests something encountered in a school room. "Required reading" is the immediate reaction of the unconscious mind. But call your essay a newspaper column and the curse comes off.

The fact that the subjects must have some hint of timeliness does not detract from their potential literary value. Indeed some of Mr. Bolitho's best pieces appeared in the daily columns of *The World*. Nor would I limit newspaper literature to the work of columnists. Many brilliant contributions have been made by journalistic dramatic critics. Book reviewing, I feel, is on a somewhat lower scale as far as the newspapers are concerned. Much news reporting is of necessity ephemeral, but, hardly a week passes in which some event does not inspire vivid and racy writing of first-rate sort.

Newspaper experience may be of great value in giving a writer the opportunity to see life and know people. It helped Mencken and Dreiser and Sinclair Lewis. But I feel that newspaper writing may be an end in itself. The literary merit of any piece of prose is neither increased nor decreased by inclusion between book covers.

The opportunities for a writer in journalism have increased in the last twenty years. We are getting away from the notion that every paper must be an organic whole and there is consequently more chance for individuality in both style and opinion. I have already cited Bolitho and I might add the names of Walter Lippmann, Franklin P. Adams, Irvin Cobb, George Ade, Frank Ward O'Malley and Frank Cobb. The editorials in the *Baltimore Sun,* the *New York World,* the *St. Louis Post Dispatch,* the Scripps-Howard papers, the *Emporia Gazette* and the *Springfield Republican* seem to me in many cases worthy of the status of essay.

Newspapers are still more addicted to the recording of life than to its interpretation. However, every newspaper "column" is necessarily interpretive and this function is exercised chiefly by special and editorial writers,—both Brisbane and Will Rogers may be cited as important interpreters of the American scene even though it may be true that their comment is frequently far from profound.

Few papers grant complete intellectual freedom to their writers. Nevertheless there is a tendency to greater liberality. This will come through the abandonment of the theory that the newspaper has but one voice. As far as I know, the Scripps-Howard papers have gone the furthest in extending hospitality to dissenting opinion by members of their own staffs.

Of the Making of Books

By Harrison Smith

Everyone has been hearing a great deal in these days in the press about that interesting profession, the publishing of books. It is the result actually of the depression in business and trade through which the country has been going since the stock market break ten months ago. The public decided that the future was uncertain, to say the least, and began, as every merchant knows, to cut down the purchase of articles that it did not strictly need. Fortunately, to a great many people books are as necessary to intelligent life as motor cars and radio sets, so that this recent decline in the number of book purchases throughout the country did not strike to the heart of the business, but affected only people who bought books occasionally through pressure of their friends and through advertising, and it also affected radically those books, too many, unfortunately, which perhaps should never have been published at all.

The publishing of books, however, no matter how efficient any individual house may be, cannot be classed with the manufacture and sale of necessities, or indeed of highly advertised luxuries for which advertising has prepared the public mind. The average book reader does not go to a book store and simply demand a book, but usually a certain specific book. This is hardly true of the readers of a standardized product like a detective story or what we call "Westerns," but it is certainly true of the great mass of books published—they are sought for and bought individually because they have been recommended to the purchaser or because the purchaser has read a previous book by the author and seeks another. The individual book publisher, unless his business is stabilized by a successful department for school and college text-books, religious books, or some other standardized product, is therefore in somewhat the same position as a theatrical producer. He brings out a series of books each season, the majority of which are theoretically a gamble with his knowledge of what the public wants. It can be seen that where the public taste has so largely entered a business it is impossible to become completely mechanized, or perhaps in the eyes of the average business man or banker, completely efficient. If a man manufactures radios or clothing or cereal he may have a very shrewd idea of just exactly what his market is going to be for the next six months. It is true that the publishers and the book stores appear to be behind the times when their business is compared with the high-pressure salesmanship and efficiency of the great businesses of the United States, but in times of depression like the present the publisher has become aware that he must in some way find broader outlets than he is reaching through the book stores of the country.

It is probable, however, that since the American public devotes most of its time to reading magazines of all sorts and newspapers, until this great public is trained to buy and read more books, the book stores with the new outlets—the chain stores and drug stores —will prove to be sufficient for the intelligent and wise producer of books. For that reason I believe strongly in every one of the methods for attaining a larger reading public, even if some of them would seem to be a definite injury to a publisher's business. An increase in the circulating libraries and the book clubs, for example, means that many more readers are found for a single volume and on the surface it would appear that this was cutting down the sales of books. On the other hand, there must be thousands of people who would not read at all if they could not find their books in the public or circulating libraries, or the Book Clubs. For a long time I believe that the publisher must have something of the missionary about him, that he must be willing to reach as large an audience as possible for his books, no matter how that audience is found.

A great responsibility actually rests on the publishers of this country. The literary output that they foster; the authors whom they help support while their early works are maturing, are actually creating the literary product of the country and consequently forming the ideas of hundreds of thousands of people. It is this fostering of new writers and first books that constitutes an extraordinary burden on the publishing business, but which is absolutely necessary for the progressive publisher. It is obvious to anyone that the older writers are declining in sale and general interest to the public and that we must continue discovering the new writers and the new books if we are not to have the business of publishing in the doldrums ten years from now. A large percentage of the dollar books and seventy-five cent books have been with us for a long time, since it is no new thing to have a successful book reprinted after its first or second year and sell in the hands of capable publishers of reprints often many times more copies than the original full-price volume. New books at a dollar are, it is true, a new experiment which everyone, publisher and bookstore manager, is watching with great eagerness. Here again it will be seen that unless the public wants a book the price makes little difference. A badly written or a dull book at fifty cents is a poor purchase. The book is literally worth nothing except the paper that it's printed on. The detective stories and standardized romances which are appearing at a low price I believe will continue to be successful. They are books, on the whole, that are read hastily, often in one sitting, and they should be thrown away. They are not worth encumbering the limited space that we have on our book shelves today.

The future of publishing seems to me to depend on two things—restoration of the confidence of the public in its financial future, so that men and women will not hesitate to buy a new book at full price if they happen to want it; and on the other hand the building up of a new group of important American writers whose books will automatically sell in the fifties and hundreds of thousands some time in the future. This we must have, and it is for this that the book readers of the country will have to look toward the editors and the heads of publishing houses who are arbiters of American literary taste. The details of the business, discounts to book dealers, the price of books, and so on, can well be adjusted after we have arrived at this successful end and it is as certain as the sun rises that we will arrive, that we will have an American literature which will make any American proud no matter in what land he finds himself, and a public here eager to buy the works of the writers they have learned to love and admire, and willing to pay an honest price that will enable the author to live as he's entitled to live, and incidentally the publisher to flourish in his own moderate way.

Learning by Working on the Job

By Boardman Robinson

Ten years of teaching painting and drawing have made me dubious of the value of the art school and of art teaching in general as currently understood. Highly accomplished and technically skilful artists are turned off by the thousand, but, in the very best of the product, the modern craze for freedom of expression tends to emphasize the idiosyncratic and the eccentric, while the material significance of form and the capacity for communicating that significance are neglected.

The sociological influences of the Nineteenth Century set the artist apart to a degree previously unknown. He became detached from the common life because society offered him so little opportunity to appeal to other than those especially interested in the arts. In short, he was not needed, and, as a result, and quite naturally, the world has come to regard him with some degree of contempt; though secretly envying him the indulgence of freedom and eccentricity, even at the expense of poverty.

Apart from the designing of textiles and various forms of ornament—for mural painting is just emerging from the trivial stage—it has come about that only in the practice of illustration and the cartoon has the painter been able to feel that he is performing any social function. In the field of the easel picture he has had no hope for a living unless he could sell for a fairly high price, with the result that he finds his product either isolated in a rich man's home or displayed in a museum, a kind of curio.

There is now much talk of Revolt in the Arts. Truly, there is evidence of some such thing; and, without doubt, the tendency is a healthy one. But, from my point of view, a new movement of any significance involves a return to first principles; as Greek art was revitalized by the Egyptian, and Italian art in turn, by the Greek. So, we must return to the main stream, the fundamental principle which lies at the root of all the ancient arts—to a true concept of the classic formula. An examination of this art of the past which we are commonly agreed to call great will reveal astonishingly little of what we refer to as the individuality of the artist. In the case of Egyptian and Chaldaean art, none whatever. These arts being produced to convey meanings, there was no opportunity for the injection of what today we call the conditioned personality of the author.

It seems to me that in a similar way our arts must reach outward instead of inward; in an effort to interpret universal principles, rather than personal reactions. Only by that recourse shall we find means of restoring art to dignity and significance. Already architects are beginning to think again in terms of materials and function instead of archaeology and picturesqueness. In association with architecture lies the opportunity of the painter and sculptor to restore the plastic arts to their historic utility, a practical value which need not be incompatible with that search for the unattainable which distinguishes the genuine artist from the mere craftsman.

Most of the great painting of the past was spread upon walls, in cooperation with architecture, in public places, and the same was relatively true of sculpture.

Now, it seems possible that in our present tendency to mass production lies a way out of the excessive state of subjectivity into which the plastic arts have fallen. The projected Chicago exposition may present an opportunity for painters and sculptors to attack enormous areas and masses with the help of trained assistants or even journeymen craftsmen. Under such conditions it is hard to conceive of artists designing without a large motive. The fact that large spaces are unsuited to idiosyncratic treatment will encourage works not merely striking but significant of something more than ornamentation of surfaces. Such an opportunity may afford a means of producing a popular art without stooping to a low level of popular taste, but, by the use of form and color, to reach deep instincts, emotions and ideas underlying all the sociological influences from which humanity suffers. Such an attitude seems to me to be the secret of the great art of the past.

Opportunity for the real school lies in such large undertakings. Big jobs require assistants, who should be pupils in the best sense of the word, *working* on the job and learning in the actual practice all the master can teach, or, better still, learning *with* him. The business of doing something that has to be done, whether it suits one's own taste or not, should be of great disciplinary value to the student, and if he possesses any real individuality it should be strengthened by such experience. Especially if, in the process, he is learning the practice of his craft.

I should like to prescribe a still wider or, rather, more fundamental activity for the student. The schools specialize him too much, and current teaching deals almost exclusively with the appearance of things. We need to learn of the *nature* of things, how materials function, and how to use materials according to their nature—to learn to understand them. Speaking for myself, I should like to have had more than a smattering of experience with stone, wood and steel. Such training among other things tends to cure the artist of the neuroticism of which he is so often the victim. Provided a youth has an aim in such labor, and realizes that his artistic purpose is being furthered and not thwarted by such activity, he cannot fail to be benefited. The best artists of the Renaissance could do almost anything demanded of them.

To sum up, I should like to substitute the shop for the studio, the job for the *concours*. Perhaps the apprentice system in the old sense is impossible today, but we may approximate it.

Art Is, Was, and Ever Will Be

By John Sloan

There is undoubtedly something stirring in the spiritual life of mankind today which is bearing and will bear fruit in every branch of man's activities, and while, of course, the art of the painter will be affected, as the painter must be, by this spirit— this spirit of revolt—I can not think that there is today, nor need be, any revolt in the painter's art.

There is, I hope, another renaissance, a return to health, after the degeneration and near death through which painting has passed during the last one hundred and some years.

Social revolution must and will come. It is a stage in growth toward humanness—we have never yet been fully human—but the one reason for life is the growth toward being human.

Art is and always has been a sign of promise. Art has always marked the progress of mankind on this road. And while social relations have always needed improvement, have always been imperfect, *this is not so of the art of painting*. No revolt is necessary —only renaissance—new beginnings—a return to a mental viewpoint, in spite of the scientific facts of eyesight brought out by photography.

As I believe art to be the product of a creative urge and the result of a consciousness of life, I am inclined to deny the possibility of any art related to the painter's art resulting from machine or mass-production. I am not speaking of good art, or bad art—just art.

Likewise, to me, the painter's art has no mission to "interpret our Machine Age life."

For my part, and in the present instance, I am strongly inclined to deny the so prevalent statement that this is the "Machine Age" or that this is any more such than any of the ages before it.

The fact that there have been multiplications and improvements in machines can not be denied, but I think this is of little concern to the painter-artist.

The great number of mechanical devices of this day have no esthetic significance whatsoever. I can find doubt in my mind as to whether they have even complicated existence. They may lead to some social improvements but—there's the place where improvement is needed! Art is, was and ever will be.

If improving machines will make for more leisure, it will make for an increased number of artists, but as long as machines are used to save wages and not to save labor-time—as long as they are not owned by the workers—they will be the foes of human culture.

It is for the scientists to decide whether the painter can help him to understand life. Perhaps he can, although I do not think that it is necessary for the artist to do so.

If the painter is life-conscious and creates in response, he does his part. It seems, perhaps, unnecessary for the painter to "understand" even his own creations.

Censorship and Puritan morality have not hindered American art. Excuses must be sought elsewhere. The painter-artist is not affected by these Americanisms.

It is unnecessary to say that such things are of no help in producing artists.

The painter's language is like other written languages, an assembly of signs, symbols or signals.

The painter, while not entirely restricted to those known to his audience, must keep his own inventions simple and often repeated in order to be understood, and, later, accepted.

Imitators are of great assistance in extending the acceptance of new signs or symbols. Many American painters have thus been of great help to what is called the modern French School.

The painter is justified in painting "for himself" to any extent. The "consumers" of good pictures constitute such a small audience that he may never be conscious of their existence. Many failures can be accounted for by the mistake made by a painter who produces work in search for an audience. A mother does not use her children for bait.

Many energetic and creatively active American painters today are eager to turn their efforts to mural work, and this is a tendency of promising significance. Architects and owners control the situation, but there are painters who will be able to provide as good wall pictures as the architects may desire.

In this branch of painting, Mexico leads this hemisphere, if not the world. A nation of artists at our doors—and we seek France!

The importance of mural paintings, as an expression of the general interest of the people in art, and as a stimulant to that interest, is very great, and if architects will cooperate with painters, they may come into more general use. Conservative timidity is a factor that must be overcome.

The general trend of the time, while not of the best for the utilization of our painters, has elements of hope for the future. In fact, it may not be too much to say that we are about to do our share. We are the great unspanked baby of the world. We will become adult.

When we do, we will use our artists. They will be on hand.

To be without interest in paintings is to be without contact with about one fourth of the means of spiritual intercommunication. The American people will find that they need pictures.

The Sculptor Waits on the Architect

By Mahonri Young

THERE is nothing new and all our own in the modernistic development of sculpture in Machine Age America. What has come out of America has been a reflex of the development in Europe. It seems that we have to get our inspiration from Europe, no matter what we originate here.

In architecture, of course, the case has been very different. Beginning with Louis H. Sullivan, we had an architect who found his problems in the conditions of modern life and who created his new forms to meet the new conditions, helping thereby to develop the modern skyscraper. If Louis Sullivan had received enough support we would have had by now our own architecture, for out of Louis Sullivan grew Frank Lloyd Wright and Dwight H. Perkins and a group of other men, mostly from Chicago. Wright has used some sculpture designed in his own office and made to fit his own architecture. Sullivan did beautiful modeled decorations for his structures. Goodhue gave Lee Lawrie all kinds of opportunities on his churches, his public buildings and other structures, of which the Nebraska Capitol is perhaps the best known example. But as a general thing there has been little use of the art of sculpture in connection with architecture in America.

When architects use sculpture they seem to prefer the machine-made sculpture from the modeling shops. The main reason for this, in my opinion, is that most of our architects today have very little conception or understanding of what the other arts are or can do. Contrast the use of the best men of their day by McKim, Mead and White.

One of the unfortunate aspects of the practice of all the arts in the Machine Age is the desire for speed. This can be understood in the case of buildings where it is necessary to get them up in a short time and earn profits on the money invested. But why in monuments—things which are supposed to last forever? Why should they be done within six months or a year or even in a month or so? I don't see the need. There is no reason why the work of the sculptor and the mural painter in the modern world cannot be fulfilled after the owner has finished and rented his building. This would make for very much better quality of work.

Our buildings have a real picturesqueness at a distance. From afar, there is a great deal of beauty in the Daily News Building. But on closer inspection our structures fall down lamentably. The sculpture, the mouldings, the ornaments, and so forth, look as if they have been bought, not made. Few have seemed able to find ornament or ornamentation to fit our box-like, set-back buildings and give them a semblance of beauty and interest. Too often what is done is taken from copy books, old and new. All one needs to do is to look at our buildings to find whether they have a treatment at the top adequate to their height and significant for their use. And yet there should be innumerable opportunities for sculpture in this age.

Of course, people have tried to do things and God bless them for their tries. They don't try often enough. There is some good architectural sculpture on the porch of St. Bartholomew's done by Andrew O'Connor. This porch is purely derivative but beautiful.

The sculpture is not derivative in a derogatory sense but is rather a little too much of its exact time. Gutzon Borglum did some figures for the choir of St. John's which helped to make that part of the building triumph. There is certainly enough in American life for American art to express that ought to go on these buildings. Couture said years ago that we did not want the Apollo Belvederes of both sexes masquerading for all the virtues. There is such a thing as character and fitness. Painting and sculpture can mean something as well as being beautiful and can carry a lot of meaning. Mere symbol is not enough. It can be significant symbol with character or it can be absolutely meaningless symbol.

It is well to remember two or three facts. To begin with, the American people are not a new people; American civilization is not a new civilization; the American civilization is a continuation of the civilization of Europe; the people are a continuation of the people of Europe; and all we do here has been, and will be, a growth out of that continuation. We can't help taking on new characteristics, new aspects, and therein lies our opportunity. But to expect, as so many people do, that we over here will make an art resembling nothing gone before out of our clear, brilliant American air, is asking the impossible. It just can't be done. We do not lack national characteristics. The American is recognized almost immediately in any crowd in Europe as quickly even as any other European nationality. There is an expression running through our people, our literature, our art, which is definitely American. It is this which has been and will be our difference. We lack a little more universal quality. We ought to develop. We can't help changing. The American has taken on a different look, but he is still man. Fundamentally, sculpture is sculpture; architecture is architecture. Their aspects will change with changing needs of beauty and use. They aren't made out of air, they are made out of stone and steel. The fundamental things don't change.

We shall never get a working union of the painter and the sculptor until our architects have a clearer conception of the uses of sculpture and painting. As long as they are content with dead, machine-made replicas, we are going to have buildings which lack interest when viewed at close range. St. John the Divine could have had some ghastly stuff put on it if the sculpture had been entrusted to artists, but it would also have had, very likely, some masterpieces. It might be well to suggest that sculptures should be put up in plaster and left up for six months before they are cut in stone.

Since the very beginning, the tools of sculpture and of most of the other arts have changed but little for the better. In recent years the electric and pneumatic drill and hammer have been added to the sculptor's kit. They facilitate speed and can be used to great profit in architectural or monumental sculpture. One can cut such hard material as granite and marble with comparative ease and great speed. If the models are properly modeled, there is no reason why these tools should not be used in the execution of larger works. They do not seem to be such a great help on smaller sculptures, for there the quality of the actual surface is of primary importance.

Photography is another of modern inventions which has expanded the subject matter of the artist's studio. The camera is essentially a machine. For a time, it threatened almost to destroy the art of drawing and the arts of design. It was so easy to take a photograph and copy it that the quality obtained from studying nature was not considered worth the time it cost. Many could copy but few could draw. Modern tendencies have corrected this mistake; we have come to recognize that art's primary function is design, and the mere copying of nature by the artist has been rendered almost obsolete by the facility with which the camera gives us a record. But it will be a long time before what nature offers ceases to interest.

What is the future of sculpture in America? Who knows? With patronage anything is possible. In public works all depends on the person in charge at the moment. In private life there will always be a few people who care enough to pay the artist to cast more than one small bronze. Here in America we can have anything if we want it eagerly enough. There is plenty of talent. We have had geniuses and great talents in sculpture in America. But the architect is the one who holds the key. It is up to him to provide the opportunity.

Architecture—"In Between"

By Frank Lloyd Wright

THE first declaration—that I know anything about—of the value of the machine as an artist's tool was made twenty-seven years ago at Hull House, Chicago. I read a paper there called "Art and Craft of the Machine," since translated into many languages, making the assertion.

Today, Holland, Austria, Germany, Switzerland and recently France have contributed work that not only subscribes to that ideal, but is more "protestant" than my own. There is distinctly now a modern architecture,—in world-wide preparation. America has less in quantity to show.

Among the forces, factors and circumstances which stand in the way of complete and general recognition of architecture as an art are: "Tradition" as the refuge of the incompetent. Academic sentimentality. "Art" in quotation marks. Unqualified wealth. A government, the helpless creature of the majority.

The immediate future of architecture in America will probably consist of a superficial emulation of the work of certain protestants. Eventually, we may have an organic architecture.

The revolt in architecture has little if anything to do with the general revolt in the arts, except as life in general insists upon itself and birth in some form is inevitable. Not much can be accomplished of a revolutionary character except in, and as, architecture because architecture is the synthesis of all arts.

Form is determined by function and modified by use when the forms are living-forms. "Renaissance" is impossible. Real forms, even *once* "re-born," are put on or taken off like garments. The machine ruined even these vestiges or vestments of the old order. New forms became imperative. They must be created.

Of course, all arts are subject to the same law. Principle in one is principle in all. Only technique changes, although, strangely enough, few artists know anything about architecture. Anatole France was only annoyed by music.

We in America have no outstanding modern achievements as "architecture" except as Europe accepted the early work of Sullivan and myself and some few of our architects subsequently learned from Europe to accept their acceptance. (This is frankly immodest. But if I must answer—it is at least true.)

There is no leadership in American architecture at the moment, at least, none that is sound and honest. A timely confusion may be seen everywhere.

The old leadership, if it can be called leadership, included: The Schools; the medievalists; the pseudo-classicists and their plan-factories. Last, but not least, the "modern" modistes themselves, may be seen as falsely assuming the role.

Public appreciation may be enlisted in the interests of better architecture by letting the people actually see some of it. Photographs can not show it nor advertising "tell" it. Nor does the propaganda of the half-baked architect and snap-shot critic do more than harm.

The economic obstacles in the way of better architecture include: the natural timidity of vested "Interests"; the women paging Culture; the frailty of the architects themselves.

The American Business Man, unintimidated by "candy"-culture

328

or "rocking-chair" esthetics, should be an asset to architecture. He has been the *only* asset, so far.

There is no trouble in the relations between client and builder. It is the architect who is in difficulties,—in that triangle.

Cooperation with the architect is the only real opportunity either painter or sculptor will ever have—or ever had, for that matter.

The work of the architect does not yet in any way correspond to mass-production. In a period of revolt, no leader of the Old can guide the New or should do so. Youth is a quality—in art as in life. The New is simply Youth—with all that is thereby implied. The Old is Old—that is all, and the Old may be found with a *"new-esthetic"* in modern architecture. The only possible analogy at the present time with "machine-made" and "hand-made" in industry is the "machine-made" structure itself and the "hand-made" ideals of "Exterior or Interior." Result: Architecture as a bad form of surface-decoration.

Form and Color in the Home

By Eugene Schoen

INTERIOR architecture and decoration have been freer from educational dogma than most of the other arts because universities have regarded them as unworthy of special consideration. They have been looked upon as inferior, as part of the "Arts and Crafts" and therefore belonging to "labor" which has no place in an institution of higher learning. On the other hand, since they are really fully creative, a demand that their essentials be taught has brought into existence many lesser schools where they are haphazardly taught. As these schools give no degrees, their supervision is perfunctory and their graduates are of all degrees of knowledge, culture and preparation. The careful study of the past is superficial and the impetus to real creation practically nil. These schools, however, have been responsible for greater art appreciation than any other agency. But with their limited training and the absence of a high standard, the decorators of today exert very little influence on creative arts, except on the continent of Europe where cooperation between designer, craftsman and manufacturer has become a reality. In this country, however, the practice of architecture, esthetically, has been mimicry and archaeology, and it is only very recently that the revolt on the part of the student body against traditional architecture has begun to take effect.

We are today faced with the distressing spectacle of architects of repute floundering between the traditions of the past and indiscriminate copying of anything that looks new whether it is good or bad. Such a thing as sound principle or formula for real creation seems utterly wanting. Naturally this lack of understanding and the use of archaeological tradition has had its baneful effect upon decorator and manufacturer alike. No manufacturer can afford to spend money on tooling up for a large production of individual creations if the demand for such products does not compel it. This will be true as long as architects are obsessed with reproduction of period furniture and fabrics. Yet economic causes have had a compelling effect to change this in that our troglodyte homes cannot be made comfortable or convenient with only the corpses of past civilizations. When the home must be small and cannot be maintained by the constant and daily ministrations of servants, the innate craving for beauty demands satisfaction in a way different from what the past can furnish, hence the great masses who live in apartment houses must have their needs satisfied by new creations. The attempt to do this has been chaotic and ludicrous, as have been our efforts at readjustment to new social and economic conditions. Yet out of all this will emerge a living thing that will be the esthetic expression of our dynamic epoch. Manufacturers will absorb the ideas of artists for their models for mass production and will have their own designing forces properly trained to crystallize our civilization.

Among the changes which will most clearly differentiate us from the past will probably be artificial lighting. Practically all illumination today is reminiscent of the tallow candle. When its hot flame was replaced by the equally hot incandescent light very little could be done but to change the unessential external appearance of the lighting fixture. Even though the point of light application is very flexible in the electric wire, the heat of its light has been a serious handicap. The high cost of electric current is also another deterrent to change. It should, however, be possible to illuminate indirectly and to simulate daylight much more than we do. As this demand becomes conscious, lighting will be very different from what it now is, and the lighting fixture will disappear and with it the annoying glare of the electric bulb. When development of "cold light" through tubing is considered, the probability of revolutionary changes is greatly enhanced, and of course the communal ownership of water power for electric development will make it possible to proceed to, what seems today, unheard-of extravagance without being wasteful or uneconomical.

There will also be a decided change in color in the home of the future. As freedom from puritanical restraints and inhibitions gains headway, the full appreciation of color will come to its own as it has always done in great epochs of the past. It is a curious thing how personal color is and how much of its use depends upon personal liberty and freedom. It may safely be said that color in decoration diminishes or increases as public impertinence, in purely private matters, advances or recedes. With free self-expression, the glories of color come into their own just as surely as drabness follows an overzealous concern about the purely personal affairs of others.

Throughout the world, the failure of political democracy to produce happiness and freedom has caused a revolt against it, and the false values which it has created. Should these be corrected, vast repressed emotions will be released and, with the aid of the machine (the great good which capitalism has produced and which will survive it), humanity will direct a highly industrialized civilization into the channels of usefulness for the creation of individualized beauty.

The present trend is indicative of this. The architect of interiors today uses many new vehicles to express form and color, the fundamentals of objective art. New applications are found for glass, cork, coal-tar products and metals, and, while at the moment, perhaps, unduly stressed, beautiful creations result from the study of function. The designer approaches a problem from the viewpoint of need, comfort and convenience and a chair, sofa, table, bookcase, carpet or piece of drapery is placed where it will best serve its purpose. Upon the memories of the past as a foundation is now being built a structure which will have historical value; but the past, painstakingly studied and absorbed, can no longer serve any other purpose.

The Challenge of Industrial Design

By Norman Bel Geddes

Any progress, in any Art can be traced directly to the predominant influence of the age in which it is created.

In 300 b. c. the Greek theatre reached a state of the highest perfection and attracted to its service some of the best minds of the day. Not because it offered great pecuniary rewards, but because it was an important part of the life of the time; as important as our newspapers are today.

In the Thirteenth Century, on the contrary, it was the Church that answered all the emotional and intellectual needs of the people. Consequently the art of Giotto, Michelangelo, and Leonardo da Vinci is expressed in terms of religion; magnificent cathedrals, impressive tombs and inspiring ecclesiastical paintings, all bear witness to the great, vital spirit that actuated these men.

In the Twentieth Century, the dominant force is neither religion nor the theatre. It is Industry. It is the realization of this fact that has given the necessary impetus to the movement, which is taking place today, toward better design in industrial projects of all kinds. While still in its infancy, this movement is a vital, dynamic thing, for it has been born out of a living and ever-growing necessity. It is spontaneous, and therefore in no way dependent upon the personal vision or will of any single individual. Conscious leadership is unnecessary. A direct manifestation of the Machine Age, it is machine-like in the relentless inevitably of its advance, incalculable in its eventual scope.

Industrial concerns, whose very existence is dependent upon their correct interpretation, and instant satisfaction, of public demand, are realizing that there is a definite demand at the present time for better design in their products. They are discovering that beauty is not, as they have thought, incompatible with mass-production. In ever-increasing numbers they are turning to the artist for guidance. Here then, lies the challenge of industrial design. It remains to be seen whether artists can not only accept the challenge, but triumph in the ensuing battle.

That it will be a battle is undoubted, for in entering this new field, the artist must draw upon his own resources. He must break new ground—accept the challenge of treading where it has been said he would be out of his element. Now is no time to look to the past for inspiration. On the contrary, there must be present, always, consciousness of the fact that here is his chance to create something new, something that is of this age, and of the future.

The problem of industrial design is, to the artist, fraught with interest. He is working in a medium, and with forms which hitherto have not been associated with artists, he is standing on the edge of a vast tract of unexplored territory. Industry, having recognized him and accorded him a place in its scheme, is proving a generous master. It takes for granted that he can create something beautiful; it insists upon but one quality—practicality—and it is this very insistence which is not only producing the best in contemporary design, but which hands to the artist the key to his problems.

It has long been recognized that the article which perfectly fulfills its purpose, is well on its way to ultimate beauty, but only today is the precept becoming common practice. Misunderstanding of each other's aims has kept the business leader and the artist poles apart, with the result that not only the esthetic value, but the utility of the commercial product has suffered. Now, the former enemies meet on the common ground of progress.

No longer can the manufacturer complain of intolerance on the part of the artist. No longer can the artist bewail the lack of chances to carry out his ideas in concrete form, so that the world may see them. Everywhere hands are being held out to help him. Two things only are demanded of him; that his designs be created out of the elements, characteristics and needs of contemporary life, that he remember always, that behind all this progress and movement looms the Machine—tireless, omnipotent, and yet obedient to every whim of its controller—the Machine, the symbol of the age.

THE CONTRIBUTORS

GEORGE PIERCE BAKER
Director of the 47 Workshop at Harvard University from 1905 to 1924. Director of the University Theatre at Yale. Author of "Dramatic Technique" and other books on the drama and playwriting.

DAVID BELASCO
The dean of the American theatre. Dramatist, director, producer. Author and producer of "The Return of Peter Grimm," "Du Barry," "The Girl of the Golden West," "The Darling of the Gods" (with John Luther Long); producer of "Deburau," "The Merchant of Venice," "Mima" and other outstanding productions.

MONTA BELL
Motion picture director. For a number of years with Paramount-Famous-Lasky Corporation, and now associated with Universal Pictures Corporation. Among his films are "The Bellamy Trial," "Young Man of Manhattan" and "East Is West."

MAJOR EDWARD BOWES
Managing director of the Capitol Theatre, and vice-president of Metro-Goldwyn-Mayer Pictures Corporation. As director of "Major Bowes' Capitol Family," a pioneer in radio broadcasting.

GAMALIEL BRADFORD
Biographer, historian, poet. Author of "The Soul of Samuel Pepys," "Darwin," "Bare Souls," "Wives," "D. L. Moody—A Worker in Souls," "Life and I," "As God Made Them."

LOUIS BROMFIELD
Novelist. Winner of Pulitzer Prize for 1926 with "Early Autumn." Other novels are "The Green Bay Tree," "Possession," "A Good Woman," "The Strange Case of Miss Annie Spragg," "Twenty-four Hours."

337

HEYWOOD BROUN

Author and newspaper man. Columnist on *The New York Telegram* and dramatic critic of *The Nation*. Author of "Gandle Follows His Nose," "Seeing Things at Night" and, with Margaret Leach, "Anthony Comstock: Roundsman of the Lord."

MAURICE BROWNE

Playwright, actor, director and producer. Pioneer in the Little Theatre movement and founder of the Chicago Little Theatre. Author, with Robert Nichols, of "Wings Over Europe." Noted particularly as producer of "Journey's End."

RUTH CHATTERTON

Actress on both stage and screen. Attained distinction as co-star with the late Henry Miller. Since the coming of talking motion pictures, has risen to a foremost position with such films as "Madame X," "The Doctor's Secret" and "Anybody's Woman."

ALBERT COATES

Formerly conductor of the Imperial Opera of Petrograd, the London Symphony Orchestra and the Royal Philharmonic Society of London. Guest conductor of the New York Symphony and Philharmonic orchestras. Also composer.

HART CRANE

Poet. His published collections are "White Buildings" and "The Bridge."

ELIZABETH DUNCAN

Sister of Isadora Duncan. Director of the Schloss Klessheim School of the Dance, following the ideals of Isadora, which has headquarters in Salzburg and branches in Paris and New York.

JOHN ERSKINE

Novelist, college professor, lecturer, pianist. President of the Juillard Musical Foundation. Author of "The Private Life of Helen of Troy," "Galahad," "Adam and Eve," "Sincerity," "Uncle Sam."

NORMAN BEL GEDDES

Stage and industrial designer. His outstanding theatrical productions are "The Miracle" and "Lysistrata." Architect of industrial plants and designer of industrial productions. Associate of the Architectural Commission of the Chicago World's Fair of 1933.

GEORGE GERSHWIN

Composer of orchestral scores and musical comedies. Among his most notable serious works are "Rhapsody in Blue," "Concerto in F" and "An American in Paris."

LILLIAN GISH

Long distinguished record with silent motion pictures. Star of many of D. W. Griffith's finest films. With other directors, "The Scarlet Letter," "The Wind," etc. Reentered the theatre for the first time since childhood in Tchekhoff's "Uncle Vanya."

MARTHA GRAHAM

Concert dancer and teacher. Associated with the Neighborhood Playhouse and the Dance Repertory Theatre.

PAUL GREEN

Playwright. Winner of Pulitzer Prize for 1926 with "In Abraham's Bosom."

ARTHUR HAMMERSTEIN

Theatrical manager and producer of musical plays. Son of Oscar Hammerstein. Among his outstanding successes have been "Rose Marie," "The Song of the Flame" and "Golden Dawn."

ARTHUR HOPKINS

Director and producer of many notable plays, including "Anna Christie," "The Old Soak," "What Price Glory," "In a Garden," "Burlesque," "Paris Bound" and "Machinal."

ROBERT EDMOND JONES

Designer of "Anna Christie," "Redemption," "Richard III," "Macbeth," and many other productions for Arthur Hopkins and other producers, both dramatic and operatic. Associated with Eugene O'Neill and Kenneth Macgowan in the management of the Provincetown Playhouse and the Greenwich Village Theatre, 1923–1925.

JESSE L. LASKY

Veteran motion picture producer, and vice-president of Paramount-Famous-Lasky Corporation.

EVA LE GALLIENNE

Founder and director of the Civic Repertory Theatre, New York, previously appearing in the leading roles of "The Swan," "Liliom" and other plays.

ALFRED LUNT

Actor. Member of the permanent company of the Theatre Guild since 1924.

WILLIAM LYON PHELPS

Author, lecturer, critic. Lampson professor of English Literature at Yale University since 1901.

BOARDMAN ROBINSON

Cartoonist, illustrator, art instructor and mural painter. Awarded the Architectural League Medal in Mural Painting for 1930.

HERMANN ROSSE

Scenic designer, illustrator and decorator. Noted for mural paintings in the Peace Palace at The Hague, and for stage and motion picture designing, his outstanding work having appeared in Balieff's Chauve-Souris, John Murray Anderson's "Greenwich Village Follies" and the Paul Whiteman picture, "King of Jazz."

DAVID SARNOFF

President of the Radio Corporation of America. Chairman of the board of the Radio-Keith-Orpheum Corporation.

EUGENE SCHOEN

Architect. Specialist in modern interiors. Designer of modern furniture. Architect for Leviathan Night Club and many bank interiors.

JOHN SLOAN.

Artist, noted for landscapes and etchings. Instructor at the Art Students League since 1914.

HARRISON SMITH

Book publisher. Vice-president of the firm of Jonathan Cape and Harrison Smith, Inc.

ALBERT SPALDING

Concert violinist and composer of music for the violin.

The Contributors

JOSEPH URBAN

Artist, architect and scenic designer. Architect for interior of Municipal Building, Vienna; Troitsky Bridge over Neva River, Leningrad, and the Palace of the Khedive of Egypt. Operatic, dramatic and cinema designing in Vienna, Paris, London, Boston, New York and Los Angeles.

J. L. WARNER

Vice-president of Warner Bros. Pictures, Inc., in charge of production. With the introduction of Vitaphone, pioneer in the talking picture field.

FRANK LLOYD WRIGHT

Architect. Noted especially for Imperial Hotel in Tokio, Japan. Author of several books on architecture.

MAHONRI YOUNG

Sculptor, painter, etcher. Winner of numerous medals and awards for sculpture.

INDEX

343

347

348

Index

351